JUICE

JUICE

The Creative Fuel
That Drives
World-Class Inventors

Evan I. Schwartz

HARVARD BUSINESS SCHOOL PRESS
BOSTON, MASSACHUSETTS

Printed in the United States of America
08 07 06 05 04   5 4 3 2 1

Library of Congress Cataloging-in-Publication Data
Schwartz, Evan I.
    Juice : the creative fuel that drives world-class inventors / Evan I. Schwartz.
        p. cm.
    Includes bibliographical references.
    ISBN 1-59139-288-8
    1. Creative ability in business. 2. New products. 3. Creative ability in tech-
nology. 4. Technological innovations. 5. Inventions. I. Title.
    HD53.S39 2004
    658.5'75—dc22

                                                            2004005827

The paper used in this publication meets the requirements of the American
National Standard for Permanence of Paper for Publications and Documents
in Libraries and Archives z39.48-1992.

For Amy, and Lily, and Michaela

Contents

Foreword

Nathan P. Myhrvold

INVENTION IS THE ULTIMATE SOURCE of all that's new. Every gizmo, gadget, technique, or tool was born in a flash of inspiration in somebody's head at some point in time. Invention is to technology what conception is to reproduction—the moment that makes something original and unprecedented. As such, it is the highest-value activity that any individual or company can engage in.

The history of our world is, to a large extent, the history of inventions. Some inventions were small incremental improvements, while others were radical and transformative breakthroughs. James Watt's steam engine powered the industrial revolution. The nineteenth century saw advances such as the internal combustion engine, steel production, railroads, the telegraph and the telephone, photography and cinema, the elevator, incandescent lighting, electric motors, and the power grid. The twentieth century was driven by the automobile and the airplane, radio and television, atomic energy, electronics, and the digital computer. We may not know exactly which inventions from the worlds of biotech and nanotech will shape the twenty-first century, but we cannot doubt that there will be such inventions. Our world is no longer just inherited from nature—it is an invented world.

Despite the incredible impact of invention, it is given short shrift in many circles. Engineering tends to focus on the subsequent development, refinement, and deployment of an idea, paying relatively little attention to invention itself. The bulk of the time, effort, and cost involved in engineering is consumed in these more prosaic, but necessary, steps. In the process, something strange has happened. The attention given to implementing and marketing inventions has, in most organizations, eclipsed invention itself. We take for granted the wellspring of technical innovation that makes all the other hard work possible. Often, this situation is bad enough to actually impede invention. The cart is squarely in front of the horse, and it is seriously getting in the way.

A telling point is that we tend to lump all technology work into the phrase "R&D"—Research and Development. Where is the "I" for Invention? Apparently it isn't important enough to mention. Along the same lines, virtually nobody lists invention as his or her primary job task. Engineers are paid to develop products as their first and highest priority—they either develop products or engage in design and analysis activities directly in support of products. Engineers do make inventions, but it is almost always as an adjunct or side effect of their real mission—design and analysis. When their main mission gets into conflict with invention, guess which one wins? Stories of great inventions are rife with examples of the almost subversive nature of the activity. Inventors in large companies generally do their work despite, not because of, their jobs.

Start-up companies, on the other hand, must innovate to survive, and this imperative fosters a lot of invention. A lot of the progress in Silicon Valley is made late in the night before a big demonstration or product shipment. Nevertheless, invention is still a sideline activity, and the bulk of the effort is focused on making products and getting revenue. The product imperative that stimulates a certain set of inventions also impedes many others. It's hard to have time for a breakthrough when you're rushing another product out the door. Invention gives rise to start-ups, but new ventures must quickly develop a singleminded focus on product and customers, or else they flounder.

Research organizations tend not to do much better. At its core, research is about learning new things about the world. This can involve invention, but it doesn't have to, and in most cases the primary impetus of a researcher is to produce research, not inventions. I started Microsoft Research in 1991, and I'm proud to say we did a tremendous amount of pioneering work—which is continuing today. But at most big R&D labs, invention is a by-product, not the main product. The same is true in academic settings. Peer-reviewed papers and graduate theses are the main products. Invention is welcome only insofar as it does not get in the way of these primary goals.

Invention isn't easy to do, but it is even harder to manage. Design and analysis tasks have the advantage in that they tend to be predictable—at least within bounds. You can ask an engineering manager to produce a schedule for a product design, at least in a reasonably well-known area. The schedule may or may not turn out to be accurate, but it is common practice to at least *talk* about such a schedule. But ask for a schedule for a dramatic new invention and you'll get a blank stare. The same thing occurs in education. It is straightforward to teach analytical methods like stress analysis or to understand the principles of old inventions. As a result, that is mostly what is taught—analysis and old recipes. Nurturing the creativity of invention is an afterthought, if it occurs at all.

So invention, which is the most important part of technology creation, is systematically given the least attention. You can view this as a problem, but as any inventor will tell you, "problem" is another way to spell opportunity. That is how it seemed to me and my colleague Edward Jung, the former chief software architect at Microsoft. We began imagining what our dream laboratory would look like and do. We asked all kinds of questions: Why can't invention be the goal in and of itself? Why can't we hire inventive people and let them cross-pollinate ideas across infotech, biotech, nanotech, or whatever interests them? Do they even have to work in the same physical location? How about having no mission other than to invent, to have fun inventing, and hopefully to produce great big transformational ideas? Why can't we just license our inventions to corporations that would be excited about building them and taking them to market? Could we remain focused only on invention for its own sake?

The result is our invention laboratory, which we call Invention Science. The model for what we are doing now was set in the nineteenth century. Thomas Edison, Alexander Graham Bell, Nikola Tesla, and many others were full-time inventors, running full-time invention shops. It worked amazingly well; they created the foundation for the twentieth century. Perhaps it is time for this old business model, with a few modern twists, to make a comeback.

Our experience to date is that invention is just about the most challenging and rewarding thing you can do. It is great fun, but also a lot of work. Just like any sort of work, it's something that you can get better at with training and experience. That is true for both individual inventors and for organizations.

There isn't a manual or textbook for invention, but you can get insights into the process by reading *Juice*. Evan Schwartz gets inside the minds of some of today's best inventors, delves into their stories, explores how they thought up their inventions, and follows the battles they fought to do their work and get it recognized. These stories—and the thinking strategies they illustrate—put you at the front lines of modern inventing. In seeing how these pioneers saw the future, then made it happen, you'll gain insights that will help you or your organization take the next bold step forward. Basic science is changing at its most rapid rate ever. We have incredible information and communication tools at our disposal, and that alone is transforming the possibilities of invention. There's never been a better time to have big ideas.

What Drives Invention?

There's no thrill that can go through the human heart like that felt by the inventor who sees some creation of the brain unfolding to success.

—NIKOLA TESLA

HYBRID CARS. Portable digital music players. Handheld computers powered by fuel cells. Experimental gene therapies. Drug-dispensing nanobots. We're impressed with breakthrough inventions when we first come into contact with them—before we begin to take their existence for granted. But understanding invention itself is another thing. Invention is the core of innovation, the process by which new products or methods or entire new companies are evolved and introduced. Inventions can create value in the marketplace or create entire new marketplaces.[1] These growing markets, in turn, drive national economies.[2]

But what drives invention? How does the mysterious act of invention happen? Where does the mental leap, the breakthrough, the "Aha!", the "Eureka!", come from? What makes a person or a company or a society more inventive than another? What motivates someone to search for a problem, brainstorm a solution, and create that highly sought-after something that has never before existed? Can we better understand and stimulate inventiveness? If we could map the contours of the inventive mind, what would we see?

We can begin by glimpsing new ideas as they come about. To neuroscientists, the mind and the brain are one. Wielding inventions such as the PET scan, the MRI, and the EEG, neuroscientists have shown that the mind works via electrical and chemical impulses. The brain's hundreds of billions of neurons, or nerve cells, fire signals across tiny gaps known as synapses. These neurotransmitter signals travel across billions of pathways, often making new connections along the way. One of the mind's many astounding feats is that this network of neural circuits can operate and grow while consuming only about a quarter of the electrical power that drives a modern microprocessor, or about twenty watts.[3] This internally produced electricity is our juice. Neuroscientists can actually watch our circuits in action, seeing the mind "light up" in places where language happens, where memories are stored, where spatial judgment occurs, where dreams are projected. Invention may happen when the brain makes an unexpected neuronal circuit.[4]

Twenty watts. Seems like a pretty dim bulb. But the light bulb itself, which has served as the symbol of inventiveness since the days of Thomas Edison, is not only an outdated metaphor for invention but also a very poor example of technology. Incandescent lamps blow out after only a few months of use. Worse, the bulb as we know it converts less than 10 percent of its inflow of juice into light, while the rest of the energy is lost to heat. That's why it's never a bright idea to grab a lit bulb. Those who know how a light bulb works are hyper-aware of how inefficient it is. Just think of all the coal that's burned just so our lights can produce heat we don't want or need. A visitor to Edison's basement laboratory in West Orange, New Jersey, still comes across signs hung by the legendary inventor himself that admonish: "Save the juice, save the juice, turn off the lights when not in use!"[5]

REINVENTING INVENTION

Our basic understanding of invention needs to be reinvented, moving beyond Edisonian homilies such as "genius is hard work, stick-to-itiveness, and common sense" because it's clearly more than that. And what better place to start than with the invention metaphor itself?

An inventor named Nick Holonyak has actually spent his entire career working on replacing the light bulb. The son of Hungarian immigrants, Holonyak grew up in a coalmining town in southern Illinois where literacy was the exception. He saw the devastation of the coal miner's life up close—including violent strikes, Depression-era layoffs, deadly explosions, and black lung disease. When Holonyak was ten years old, his father gave him a pocketknife and said, "Make what you need." He learned to apply his mental capacity to his everyday problems and desires, first by whittling, then by taking apart telephones and fixing car engines. He ended up receiving his degree in electrical engineering from the University of Illinois. In the early 1950s, Holonyak became the first graduate student of John Bardeen, who had co-invented the transistor at Bell Labs, a breakthrough that led to the first of Bardeen's unprecedented two Nobel Prizes in physics. The opportunity to have the serene and brilliant Bardeen as a mentor and role model "was pretty lucky for me," Holonyak recalls. "I was not 100 percent smart."

Now in his seventies, Holonyak is spry and silver-haired, and looks a little nerdy when he wears his large glasses. But he still comes across as that hardscrabble country boy when discussing the advent, some four decades ago, of the biggest of his "Aha!" moments. After stints at Bell Labs and in the U.S. Army, Holonyak joined General Electric in Syracuse, New York, where he was supposed to be working on improving semiconductors under an Air Force contract. He heard something odd that distracted him from that work. Semiconductors, he had learned, could produce invisible infrared light energy. That got him wondering whether it would be possible to make circuits that produce light you could actually see.

He created this opportunity in his mind. "My colleagues thought I was a bit nutty," he says, and he had to keep his experiments secret from his boss. "I worked on the sly for two years," he says, noting that if management found out, "I would have been in trouble and gotten fired."[6]

His breakthrough came one day as he was testing a semiconductor material called gallium arsenide phosphide. When juiced with electricity, the circuit emitted a speck of red light.

Holonyak had invented the light-emitting diode—the LED. "Once I created a red one, I was constantly thinking, why can't I create an orange, a green, and a blue one?" He and other inventors later discovered different materials that produced the different color frequencies. The blue LED was created by a Japanese inventor in early 1990s, and the race to perfect a bright white one is on right now.[7] But LEDs of any color can last ten years or longer. They also produce almost no heat. Now used as standard indicator lights for everything from digital clocks to appliances to car dashboards, LEDs are also the basis for new flashlights, car taillights, traffic lights, and the giant NASDAQ billboard in Times Square. Each year, there are twelve LED-based products sold for every person on earth, and LEDs are already becoming a source of general lighting. Holonyak waves at incandescent lamps and fixtures. "All of this," he says. "Doomed."

On a symbolic level, Holonyak has replaced an obsolete metaphor. For every watt of power, an incandescent bulb produces only about fifteen lumens, a measure of brightness. The light-emitting diode, by contrast, can produce up to five times the lumens per watt, in the range of fluorescent lighting, but with a more pleasing glow. That brings us back to our twenty watts of internal juice. "I can generate a hell of a lot of light with twenty watts," says Holonyak. "With twenty watts, you'd be walking around like a lighthouse. You'd be totally lit up." That's why the LED must be seen as the new symbol of invention.

We all may have pretty much the same amount of juice powering our minds. But if we channel it the right way, if we keep making new and unexpected connections, we can produce that special form of creativity known as invention, and cognitive LEDs will start popping up in our heads more and more often. As Nikola Tesla, the inventor of alternating current, noted, the electrical energy of invention races through your heart as well as your brain, and there's no feeling quite like it. After you come up with an invention once, says Holonyak, you have enough confidence to keep doing it. Indeed, you can become addicted to invention. This ability to receive meaning and pleasure from the act of thinking differently begins to explain why some people are more motivated to invention than others.

PLAYING THE INVENTION GAME

To get a sense of how invention works, try playing the invention game for yourself. Think of something that people would need that doesn't now exist. Something that would make you rich, or something that would help people live better, or something that would transform your company or your industry. Take as much time as you want.

Many people will first think of something in the realm of zany science fiction: an antigravity pack that lets us hover above the treetops, an anti-aging pill, or a brain implant for reading other people's thoughts. Others will think of something more practical: car keys and sunglasses with radio-frequency chips that let you locate them when they're lost, or chairs and tables that never grow out of balance and develop that annoying rocking. Others, with more knowledge of what's happening in certain fields, might name something that sounds impossible but that's actually under development: a "cellfixer" nanobot that swims in your blood and repairs damaged cells, or a "clonemaker" machine that synthesizes genes and proteins and builds new life from scratch. Finally, there are inventions of the whimsical variety, such as the ones showcased on *Futurama*, Matt Groening's cartoon series in which Professor Hubert J. Farnsworth unveils his smell-o-scope, his cool-o-meter, and his what-if machine—the ultimate invention because it enables the user to visualize anything. (Of course, we already have one of those between our ears.)

These visions aren't bad places to start. But what would you do next? The point of this game isn't to get you to become an inventor.

That's not necessary. You already *are* an inventor, or can be. As Emerson wrote, "An inventor knows how to borrow, and everyone is, or should be, an inventor."[8] Contrary to popular belief, an inventor is rarely the person who first conjures up the basic idea for a hit product. Today's inventors combine different ideas from different knowledge domains to make the visions of others become a reality. Inventors are often inspired by one another, and they often work best in cross-disciplinary teams. Nature invents too, and some of the most unlikely breakthroughs in medicine, materials, and artificial intelligence are inspired by analogies to how nature works.

A highly focused form of human creativity, invention is an enduring essence that we've all inherited, part of what Ecclesiastes, the Bible's book of wisdom literature, calls "the immortal mind." Prehistoric handtools recovered by archeologists are some of our earliest evidence of the human mind at work, reminders that people were exercising their inventiveness long before we came to subsequent milestones—writing, agriculture, science. But that doesn't mean we're aware of how this concentrated kind of ingenuity happens and can best be put into practice.

We all suspect that invention has some degree of overlap with artistic creativity and scientific thinking. Many books and studies lump these domains together, trying to find the commonalities among the Eschers, the Ellingtons, the Edisons, and the Einsteins. But what if we remained informed by the artists and the scientists but simply made it our main goal to understand invention? What if we could learn how inventors spot new opportunities in surprising new ways and how they approach problems from unexpected angles? What if we could drop the conventional view of products and markets, and if companies began thinking more like inventors who had already brought forth incredible things? What if invention were a discipline that you could discover and apply—to any domain?

The first thing you'd need to do is to stop thinking like a consumer for a long moment. In our current social context, we are trained to ask: Do I want that? How much does that cost? Would I impress people if I had that? What can that product do for me or for my company? This consumer-centered attitude toward the objects in our world is so pervasive that humorist Dave Barry mocks it in one of his columns. "Without question, the greatest invention in the history of mankind is beer," he writes. "Oh, I grant you that the wheel was also a fine invention, but the wheel does not go nearly as well with pizza."[9]

Thinking more like an inventor requires a different perspective: How does this work? Why does it work? What is the thinking that went into making it? Why wasn't it made at an earlier date, in a different place, by someone else? What's wrong with it? How can it be improved? How can it be made obsolete? What else is needed? Who says it needs to be this way?

The good news is that you don't have to be a scientist or an engineer to be more inventive. We typically think of invention in certain contexts: in computing, chemistry, consumer products, biotech, medicine, materials, aviation, energy, electronics, defense, and so forth. But invention is transdisciplinary and therefore can be extracted from any technological realm and applied to problems in any area.

The bad news is that invention isn't easy. The bar is set high by three rules. First, an invention needs to be new. It's not enough for you to be creative and imaginative, you must originate something that no one else has created before. An invention also must be non-obvious. For example, you can't take someone else's idea, put it on the Internet, and call it an invention. The third rule is that it must be useful. A sculpture can be original and entirely non obvious, but it isn't an invention in the literal sense because it isn't used to perform a practical function. That thought, however, might be open to challenge. In fact, every assumption is open to challenge. That's also how invention begins.

BEING INVENTIVE

In addition to being an enduring part of human history, invention is vital for the human future. There are thousands of problems out there than can be solved by inventive thinking. And most of the value in our economy is now based on creating opportunities and solving problems in some form. Drudgery gets outsourced to the machines that we invent or to the people in places where knowledge work doesn't yet dominate the economy. Invention is the ultimate knowledge work. The best jobs of the future will involve invention in some way. Good inventors can't be unemployed. They may be struggling, or they may have attained such great success that they no longer need to work, but they will never suffer for a lack of things to do. Invention never stops, and inventors never stop inventing.

In this book you are going to meet some of the world's most accomplished inventors. These inventors express the belief that "the idea is the thing" through their actions, by inventing mainly for the sake of inventing. Most of these people have become wealthy, and that is indeed their desired outcome. But that's not why they invent in the first place. They could have chosen other ways to make money, and they still can. They invent because they are inventors. They have that same inner compulsion to create that has marked the advance of civilization since the beginning of humanity.

Where does that compulsion come from? What can we learn from these people? One hint comes from Nick Holonyak's childhood pocketknife and his fixing of clunky telephones and noisy car engines. Virtually all the inventors we'll meet in this book were seized by something similar when they were kids: playing with erector sets and chemistry kits, taking apart radios and televisions, and so forth. It's why dissecting a foul-smelling frog in biology class tends to drive home the biology lesson itself. There is something visceral and multisensory about delving into physical objects. This childlike tendency to phyically explore why something works and why it can be made better sometimes gets lost in our current world of symbolic experience. It goes back to the truth at the heart of the famous Confucius quotation: "I hear and I forget, I see and I remember, I do and I understand."

The conventional view is that the people who tackle these hands-on projects are nerdy and quirky and that much of their inventing can be explained by their personality traits—that Edison was an autodidactic, workaholic, attention-deficit-disordered savant, and there's no sense in trying to become like that. Because there are so few famous inventors living today, there is little to counteract that image. If you try to name well-known living inventors and count them on one hand, you will likely have several fingers left over. Inventors used to be national heroes in the days of Edison, Bell, Tesla, and the Wright brothers. But the new industrial corporations that these and many other individuals spawned went on to build giant and successful corporate R&D laboratories, and the creative, highly educated, technical professionals who worked there were reclassified as "researchers." In 1940, the U.S. Census Bureau actually eliminated "inventor" as a separate job category.[10]

These days, most popular notions of what an inventor is come from works of fiction that show inventors with superhuman talents. Epitomized by the mythical Dr. Victor Frankenstein, by Willie Wonka, by Doc Brown in *Back to the Future*, or as creators of destructive robots in *The Terminator* series, such portrayals have inventors working outside mainstream social and academic contexts, and they depict inventors as irrationally passionate, emotionally unstable, or downright mad.[11]

Inventors are only a little bit like that. They tend to have personality quirks, but so does everyone, and because those traits are varied, to focus on them would only be a distraction. You'll get a sense here of the intellectual background of the inventors profiled within these pages, as well as a taste of their personalities. But that is not the focus. The focus is on their strategic thinking patterns, the series of "Aha!" moments that leads to the final products we recognize as inventions.

Invention is highly path-dependent. To understand an inventor's breakthroughs and contributions, you must understand what came before them: the inventor's motivation for tackling a problem, the series of choices the inventor made, the chance events that shaped the inventor, and the knowledge available to the inventor—as well as the knowledge that had to be abandoned as wrong or in the way. Invention is also highly contextual. You need to know the environments inventors have been working in, and the needs of society at the time of their inventions. The case studies here are of inventors working today. They have been chosen because they are interesting, because the inventors were available for in-person interviews, and the inventions described in each case have always been ahead of their time. For contrast, these stories are juxtaposed with classic cases.

Where and when do inventors come up with breakthrough ideas? They do it everywhere and all the time. They're assigning themselves problems at bedtime and dreaming new ideas as they sleep; they're having epiphanies in the shower; they're incubating concepts while driving; they're brainstorming while exercising on treadmills, riding bikes, climbing mountains, and jogging through canyons; they're informally bouncing possibilities off of colleagues; they're reading constantly; they're observing everything around them, looking for clues; and they're often absorbed in their own thoughts. But they'd be the first to tell you that most of their ideas aren't brilliant. They need to generate a lot of ideas to come up with the fewer viable ones. They rely on a messy yet systematic process for doing what they do, and when they stop to reflect on it, they can sometimes tell you how this special kind of thinking actually works.

I'm not saying that you can pour their thinking into a glass, drink it, and become an expert inventor tomorrow. But the inventors profiled in this book tend to agree: Invention is a set of strategic thinking tools that you can teach, learn, and practice, just as you can with other skills like cooking, acting, or sailing. Unfortunately, the practice of invention is rarely taught in schools, perhaps because it requires so much independent thinking, or perhaps because it has been steeped in myths such as the notion that invention is purely accidental or that inventors are born, not made. The hope here is that you will be able to use this book as a tool to help you turn on the juice of your own inventiveness. We know that brainstorms are electrical, and you need to have many of them if you want to change the world. Here, at least, are a blend of examples to get you started.

1

Creating Possibilities

To raise new questions, new possibilities, to regard old questions from a new angle, requires creative imagination and marks real advance.

—ALBERT EINSTEIN

BEFORE THEY CAN MAKE new products, inventors pose new possibilities. An inventor can be sitting on an airplane and suddenly become entranced by the floor tiles, the lighting system, the magazine rack, or the food cart. An inventor might observe people playing games or working on their computers, or perhaps gaze out the window to view an entire civilization from a distance. Whatever it is, an inventor will zero in on the one object or task that is primitive compared with what it could become. The potential seems so great that the thing seems to be malfunctioning, at least in the inventor's mind.

When most people think that everything is working normally, an inventor will home in on the absurdity, the utter foolishness of the way everyone seems to accept the world as it is. Others won't even see what's wrong—until the inventor stumbles across it. By isolating a problem in a new way, by redefining it, by focusing it down to something more specific than meets the average eye, the inventor constructs a new possibility where none was thought to have existed. This thinking strategy doesn't just appear out of nowhere, and we can't just start practicing it well without some guidance. By the same token, those who are rehearsed in imagining one possibility after another couldn't break the habit if they tried. Once they are possessed by this inner drive, it tends to stay with them.

Elwood "Woody" Norris has been creating opportunities his entire career. But like many inventors, Norris didn't initially set out to become one. A tall man with a big smile, and childlike enthusiasm for just about everything, Norris looks more like a high school gym teacher than a man of science, and he tells his story with aw-shucks expressions such as "in'dat cool?" Growing up in rural Maryland in the 1940s and 1950s, his family was so poor that they lacked indoor plumbing. His father was a Cumberland coal miner, and his mother had only an eighth-grade education. Out in the backyard was a foul-smelling chicken coop. "I remember it quite vividly," says Norris. That's where he played with radios. Along with old tube consoles, he'd scavenge discarded televisions and anything else electronic. He'd bring the gear back to the coop and then dissect and reassemble it until he unlocked the mystery of how these things worked. "I always had an interest in tearing things apart," he says.[1] At night, he'd cover his makeshift laboratory with a tarp to keep it dry.

Unable to afford college, after high school Norris entered the U.S. Air Force, where he learned more about electronics, especially Doppler radar. His parents, meanwhile, had gotten a divorce, and his mother moved to Seattle and remarried. One day, she telephoned her son in the middle of a nervous breakdown. Her second husband had been declared a missing person after failing to come home from work. Norris got a discharge from the service and went to care for his mom, landing himself a $400-per-week job as a technician repairing electronics at the University of Washington, where he was free to hang out at the library.

Norris's invention career literally began as a joke. In April 1960, he was in the UW library reading an article in *Radio & Television* magazine about a new electric shaver that ionized whiskers without making any contact with the face. He was amazed—until he read the editor's note, which revealed that the article was an April Fool's prank. Furthermore, there would be a $300 prize for the person who could write the most convincing story about a fake new gadget for the next year's issue. "I sat down to write an article about a phony invention," he recalls. What could it be?

LIGHTING THE INNER FIRE

Creating a possibility in your mind doesn't necessarily mean that the underlying problem you're trying to solve is new. What's new is your particular representation of the problem. Successful inventors often aren't the first to come up with the basic concept of their own invention. Alexander Graham Bell wasn't the first to discover the need for the telephone. Other inventors had been working on the problem for at least fifteen years before he made his first call. Thomas Edison didn't discover the need for the electric light. The need had been burning in the minds of other inventors for at least thirty years before he switched on his first bulb. Wilbur and Orville Wright didn't discover the need for the airplane. The race to build a flying machine started at least a century before Kitty Hawk. In the same vein, the future inventor of the first quantum computer, the first portable genomic scanning machine, the first nanotech cell-repairing robot, or the first antigravity machine won't be the first person to have imagined those possibilities. The original dreamers were also demonstrating inventive behavior.

The most common explanation of what drives inventive activity is the age-old maxim, "Necessity is the mother of invention." But that aphorism explains almost nothing and is wrong in most instances. Because new scientific discoveries or technological possibilities often give rise to new desires, it's usually even more correct to say the opposite: "Invention is the mother of necessity." Although successful inventions seem in retrospect to fill a clear human need, what they really do is to generate the demand in the first place. Only a handful of people imagined the telephone, the electric light, and the airplane beforehand. After these things existed, however, masses of people suddenly couldn't do without them.

The task of choosing or finding the unrealized possibility isn't as straightforward as saying, What would people want? Ask yourself that question, spend some time thinking about an answer, and you'll see that there's a special habit involved. Inventors are attuned to finding the problem *inside* the problem or finding the problem *outside* the problem. They frame the challenge in such an original way that they've redefined a need and turned it into something new. That is the key: The new potential begins life in the inventor's mind.

This is where the process of invention is misunderstood. People often look at the invention and then work backward. When they see a successful new technology, they immediately relate it to the trouble it has alleviated. But you can't understand the process of invention by looking only at the inventions. You must first empathize with the inventors, the people who stirred up that trouble in the first place. The "mother of invention" adage doesn't explain why certain individuals take on a life of creative problem solving, some to the point of obsession, whereas others don't consider it. "The crucial question is why some groups respond in a particular way to the same human needs or wants that in some other groups remain unfulfilled," writes technology historian Carlo Cipolla.[2] What motivates inventors to do what they do, and why are some people, companies, and societies more inventive than others?

Psychologist Carl Jung suggests that the drive to create possibilities is actually something that comes from *within the individual* rather than from the pull of an unmet need in the marketplace of human activity. "The creative mind plays with the objects it loves," Jung argues.[3] The impulse derives from childhood experimentation and imagination. "The creation of something new," he adds, "is not accomplished by intellect but by the play instinct acting from inner necessity."

This instinct to play describes what keeps happening with the inventors you'll meet in this book. Inventors don't have to be intellectually advanced, at least in terms of formal education. Many of them insist that they aren't especially smart. But they all display flashes of genius, and that genius is derived from their childlike proclivity to play with the things that interest them. That's the source of their urge to invent, their compulsion to create, their creative juice. In Jung's terms, inventors develop an *inner necessity* to imagine new possibilities and realize them. They make their own fuel and keep it burning.

STARTING SOMEWHERE

In 1960, Woody Norris, thinking about how to win the $300 April Fool's prize, quickly narrowed his possibility search to what he knew best: audio systems. Taking a close look at the high-fidelity systems on the market—known then as hi-fi—it struck him that the tone arms on phonographs were ridiculous. The end with the needle would sweep about six inches across the record while the wires at the base of the arm barely moved. The angle by which this apparatus moved seemed absurd. No wonder the needle skipped and scratched the record if someone in the room jumped or if someone touched the system. But as Norris notes, "The brain has all these different, disconnected things vying for your attention." To focus and to overcome this distraction, Norris developed a technique of verbalizing the problem. "It goes out of my mouth, and around the side my head and into my ear. Talk about the problem. Don't just think of it."[4]

Norris imagined a new possibility: incorporating radio as part of the record player itself. His potential solution seemed absurd enough to win the April Fool's prize. Norris decided that the problem lay in the wires that carried the electrical sound patterns from the needle to the amplifier. The wires had to be eliminated. He envisioned a wireless cartridge that would hold the needle and move from the outside of the record along the radius to the inside. A built-in radio transmitter would send the sounds to the amplifier. In radio, he saw a new possibility for changing the record player. He called his idea the "radial tracking tone arm."

But before sending his hoax story to the magazine, Norris called a local hi-fi dealer and pretended he had read about this invention. The store owner was interested in seeing it and perhaps selling the product. Based on this, Norris decided not to send the story in as an April Fool's joke but instead to build a prototype as specified. "That was the first time in my life I'd ever thought of anything new," he recalls.

What happens to his inventions after he creates them doesn't interest Norris very much. In this case, he ended up building a working model for an electronics company under a lucrative contract and patenting his concept. The device was eventually marketed, with limited success. Eventually, of course, the turntable itself was rendered obsolete by the laser, digital audio, and the compact disc. All inventors must start somewhere, and they usually can recall the precise details of their first invention, even though the invention itself is usually not very significant. The larger point is that Norris came to believe that he may have come across a method of spotting possibilities missed by almost everyone else.

CONSTRUCTING MENTAL MODELS

Spotting new possibilities happens not in physical space but rather inside what can be called the mental model of the inventor's creation. After observing the world, inventors take all the information they have gathered about the system they are considering. Then they combine this information with their technical experience and background, however limited that may be. "Through interaction with a target system, people formulate mental models of that system," suggests cognitive psychologist Donald A. Norman. "These models need not be technically accurate, but they must be functional."[5] After the model is constructed in the mind, the inventor can make changes to it. The process of modifying the model is what generates additional possibilities.

After doing this for the first time, Norris wanted to see whether he could do it again. One evening several years later, he was heading home from the university when he ran into some buddies who were starting a company. It was the mid-1960s, and the stock market was hotter than it had been in a generation. Entrepreneurial fever was breaking out everywhere. The leader of the group, Grant Heaton, told Norris that he and his friends were developing a sales strategy, a marketing strategy, and a financial strategy. There was only one thing they lacked: a hot new product to sell. The entrepreneurs had a vague notion that selling new medical devices would be profitable. Norris told them he would invent something for them in that realm.

Again, he needed to create a new possibility. And again, he focused on what he knew most about: sound and how it is transmitted. What about listening to what was happening inside the body? The idea of trying to hear internal organs can be traced to Hippocrates in the fifth century B.C., but it wasn't until 1816 that French inventor René Laennec created a wooden tube for isolating and reverberating the sound, a tool that evolved into the stethoscope. But the stethoscope was a mechanical device limited to detecting vibrations.[6] Norris saw this as an unreasonable constraint. The X-ray machine, meanwhile, enabled visual representations of the body's interior, but evidence was piling up that the high-frequency light beams it emitted were inappropriate or harmful for certain applications, such as observing a fetus in the womb. In addition, X-ray images were like photographs: They didn't show movement, and they certainly didn't detect sound.

Norris was constructing a mental model of a new possibility. Why wasn't there a better way of hearing what was going on under the skin? Why not invent a device based on the basic principles of sound and see whether it could do more than the old stethoscope?

From his Air Force training, Norris knew about the Doppler effect, in which delays in successive sound waves seem to grow more frequent as the sound source approaches the listener. The pitch, or frequency, keeps changing. The buildup of the waves reaches a crescendo when a train, airplane, or other sound source passes by, and then the pitch wanes as the source gets farther away and the interval between the waves grows longer. As a result, you don't have to *see* the train to know it's passing by. Why not apply this knowledge to this problem?

Why not use sound to see inside the body? Why not shoot high-frequency sound waves through the skin? Norris knew about ultrasound, electromagnetic energy that beats more than twenty thousand times per second—too frequent for the human ear to detect but strong enough to penetrate most forms of matter. "The idea was to create a thing that would emit ultrasound into your skin," he says. "Because of the Doppler effect, if something in there was moving, there would be different frequencies. The shifts would create movements that you would be able to hear."

Norris was engaging in a common habit of inventive engineering: taking a technology or technique that works in one domain—in this case Doppler radar detection of aircraft or weather patterns—and then repurposing it for a new problem space.

Was Norris the first inventor to think of this basic idea of diagnostic ultrasound? Hardly. But he imagined the possibility without knowledge of other efforts. Throughout history, most epochal inventions have been born in a rush of nearly simultaneous discovery. Ultrasound technology was certainly in that groundbreaking category. Aside from the birth control pill, one would have a hard time coming up with an invention in the past half century that revolutionized obstetrics and gynecology more than diagnostic ultrasound. In this case, doctors, engineers, and inventors all over the world were constructing their own mental models of the possibilities at roughly the same time. "There were others, as often happens, working on the same idea," Norris says. "I never really researched it."

If he had, he might have found that John J. Wild, a British surgeon working at the University of Minnesota and later for Honeywell, had developed a technique in the 1950s for bouncing ultrasound pulses off of internal tissues, finding that muscles, tumors, and organs deflected different echoes. But this technique is borrowed from underwater sonar, which itself is modeled on the way whales and bats sense their surroundings. Norris's idea of detecting Doppler shifts to pinpoint internal movement was different from Wild's idea of measuring echo patterns, and each method had different applications and created different possibilities.

Others were approaching the problem from their own frames of reference. Karl Dussik, an Austrian doctor, and Ian Donald, a Scottish doctor, were lead authors on seminar papers on medical ultrasonics in the 1940s and 1950s, respectively. New centers for the study of ultrasonic diagnostics were also cropping up in Australia,

Denmark, Germany, Japan, and Switzerland.[7] There was even a medical ultrasound project at the University of Washington, where Norris had been working. Leading that effort was Donald W. Baker, then director of a campus lab within the electrical engineering department. Norris says he is surprised to learn that there was such a project at UW or elsewhere. For his part, Baker, now retired, says he doesn't remember Norris specifically but supposes that anyone on campus could have been influenced by talks and papers he and his colleagues were giving. At the time, most universities prohibited professors from receiving patents on medical devices because such advances were considered to be detached from the world of for-profit commerce. "In today's world," says Baker, "ideas like this would definitely be patented."[8]

In this respect, Norris was ahead of his time. Over a weekend, he developed a crude prototype using materials from Radio Shack and other electronics stores around Seattle. He gutted a flashlight and fitted it with a radio receiver and an ultrasonic emitter adapted from an early TV remote, which operated at 40 kilohertz. He smeared petroleum jelly on his skin and began using the device to detect frequencies inside his body. Boundary layers deflected back different density patterns, and any internal movements would come back at frequencies other than 40 kHz because of the Doppler effect.

Norris's mental model worked in practice, as good ones often do. Norris wrote up descriptions and created sketches of his idea for what was eventually called a Phase-Lock Doppler System for Monitoring Blood Vessel Movement, later known more generally as the Transcutaneous Doppler. "You could use it to hear sound in a much more isolated way," he says. "You could separate the different sounds under the skin and inside the body. You could slide it up your arm and your leg. You could hear blood clot. You could hear the fetal heartbeat, which was separate from mom's heartbeat, and which was often difficult to pick up with a stethoscope." The range of possibilities was mind-boggling.

Norris assigned his concept to his friend Grant Heaton's new company, Medical Development Corporation, in return for a promise of equity in the venture. Two years later, Norris received an unexpected call. The invention was now considered to be a valuable piece of intellectual property. The patent was issued in January 1972, listing Norris as the inventor.[9] If this exact technique had already been described in existing patents or in published papers, it wouldn't have been eligible for patent protection. Norris was told he had forty thousand registered shares in the start-up. "I said, 'Great! What are they worth?'" The answer was $8.50 per share, or $340,000.

As with the case of most inventions, however, it would take years to find out just how useful or valuable this one was. It wasn't until the 1980s that this technique would evolve, be combined with other techniques, and result in the ultrasound devices and sonogram images now familiar to virtually all mothers-to-be in developed countries. Diagnostic ultrasound is now used for hundreds of applications, and equipment sales are part of a multibillion-dollar industry controlled by companies such as Philips, Siemens, Toshiba, and General Electric.

As it turned out, Norris's contribution to the field was a relatively small one. But the invention was the launching pad for his career. After selling his stock and paying a 15 percent capital gains tax, Norris quit his job and set up shop as an independent inventor. Years later, Norris would hit upon an even more original breakthrough in the sphere of sound. Yet his proclivity for creating possibilities in his mind was honed early on. "I just look at things differently," he says, "and I developed a process for doing that."

Reframing Possibilities

There is more than one way to create a new possibility, and of course not all such ideas are of the same magnitude. We can adopt a useful shorthand for classifying inventions into four types according to the nature of the process that brings them into the world. Let's look at each of these types.

First, an inventor might try to find fault with something people already use and imagine a valuable improvement—for example, the flat panel computer screen or the portable kidney dialysis machine. That's the better mousetrap.

Second, inventors sometimes recognize a latent opportunity that others miss. They dream up something that people didn't know they needed. Examples are the Sony Walkman or the Segway human transporter. That's the hopeful niche.

Third, inventors may reframe a previously insurmountable problem, sensing a fresh approach for creating something that does not yet exist but that would clearly be in great demand—for example, the electric light or the airplane. That's the epochal breakthrough that might transform the world.

Now and again, there are surprises, and an invention from any of the first three categories ends up having a much wider application than even the inventor dreamed. The steam engine or the laser are examples. That's the lucky strike.[10]

To see how all these kinds of approaches work in practice, let's explore how Alexander Graham Bell created possibilities in his mind. His most famous invention fell into one or another of the preceding categories at different times. It started as a better mousetrap problem then became a hopeful niche, a way of delivering urgent telegrams by voice. Then it became an epochal breakthrough, and in retrospect it was certainly a lucky strike.

The central mystery surrounding the invention of the telephone has always been why someone else didn't invent it much sooner. Why did more than four decades pass between Faraday's discovery of electromagnetic induction in 1831 and Bell's breakthrough in 1876? The demand for the telephone may have been a latent one, but it was there for inventors to find. All the needed scientific knowledge and physical components existed. What took so long? "The answer," suggests Bell biographer Robert V. Bruce, "lies deep in the working of the human mind."[11]

The story of the invention of the telephone is one of reframing a possibility in a unique way. Others had thought that the telephone would work like a telegraph; a circuit would be made and broken in patterns that represented the content of a message, as in the dots and dashes of Morse code. This was the model for an apparatus invented in 1861 by German inventor Philipp Reis. The user would speak or sing into a diaphragm, which would vibrate a metal needle on its surface, creating a series of rapid but discrete electric pulses. The term *telephone* (meaning "far-speaking") had already been coined, and Reis used it to name his device.

The representation of the problem seemed to be on the right track, but it got inventors stuck on the wrong mental model. The electric current that the Reis transmitter produced didn't vary in relation to the sound's amplitude—its degrees of loudness. Therefore, the device would never be able to send speech, only musical monotones. It should have been called the tele*tone*. Still others picked up where Reis left off, viewing the telephone as a generalized version of the telegraph. Thomas Edison, for example, later used a Reis device as the starting point for his own mental model of a telephone system. He, too, got trapped.

Bell, on the other hand, knew very little about Faraday, electricity, or the telegraph. Instead, from an early age he had developed a mental model of how speech works. His mother was almost completely deaf, and while growing up in Edinburgh, Scotland, "Aleck" would often play the piano while his mother pressed her hearing horn against the instrument's sounding board. Bell's father and grandfather were accomplished speech therapists and elocution coaches, his father going so far as to create *Visible Speech*, a best-selling catalog of images representing every sound the human voice could make. Bell's father devised these symbols for teaching children, illiterates, and nonnative speakers to read English. But this new alphabet—based on lip, tongue, and larynx positions—inspired Aleck, at age nineteen, to experiment with drumlike membranes that measured the air vibrations caused by human speech. A year later, Aleck began using Visible Speech to teach a class of deaf kids in London to speak. In this way, he recalled, he "was thus introduced to what proved to be my life's work—the teaching of speech to the deaf."[12]

For the young Bell, new possibilities arose from his inner drive to understand hearing and speech, and follow-on ideas always seemed to arise from current ones. He noticed, for example, that when he pressed the foot pedals on his family's piano and sang notes into the instrument, the corresponding piano strings would resonate. He was amazed at this phenomenon of "sympathetic vibration," and it would later play a big role in his inventions.

Bell initially didn't set out to invent the telephone. More experienced inventors, meanwhile, did set out to do so and failed. Instead, Bell came up with a new theory, and it was a theory that began as a series of possibilities he created in his mind. Those possibilities led to his experiments with converting sound into continuously undulating electricity, which soon led to the telephone we have come to know.

CONNECTING MULTIPLE POSSIBILITIES

Bell's compulsion to understand the ear and the nature of sound seemed to serve as an endless wellspring of ideas. In 1871, after his family emigrated from Scotland to Canada, Bell traveled to Massachusetts and began teaching at the Boston School for the Deaf; two years later, he won an appointment as a professor of elocution at Boston University. It was during this time that his teaching interests and his passion for invention converged. Gardiner Greene Hubbard, a Cambridge, Massachusetts, patent attorney who pioneered deaf education in the state, enrolled his teenage daughter, Mabel, in Bell's class. Hubbard was also an outspoken critic of Western Union, the telegraph monopoly, and he encouraged Bell to create a "multiple telegraph," a machine that would send many messages at once over an existing telegraph wire. The need for a multiple telegraph was obvious. Thomas Edison, among others, was already working on the problem. Bell made it his goal, too. He set out to build a better mousetrap.

Bell had several experiments going at any given time. He'd work late into the night on his inventions in his Boston apartment, teach in the mornings, and attend or give lectures in the afternoon. As a result of all this activity, he quickly made key contacts within the world's leading scientific community. Through colleagues at the Massachusetts Institute of Technology, he was given access to a Helmholtz machine, which employed electromagnets to vibrate a set of tuning forks. In this machine, designed by the great German scientist Hermann von Helmholtz, Bell saw a parallel to the way different vocal pitches caused his family's piano to resonate. In his investigations, he created a new possibility. Why is this machine being used only to generate pitches in a room? Why can't a series of harmonic sounds be transmitted over a wire? If that were possible, it would create an additional problem. You'd need a way to unscramble the resulting electric signals on the receiving end, converting the signals back into continuous sound waves that the ear could process.

In his own lab, Bell built wild and dangerous machines in which the human voice would modulate gas-fueled flames, a crude attempt to enable his students to "see" sound. One of his follow-on experiments involved a human ear cut from a corpse. As he spoke into the ear, he would watch the tiny bones inside vibrate. He attached a piece of straw to one of the bones and rigged the other end of the straw so that it would trace the vibrating patterns on a charcoal slate. All the puzzles and possibilities that Bell created were building up in his mind. If sound waves themselves were powerful enough to move the straw, Bell wrote in his journals in 1874, why couldn't they control an electrical current? He had arrived at his breakthrough concept.

Bell's half-successful experiments led him to believe that he had found a way for *continuous* patterns of electricity to carry almost any type of sound over wires. Edison and others took other paths toward the same end at about the same time, but it was Bell who seemed to understand the potential most deeply. His unique perspective gave him the edge he needed to compete with the more professional inventors. With the assistance of Hubbard, who soon became his father-in-law, Bell in 1876 filed for a patent on his "improvement in telegraphy," only hours before rival inventor Elisha Gray, co-founder of Western Electric, filed an affidavit stating he intended to build something remarkably similar. Bell's application would go on to become the single most valuable patent in history.

Bell's method, however, was anything but a linear progression—the first problem leading to a second, leading to a third, and so on. Instead, his diverse investigations led to an explosion of puzzles, a simultaneous eruption of new possibilities that sent him down parallel paths that he eventually connected. He saw that all these small problems were part of a bigger opportunity that pointed to a new solution. His work with the deaf, his observation of acoustical instruments, and the development of his own instruments gave rise to possibilities that Bell was able to join together in his mind. In retrospect, he seemed destined to be the one to make sense of it all, channeling all this creativity into the telephone. But none of it was predestined, as he would later attest. Aleck Bell got there only because he kept creating the right kind of possibilities along the way.

MINDING THE GAP

The better mousetrap, the hopeful niche, the epochal breakthrough, the lucky strike—all kinds of inventions can emerge after a possibility is created. In each case, it's also essential to exaggerate the potential of the invention—not to fool people but to make the strongest possible case for undertaking the project in the first place. The key to creating radically new possibilities worthy of equally radically new manifestations is to imagine a giant gap between what is there before your eyes and what one day might be. That's what Aleck Bell did, and it is what Woody Norris is still doing.

Norris was certainly not the only person to conjure diagnostic ultrasound. But he did see just how primitive the stethoscope was. The gap between what was and what could be was enormous, as he saw it back then. Yet he readily admits that when he was building his flashlight-sized ultrasound emitter he didn't envision the final product or most of the implications of the revolution he had a small hand in starting. "To me, it was just for listening," he says. "I didn't even know that they'd one day put pictures on it."

The careers of Norris and Bell have interesting similarities. Both began as amateur inventors. Both lacked advanced training in their chosen field. Both went about creating possibilities in the realm of sound and hearing. After filing for his seminal patent, Bell spent the next fifteen years developing follow-on improvements to the telephone. Norris, meanwhile, also stuck to problems in the same general area. In 1980, he started American Technology Corporation, based in San Diego, California, to develop and market his inventions.

Shortly thereafter, his work on the radial tracking tone arm led to the creation of another possibility in his mind. He had loved transistor radios from the moment he saw his first one more than a quarter century earlier. But he recognized that these devices were still too big and heavy because the batteries took up too much space and weight. Why not eliminate the batteries, and see how small and light a radio could really be?

The possibility he imagined was this: Adapt the radio transmitter that he had created for the tone arm to create the world's smallest consumer radio. "Here's where I came up with the idea," he recalls. "If you've got a guitar, tune two strings to the same note. Pluck one. The other will start to vibrate. Since nothing is free in the universe, the second one had to derive energy from someplace. So the first string has got to be losing energy. What if I did that with an electronic circuit?" Norris was noticing the phenomenon of sympathetic vibration, exactly the same principle that Aleck Bell noticed in his family's piano, knowledge that led to the invention of the telephone.

Now Norris was going to apply that same knowledge to the creation of another possibility. He knew that electromagnetic waves—radio waves—are a form of low-level energy in and of themselves. Why not use that energy to replace the batteries and actually power the radio? "What if I built a little radio transmitter? I have a little rod that picks up a radio signal." Just as a guitar string or a piano string steals energy from voices or notes in the air, the rod would be stealing energy from the airwaves.

The result was indeed the world's tiniest FM radio; it was tuned by pressing a button that scans for the next strongest signal on the dial. Shorter than your thumb, thin enough to clip inside your ear, the device weighed a quarter of an ounce. Norris distributed the product through Technoscout (formerly Comtrad Industries), a catalog company that sold thousands of these FM Sounds branded devices, at about $29 each. This invention didn't change the world, but Norris had created a new possibility, and it turned out that lots of people wanted this better mousetrap. Invention proved again to be the mother of necessity.[13]

But that product and others were merely warm-ups to what would become, by far, his greatest invention in sound. Employing the same method that he discovered within himself as a young man, Norris in 1988 created another possibility for a radically new hi-fi system. Everything in the system, he observed, was composed of microelectronics and digital components—everything, that is, except the speakers. In Norris's mind, even the best and the smallest speakers on the market remained crude, mechanical, bulky, and subject to distortion. He set out not to improve speakers but to eliminate them. As we'll see when we pick up the story of Woody Norris again in chapter 7, it would take him fifteen years to deliver on this new possibility.

TAKING FLIGHT

Perhaps the most uncanny similarity between Bell and Norris has nothing to do with sound. Both inventors, oddly enough, suddenly turned from that field toward one that seemed totally unrelated. From the 1890s onward, now wealthy and world-famous for his invention of the telephone, Bell lived year-round at his "dreaming place," his Victorian estate in Braddeck, Nova Scotia, high on a bluff overlooking the ocean. There, he built and launched multidimensional kites aimed at an understanding of the problems and principles of flight. He was beaten to the solution, of course, by a couple of brothers from Ohio who also started as amateur, part-time inventors. But the possibilities of flight continued to fascinate him for the rest of his life.

A century later, Woody Norris would also take up his own imagined possibilities for flight. If an inventor could find a new way to make sound travel through the air, why not find a new way for objects to do so as well? One day, Norris happened to be on an airplane flying to Hong Kong, sitting next to a man who was saying how cool it was that people could travel around the world in a matter of hours.

"You really believe that?" Norris said.

The man nodded.

"Let me tell you what I think," Norris said. "This bucket of bolts is screaming through the air in order to stay airborne. In order to *get* airborne, it has to go the better part of a mile down a runway like a goose trying to get out of the water. It is pure brute force. Then when you land, you are taking your life in your hands. This thing is practically vibrating the luggage out of the overhead racks. The wheels are smoking. What a crude, terrible, mechanical way to get around. Here we are at the beginning of the twenty-first century, and it's truly embarrassing. I believe in the next five to seven years, we're going to figure out gravity, and . . . airports will be obsolete. We haven't even discovered most of the fundamental properties of physics yet. It's just awful."

Norris was imagining new possibilities for the airplane itself. The chance conversation helped him verbalize these ideas. Later, he would attempt to realize this possibility. But the mere fact that inventors like him can deploy their thinking strategies across different fields and different technological domains says something powerful about these habits. Inventors know how to ask new questions, pose new puzzles, construct a mental model of the predicament, and create in their minds a wide range of possible solutions. They might try to imagine how big the impact could be. But if everything works as planned, their imaginations will likely fall short.

CHAPTER 2

Pinpointing Problems

Since the advent of the cube, people all over the world have asked for help, saying that as I posed the puzzle, I must know the best solution. But this is a misunderstanding!

For me, it was more interesting to find the problem than to solve it, although, of course, I know that practice in solving problems helps us formulate new ones.

—Ernö Rubik

INVENTORS ARE USUALLY THOUGHT of as people who are good at *solving* problems, but they should be thought of foremost as people who are good at *finding* problems. Inventors spend considerable effort hunting for a challenge that matches their own set of skills. Some inventors uncover a problem that no one else has seen. Others pick a solvable piece of a larger problem. Still others redefine the predicament so thoroughly that they turn a known problem into something that was at least partially hidden. If the inventor doesn't pinpoint the problem correctly, then all the effort he and others expend pondering the solution could be wasted. The inventor might create something that no one really needs, or she might take on an impossible task. As Nobel Prize–winning physicist and inventor

Albert Michelson attested, "Knowing what kind of problem it is worthwhile to attack is, in general, more important than the mere carrying out of the necessary steps."[1]

Ernö Rubik imparts the same wisdom. "To formulate the problem and to solve it are not the same thing," he notes.[2] In posing his cube in 1974, the Hungarian industrial designer worked on a variety of construction techniques and a variety of forms, all the while asking himself the question, How can I create the most challenging problem that is solvable in a variety of ways? He settled on a three-by-three-by-three-face cube, with fifty-four squares total, as the ideal challenge. "If the number is decreased, some of these qualities will be lost," he wrote. "If it is increased, no new quality is gained." He applied for a patent on his "magic cube," licensed it to a local manufacturer, and sold one million units in Hungary alone, a number that is remarkable for a country of only ten million people. After it was exported through an American toy company in 1980, Rubik's Cube became a worldwide sensation. The lesson: The human mind likes taking on challenging problems, but pinpointing such problems requires a special skill.

Jay Walker, founder and chairman of Walker Digital, a business innovation laboratory based in Stamford, Connecticut, works constantly on developing this skill. Walker is a high-energy thinker who reads voraciously, watches no television, and seems to love nothing more than to hyperfocus on someone else's problems. Whenever Walker hires new inventors for his laboratory staff, he hands them a new Rubik's Cube to keep on their desks as a way of showing them what a tough problem looks like. It's one of the few employee policies at Walker Digital. To Walker, the puzzle's objective seems simple enough: You must align all the cube's squares so that each side displays a single color, either red, yellow, green, or blue. But solving the puzzle isn't as easy as it appears. "Here's a six-sided figure," Walker says, "and getting five of them right doesn't help you. Just when you think you've got one side perfect, another side is out of kilter. It's a perfectly accessible metaphor for what we do [at Walker Digital]. But it's just a metaphor, because most things are much more complex than a Rubik's Cube."[3]

Problems that require invention often have many sides. "If you can't find at least six sides to a problem," Walker says, "you're not looking hard enough." Over his career, he has developed a knack for finding and defining problems in original ways. He is always teaching the inventors on his staff how to do it, while picking up new approaches from them. "We focus a lot on problem definition," Walker says. "Most inventors haven't learned to spend time thinking about the problem. They're too busy thinking about the damn solution. It's a big mistake."

FINDING MULTIDIMENSIONAL PROBLEMS

To show more precisely how this process of pinpointing problems works, Walker cites a recent invention. He decided to enter the problem space of what is called *noncompliance*: the failure of patients to take medicine their doctors have prescribed. Many elderly people, for example, don't take their blood pressure pills. Why not? What can be done? "It's a huge problem," Walker says.

The magnitude of the problem is underlined by Peter Corr, vice president of research and development at Pfizer. The pharmaceutical giant spends more money on R&D than any other company in the world. At any given time, it has several hundred new drugs in various phases of discovery research. Yet it has little control over how patients use its products or whether they follow their doctors' orders. "With many medicines," Corr says, "if patients are noncompliant, the medicine is not effective."[4] He cites the anticholesterol drug Lipitor—Pfizer's top-selling product—as one example of a pill with an especially large noncompliance problem.

As it turns out, this problem has many facets, according to Walker. The most obvious facet is that patients put their own health in jeopardy. Another facet is the billions of dollars lost by drug companies because people take fewer pills than prescribed. Yet another facet is the cost to health-maintenance organizations of noncompliance, costs such as increased hospitalization and doctor visits. Still another facet is the stress at the families of patients, who are worried and upset about their loved ones.

Making this problem especially gnarly, many maladies, such as high blood pressure or high cholesterol, have no outward symptoms. Patients typically do not feel pain or discomfort. Eventually, the unnoticed damage caused by these conditions might cause a heart attack, but the idea is to alleviate the condition before that happens.

Isn't the solution obvious? "The classic M.B.A.-type solution would be to send the patients e-mail reminders to take their medicine," Walker says. "Or let's program their cell phones or PDAs to go off twice a day to take their medicine." But those ideas reveal a complete misunderstanding of the nature of the problem. "Those kinds of solutions would appeal to someone who wasn't taught how to think about problem definition," he says. "Silicon Valley is guilty of this all the time. They define problems through a technological prism." People focused on a particular technology often "ignore human behavior," he says. "During [the Internet boom of the late 1990s], anything could get funded, because [venture capitalists] didn't think about the real problems. They just said, 'This could happen, why don't we do this?'"

Thinking in a more focused way, Walker concluded that the problem wasn't that people weren't taking their medicine but rather that people were not *motivated* to take their medicine. "That's a different issue," he says. "Let's take it even further. The problem is that there is no immediate reward for taking your medicine. The medicine literally doesn't make them feel better. Most people do not behave without tangible rewards, without the feedback element. If we don't see the benefits of doing something, we will stop the behavior. That's just human nature. So the real problem is that you don't see any benefit in taking the pill."

Pinpointing the problem in this way, Walker was able to come up with a unique solution. "Our solution is to build a slot machine right into the bottle cap of the blood pressure medication, with a chip in it. So if you open the bottle at the right time, twice a day, the LCD's lights spin, and you can win a $5,000 prize immediately."

Like many new ideas, this one seems crazy. Turning medicine bottles into slot machines? What could be more ridiculous? But if you walk into a casino, you can watch all the people lined up at the slot machines. Notice that a disproportionate share of these people are over the age of sixty. Start to think about the human motivations behind the exploding use of slot machines. Walker has done this, and so has James Jorasch, the invention operations chief at Walker Digital. Jorasch spent the early part of his career in Las Vegas, studying customer behavior as an analyst and game developer for Tropicana Resorts.

Walker and Jorasch described the precise workings of this idea in a patent application. They explained how this mini slot machine would operate in conjunction with the medicine bottle and how the slot machine would be programmed to work only during predetermined windows of time. They described the operations of the slot machine itself, along with the lottery system that would administer the prize money. They explained how the winner would be flashed a special code number to use in claiming the prize. They even described how winners would receive a drug test the next day to verify that the drug was in their bloodstream.

Walker and Jorasch believe that this slot machine–activated drug bottle is a good example of their method of developing "business-driven patents." These kinds of patents derive directly from business problems and goals rather than from technology. The process of finding such problems begins with looking through a behavioral prism, not a technological prism. Walker aims to align his inventions with strong and universal *behaviorial* traits that he calls "superforces," and gambling is one such superforce.[5]

Next, the inventor must understand in a comprehensive way who benefits from the problem and who would benefit from the solution, says Walker. The inventor then determines whether solving the problem would be a good bet in terms of investment of the company's resources and the potential return. Critical to this process are feedback loops, such as focus groups or early assessments and reactions from those who would be affected by the solution. The process doesn't necessarily involve building a working prototype. It's immensely helpful to be able to demonstrate inventions, but it isn't required or necessary in order to obtain a patent.

Walker became convinced that the slot machine–activated drug bottle was a good bet that would likely be licensed and used by a drug company, a drugstore chain, or another interested party. One question that he left up in the air was where the $5,000 and other prize money would come from. But Walker is confident that so much money could be saved from reducing noncompliance that drug companies, HMOs, or employers would gladly fund this system if it prevented heart attacks and other costly health failures. The relatives of the patients may even want to contribute. "Who is financially motivated to pay?" Walker asks. "If I can get my mother to take the medicine, and all I have to do is pay $1 per month to fund the payouts, I'd do it in a heartbeat, no pun intended."

Whether or not this invention works in practice, there is no doubt that Walker found an inventive way to pinpoint a problem in a fertile area. Pfizer's Peter Corr says that 50 percent of healthcare costs are related to behavioral issues, such as overeating, lack of exercise, smoking, and noncompliance with prescription orders. If inventors can come up with solutions that alter people's behavior, they can strike gold and save lives at the same time. But that can be accomplished only by finding the real problem beneath the surface.

FINDING IT THE HARD WAY

A critical aspect of pinpointing problems is assessing whether it's a good bet to work on a given problem. Will a solution be received well by the market? Will the payoff justify the effort and expense? For his first patented invention, Thomas Edison learned the hard way about the relative merits of picking one problem over another. After working as a roving telegraph operator, traveling by rail from town to town in search of higher-paying stints, the twenty-one-year-old Edison ended up applying for a full-time position with the Western Union company in Boston. By the time he arrived in town, in 1868, he had invented various improvements to telegraph receivers, but he had not yet patented anything.[6]

In his off-hours working for the telegraph monopoly, Edison moonlighted, searching for problems that might require invention. One evening, while attending a session of the Massachusetts legislature in Boston's gold-domed state house, he noticed how inefficient the process was for tabulating votes among the representatives. The roll call was chaotic and confusing. Obtaining a simple count using handwritten ballots could take hours.

Based on his experience working with devices to record and transmit information, Edison became convinced that this was a problem he could solve. He ended up building an ingenious device: an electric vote recorder. Each member of the legislature would position a switch at his seat in one of two positions: yea or nay. The decisions would be relayed by wires to the machine, which would instantly record the votes on rolls of treated paper using a special electrochemical process. The machine would then tabulate the overall result.

But when Edison paid a sales call to the legislature, one of the senior members listened to the pitch and exclaimed, "This is exactly what we do not want!" The chaotic delays that happened during the roll call served a purpose, the politician said. This time was reserved for arguing, bargaining, filibustering, and cajoling other members into switching their votes. "Your invention would not only destroy the only hope the minority would have in influencing legislation," said one representative, "it would deliver them over—bound hand and foot—to the majority."

Edison didn't anticipate this. He failed to take into account a major facet of the problem: Who benefits from the current way of doing things? The main users of the invention might not see it as an improvement. They might push back. They might feel threatened by it. The interests of various groups of users are always key parts of any problem that requires invention. These are exactly the kinds of questions that Jay Walker has learned to ask before he chooses which problems to solve and how. How does the invention affect each of the stakeholders in the problem?

For his part, Edison encapsulated the lesson in a much more straightforward way: "Never waste time inventing things that people would not want to buy," he wrote. Of course, some inventions are simply ahead of their time and eventually will be accepted. But building and selling voting machines has always been an uphill battle. The political system is not only perpetually short of money but sometimes also corrupt, and it's usually hesitant to adopt better technologies for fear of giving one side or another an unfair advantage. Is it a good bet to attack the problem of voting inefficiency? Clearly not. This seemingly straightforward problem remains with us today. During the disputed U.S. presidential election in 2000, some commentators noted the irony that the greatest inventor who ever lived once provided a solution that was rejected by the market.

For his next invention, Edison was determined to choose a problem that had better odds of success. After giving up his Western Union job and relocating to New York City, which he considered "more commercially minded" than Boston, Edison stumbled upon an opportunity. Wandering through offices near Wall Street in search of employment, he met the manager of a brokerage firm, who was in a panic because his ticker machine was broken. The Gold Indicator Company made its living by supplying price quotes for gold to banks and traders. When Edison stepped in to replace a loose spring and got the device working again after only a few minutes, he was instantly offered a $300-per-week job to manage, fix, and tinker with the firm's machines. He quickly learned that the market for gold as well as stocks was swinging so wildly that these specialized telegraph receivers commonly failed under the strain. On Black Friday, September 24, 1869, when robber baron Jay Gould raided the gold market and set off widespread panic, Edison watched from a balcony at the stock exchange as thousands of traders lost fortunes because they couldn't keep up with current prices.

Edison had found a good bet, a problem worthy of his time and effort. He came away from the Black Friday experience realizing that selling information about the value of gold was worth more than the gold itself. He witnessed firsthand the primal superforces of greed and fear. All the players in the market wanted better information more quickly, and any technology that could accomplish that would command a huge price.

He immediately placed a notice in a trade newspaper, the *Telegrapher*: "T. A. Edison has resigned from his situation and will devote his time to bringing out his inventions." When he completed his improved stock ticker machine and filed for a patent on the device, Edison took his invention to the Gold & Stock Telegraph Company. He had planned to ask for $5,000 in return for the patent rights, thinking he would settle for $3,000. When the head of the company offered to write a check for $40,000 to back a new firm to manufacture the machines, legend has it that Edison nearly fainted. He opened Newark Telegraph Works in New Jersey, hired fifty workers, and used the profits from the venture to pinpoint and solve new problems. This was the birth of Edison's first professional R&D laboratory.

PLAYING GAMES WITH PROBLEMS

The first thing you notice when you walk into the office of Jay Walker is an authentic Edison stock ticker machine made at that Newark factory. The apparatus sits on an oak base under a glass dome. Walker purchases collectibles such as these at auctions and estate sales. Also scattered about his office are a giant roulette wheel from 1900, one of the earliest typewriting machines, an original Enigma code–breaking machine from World War II, a dinosaur fossil, a moon rock brought back by *Apollo 12*, a set of Civil War surgical instruments, and a complete atlas of the world from 1620. Hanging on the walls are original documents, including a fifteenth-century illuminated manuscript, John D. Rockefeller's controlling stock certificate in the Standard Oil Trust, President Nixon's resignation letter, and a $100,000 bonus check from Thomas Edison to his staff, paid to the order of "ourselves."

Why has Walker amassed all this memorabilia related to the power of ideas and information? Actually, it's common among the inventors you'll meet in this book to collect remarkably similar objects. "Inventors make their living on their wits," Walker explains. "They admire the way other people have solved problems. Inventors are always looking for ways to stimulate their minds and open their thinking. It's a lot like going to a writer's house and noticing he has a lot of books. Every writer I visit! I can't understand why! It must be something about writers! Yeah, it pretty much is!"

But perhaps more than most inventors, Walker collects business artifacts as well as inventions. He has always combined his interest in finding and solving problems with the associated business opportunities. Growing up in Yonkers, New York, in the 1960s, he opened a laboratory in a spare closet, where he built model rockets, ships, and airplanes. By the age of ten, he was having hot times with a soldering iron, ordering build-it-yourself Heathkits to learn how to make volt meters, oscilloscopes, radios, TVs, stereos, microwave ovens, and slot cars. Heathkits were filled with electronic and mechanical parts that could be assembled in many different ways.

As a teenager, Walker honed his skills as a door-to-door salesman, peddling greeting cards, jam, and magazine and newspaper subscriptions. Later he took a leave from Cornell University to start his own local newspaper, quickly ramping up to one hundred fifty employees and competing head-to-head with Gannett for readers and advertising revenue.

Throughout his career, Walker has consistently drawn lessons from makers of games and puzzles, on the theory that a good game or puzzle is an example of a well-defined problem. He also likes to find flaws in problem definitions. A national Monopoly champion during his college years, Walker was once sued, unsuccessfully, by Parker Brothers to prevent him and his sophomore roommate, Jeffrey S. Lehman (who twenty years later would be named president of Cornell), from publishing a how-to book that showed that Monopoly was a game of skill and not chance, as claimed on the box. "Monopoly is a balance of power game," Walker says. The skill relates to the trading of the properties. If you have three or more players, you can use trading techniques to alter the balance of power in your favor and encourage the other players to destroy one another. Having this kind of knowledge is an unfair advantage of sorts, and it might explain why Parker Brothers was upset.

That experience led to a lesson: Defining challenges in a unique way provides a competitive advantage. "As an entrepreneur, I always selected or invented businesses that were different," Walker says. "I always liked having the unfair advantage that comes when you can create your own category. Now you're not competing directly. It's like the principle from *The Art of War*. If you attack directly, you better have overwhelming force. If you attack indirectly, or solve problems uniquely, you exploit weaknesses." [7]

Walker applied that lesson to the publishing business. While working as associate publisher at *Folio*, the magazine for the magazine industry, he homed in on a problem that he believed applied to almost every consumer magazine title on the market: getting the largest number of subscribers to renew each year at the lowest possible cost. Working with a partner, Michael Loeb, Walker modeled the problem from all sides and came up with a solution: Sell a subscription discounted at a special rate for those who pay by credit card. At the time (1991), very few magazine subscribers paid by credit card, so this was a novel idea. The method also involved keeping the card numbers on file and sending annual notifications stating that the subscription was being automatically renewed and offering subscribers the choice of opting out.

This "continuous service" method indeed proved successful at retaining a higher percentage of readers at a lower cost than the method of soliciting and processing checks. Walker and Loeb eventually sold the resulting service, now called Synapse, to Time Warner in a deal worth nearly $600 million. Loeb stayed on as CEO of what is now one of the world's largest magazine subscription agencies. Walker, meanwhile, had already started his invention laboratory. Some of the first patents he filed were on certain aspects of the Synapse business model, and those patents were key assets bundled with the deal. Instead of competing with American Family Publishers, Publishers Clearing House, and other such agencies directly by using the brute force of mass mailings, Walker and Loeb chose a very specific problem and solved it in a unique way. Using a novel idea enabled them to leapfrog the competition.

Pinpointing a New Process

This approach to finding problems has found fertile ground on the World Wide Web. In the mid-1990s, Walker was among the first to understand that the Internet had attributes that could help solve a wide range of problems in new ways, provided that the problems themselves were rigorously defined. One of the areas that Walker targeted was online travel reservation services.

Obviously, consumers wanted cheaper airline tickets. But the existing systems didn't allow consumers to express what they would trade off to get those cheaper prices. Perhaps they would be willing to be more flexible about their flight times and the number of connections they'd have to make. The airlines, meanwhile, didn't have a good way of unloading unsold airline seats (called *excess capacity*) without undercutting the pricing structure of the other seats on the airplane. Walker calls this "the markdown paradox." If this paradox could be solved, then revenue could be boosted without an impact on the high fixed costs of running the business.

Although the Internet absolutely enabled the success of the idea, Walker's invention itself was the result of pinpointing this multidimensional problem in the first place. Like a Rubik's Cube of sorts, the airlines were one side of the puzzle, consumers were another side, the Internet yet another, credit cards another, traditional marketing channels such as 800 numbers another, and electronic ticketing another. Walker conceived Priceline.com as an intricate system, a process in which all the sides would click into place. In 1998, after convincing several major airlines to sell this way and after convincing millions of consumers to buy this way, Walker suddenly became famous as the entrepreneur who created Priceline.

The value of Walker's "name your own price" business method, however, has often been misunderstood. At first it was underestimated, then wildly overhyped, and then taken for granted by millions of people. Walker has been consistently amazed that many people miss what Priceline really is and the reasoning behind it. Many people view Priceline as only one of numerous Web sites where they can complete a task, but Walker considers it an invention in the classic sense.

His patent on "buyer-driven commerce" generated immense controversy in the business world when it was issued in August 1998.[8] Most people didn't realize that such an intangible service could receive patent protection. But similar concepts have been patented; chemical processes, for example, have been patentable for more than a century. The confusion stems from the fact that the patent system has been so deeply rooted in the electromechanical world that most people, including patent examiners, couldn't imagine that such intangible inventions could be protected in the same way.

To many who follow patent law, this confusion was finally erad-
icated only a month before Walker's patent was issued. That's when
State Street Bank won a patent infringement lawsuit against Signa-
ture Financial. In dispute was the bank's method of pooling assets in
an investment portfolio organized as a partnership. The decision, by
the U. S. Court of Appeals for the Federal Circuit, had revolutionary
implications: It meant that business processes such as frequent flier
programs (invented by American Airlines) and credit cards (invented
by Bank of America) could have been patented.

Yet when Walker's patent efforts came to light, people misunderstood the wider implications of what he was doing. In some circles, it was becoming conventional wisdom that you could obtain
patents on Web sites themselves. That, of course, isn't true. The brand
names on Web sites can be protected by trademarks, and the content posted on Web pages is automatically protected by copyrights,
but patents are reserved for ideas that pass the invention tests of the
patent office: The idea must be useful, nontrivial, nonobvious, and
original. The form the invention takes is not important. Software-
based inventions, for example, have been considered patentable ever
since a U.S. Supreme Court decision in 1981 affirmed that right.

Meanwhile, the buyers and sellers who began using Priceline saw
the problem only after it was solved. Like a completed Rubik's Cube,
it seemed simple. Consumers began taking it for granted, just as they
do with most successful inventions. The acclaim that Walker received
had more to do with the multibillion-dollar valuation on his new
enterprise than with his success as an inventor. "An entrepreneur is
high in the pecking order; an inventor is low," he says. "I don't think
I received acclaim because I was clever. Except maybe in business
school classrooms, where they would deconstruct the theory of the
idea. They'd say, 'Wow, what an interesting market-making exercise
to capture a unit of demand, strip it of its identity, and allow the
seller to grab the unit of demand on a first-come-first-served basis.'
But the general public doesn't view Priceline as an invention. They
view it as one of many solutions they can choose."

Yet Priceline became one of the few start-ups that thrived in the
dot-com era and then survived the subsequent market shakeout. It
did so precisely because it filled an untapped need and delivered

value to buyers as well as sellers, and because the central concept was granted limited monopoly status by the patent system. In its first five years in business, Priceline sold $4 billion worth of airline seats, rental cars, hotel rooms, and other services to ten million consumers worldwide.

After running Priceline for its first couple of years, Walker resigned from the company, transferred the service to offices in a nearby location, and went back to running Walker Digital full-time, doing what he likes best: finding new problems to solve. For now, Priceline may be the most famous of the hundreds of inventions that Walker and his teams of inventors have devised. But most of the inventions that come from this unique laboratory begin in exactly the same way: as well-defined problems.

NARROWING THE PROBLEM

Very few of the inventors at Walker Digital are engineers. Typically, they are marketers, doctors, scientists, salespeople, poets, or writers. "We hire people who like to think for a living," Walker says. "They usually have good creativity and verbal skills. They've often had a lot of failures, a lot of real-world experience. They've tried to build things that haven't worked. They know they can make it work, but they don't yet know how." When Walker does hire engineers and programmers, they are usually assigned to the operating companies that are spun off from the laboratory to take their inventions to market.

Given the diverse nature of these teams, it's not surprising that invention happens here in noisy group sessions. Ideas are hashed out on white boards with lots of flowcharts, before teams of hypercritical people. "All of our inventions are team efforts," says Walker. "If you think you've solved a piece of the puzzle, you bring it to the group, and you declare, 'I've got a piece of it!' Then we argue about how it fits into the system. We argue a lot."

By at least one numerical measure, Walker's process of pinpointing problems is well on its way toward becoming history's most successful method of inventing. To date, the record for the sheer number of inventions still belongs to Thomas Edison, whose name appeared on 1,098 U.S. patents, the first one filed when he was twenty-one and the last one shortly before his death at eighty-four. At his famous New Jersey laboratories in Newark, Menlo Park, and West Orange, Edison also convened groups of creative individuals. As the master inventor of the house, he put his name on all the filings. That's Walker's policy, too. "I serve as the captain of the inventing teams," he says. In recent years, he has been averaging about one hundred patent filings annually. With more than two hundred fifty issued patents and more than six hundred pending, he will most likely exceed Edison's record before very long. "Assuming I live long enough, I should pass that," Walker says. "It would be surprising if I didn't. But other inventors will do it, too."

Over time, Walker Digital has focused the efforts of its invention shop on several targeted problem areas. Casinos, and especially slot machines, are one strain of Walker's patent activity. He believes that current generation slot machines are lackluster. He wonders, for example, why winning is based on sheer chance. Why isn't skill a factor in winning at slots? Cash registers are another problem area. Why do cashiers give customers their change? Why not find a systematic way to offer additional products in lieu of the money? Vending machines are yet another problem area. Why can't you communicate remotely with a vending machine, or take out an annual subscription to your favorite one? Internet commerce represents another strain of problems, and healthcare is another. Often, Walker's teams invent at the intersection of these strains. That was the case with the slot machine–activated medicine bottle.

But on September 11, 2001, Walker became instantly focused on yet another set of problems. That morning, he was driving to a meeting with dozens of colleagues and business partners in the Woolworth Building, which stands only a couple hundred yards from the site of the World Trade Center. His colleagues witnessed the devastation up close, watching the horror from the office windows. Several people there that day lost friends and family members. Aside from the personal devastation, Walker had a business stake in the crisis. With the major airlines grounded and facing bankruptcy, the travel industry was devastated, and Priceline was teetering on the edge of shutdown in the weeks that followed the attacks.

Like many people, Walker wanted to do something to help. But what? During the massive cleanup over the coming weeks and months, Walker brainstormed. "Hey, we're not going to pass out coffee at the Trade Center site," he says. "It's important, but other people do that. We as a team said, 'We're inventors! This country has a history of citizens solving problems. Somebody has an idea, and says, "Wow, I can build a better bridge. I can make an air brake." If we as citizens don't step up to the plate and contribute our skills, who will? Who is going to solve the problems?'"

For the next several months, Walker and a small team pondered all the problems stemming from the events of September 11. There was no shortage of them, but the team wanted to pinpoint one that they could potentially solve. "The problems were everywhere," he says. "How do you track nuclear material? What about the two million shipping containers that the country receives each week? How do you stop five kilograms of plutonium from coming into a country that can't stop two hundred tons of drugs from coming in every month? How do you screen people trying to sneak into the city with a basketball-sized bomb? How do you prevent illegal immigrants from getting through JFK Airport? One could argue there are tens of thousands of problems, and it didn't take a genius to figure that out." He pauses and then adds, "But we're not defense contractors, so what are we going to invent? We're not going to invent a new radar, or a new detector, or a new electronic antimissile defense. That's not us."

Finally, after nine months of trying to pinpoint a solvable problem, Walker and his team of three other inventors narrowed it to something promising. To Walker, the solvable puzzle area wasn't stopping terrorism per se. Rather, the team defined the problem area as one of national security, broadly speaking. "The nation is not secure," as Walker puts it. His team further narrowed the problem of insecurity to the subproblem of trespassing—more specifically, trespassing in prohibited places where people are almost never supposed to be. Such places might include areas around chemical plants, water reservoirs, nuclear waste dumps, electrical power generators, and the perimeters around airport runways. America has some forty-seven thousand of these vulnerable infrastructure facilities.

Proposing a Solution

Walker admits that this problem is "only one piece of a larger puzzle, and not even the most important one." But his team of inventors became convinced that they were pinpointing something they could solve. To begin, they went through a precise exercise. As Walker explains it, they had to "name in priority order all the people who benefit from the problem, and why. Normally, you think of problems having negative consequences. But crime is a problem. Insurance companies benefit. No crime, no insurance. There's uncertainty in crime, which people don't want. They'd rather have certainty. So you buy insurance against the economic cost of crime."

The same is true for the lack of security around these sensitive prohibited zones. Who (in addition to potential terrorists) benefits from the fact that there is little or no security around reservoirs? One example is people who like to fish. Often they're not supposed to fish or boat in certain reservoirs, but sometimes they do. Who benefits from unpatrolled areas around electricity-generation stations? Teenagers who like to make out and not get caught. "Are these significant beneficiaries? No," Walker says. "Are those beneficiaries going to counterattack if we were to solve the problem? Not likely. But solving a problem often engenders a counterattack." This insight mirrors the case of Edison's voting machine. "You have to evaluate the counterattack. If you misunderstand the counterattack, you misunderstand the stakeholders in the problem."

As his team was devising a solution, Walker met with some of the significant stakeholders. Among them were local reservoir management officials. He found that those officials didn't want to spend money on a solution for making their reservoirs more secure. "They're the ones who counterattack," Walker says. "They say, 'This isn't necessary. We'd have to raise utility bills. The mayor and consumers will scream at us. This isn't good.'" In one meeting, Walker posed this question: "What if someone throws poison into the reservoir?" The official replied, "You don't understand water dynamics. If you throw poison into the reservoir, it would be diluted to the point that it wouldn't be unsafe."

Walker was surprised. "Let me understand this," he said. "Someone throws a satchel of an unknown substance in a reservoir, and you want to get on television and say that the toxicity seems to be well below the levels we're worried about? Everyone should drink the water? Don't worry? You clearly don't understand people, if you think anyone is going to drink the water." Again, Walker was viewing the problem through a behavioral prism—this time tapping into the superforce of security and safety.

He went through the same exercise with airport security officials. Although passenger screening was boosted and taken very seriously in the wake of 9-11, far less was being done to secure the perimeter of the airports themselves. Walker asked one security manager, "What if someone fires a shoulder-launched missile at an airplane?" The manager replied, "That's very hard to do. It's almost impossible to hit an airplane with a shoulder-launched missile." Walker agreed but added, "That's not the issue. They can miss. That's just fine. They don't *have* to hit it." "What do you mean?" the official asked. "How many people are going to get on airplanes after someone has fired a missile at one?" Walker said. "You'll knock out a third of the demand overnight. Last time I checked, you knock a third of the demand out of the civil airline system, they're all bankrupt tomorrow. You don't have to hit the airplane."

Walker continued to narrow the problem even further. The problem he could address wasn't terrorism and it wasn't security, broadly speaking. The problem was consumer confidence. There needed to be higher confidence in homeland security, at least for the areas that Walker would be addressing with his new invention.

The resulting invention, called U.S. HomeGuard, is a system that connects the thousands of current and future security cameras located in these prohibited zones to the Internet. The cameras peer out at miles of fences around plants, power stations, reservoirs, airports, and other sensitive spots where humans aren't supposed to be.

Instead of hiring thousands of security guards to patrol these areas or hiring professional security personnel at an average cost of $25 per hour, Walker suggests the use of a distributed, decentralized approach: Pay ordinary citizens sitting in their homes $10 per hour to view snapshots taken by the cameras. If they see anything suspicious, such as a trespasser, they click a button and send that image data to a small cluster of professional security people.

The HomeGuard system contains step-by-step protocols for providing security at low cost. The steps include capturing the images, concealing the location identity, uploading the images instantly to the Internet, sending the snapshots at random to thousands of people around the country, mixing the images with occasional test images of suspicious activity to verify the alertness of these citizens, collecting votes as to whether anything unusual is happening in the real images, and sending the suspicious ones to professionals who can view the location identity. For the cost of a penny a picture, humans act as "judgment filters" in this system, Walker says. "The human brain is the best pattern recognizer ever built. You know the difference between a tree and a person dressed up as a tree. You instantly know the difference between a dog and person dressed like a dog. Software can't do this."

This technology incorporates a patent-pending method called "digital piecework," which could also be applied to sending X-ray and MRI images to doctors all over the world for dozens of opinions on a patient's condition. In the case of HomeGuard, security professionals who receive suspicious images would question the intruders by speaking into a microphone that feeds to the camera. If the answer is not satisfactory, armed guards would be dispatched immediately to the scene.

One might expect a counterattack from privacy advocates. Walker has anticipated that. Because U.S. HomeGuard would capture images only from places where people aren't supposed to be, who can argue that privacy is being violated? Another issue Walker has addressed is the question of who is going to pay for it. Walker believes that HomeGuard not only would provide low-cost security to these unpatrolled areas but also would lower the insurance premiums paid by these facilities. If you lower the risks involved, you should be able to get cheaper insurance.

Who is going to fund the development of U.S. HomeGuard? Walker has met with officials from the Department of Homeland Security as well as the CIA and has offered to license his patents on the system to the government for $1. "We don't need to profit from making the nation safer," he says. If no private contractor is willing to build a pilot, Walker plans to build one himself, under government contract, just to prove it would work. But then he wants to hand it over. "Maybe IBM or EDS could run the large-scale system," he says.

Again, Walker and his team have devised something that sounds a little crazy at first. Put ordinary citizens to work keeping an eye on possible terrorism targets? It sounds promising only when you consider how rigorously well defined the problem is. All the citizens have to do is to spot humans in the photos and report these photos to security professionals. Use the Internet as a national security system? It may or may not work. Like all successful inventions, this one will sound plausible only after it's put into practice. Only then will it be taken for granted as something that was obvious all along.

CHAPTER 3

Recognizing Patterns

Invention establishes relationships that did not previously exist. In its barest essence, the element of innovation lies in the completion of a pattern or in the improvement of a pattern that was unsatisfactory and inadequate.

—A. P. USHER, *A History of Mechanical Inventions*

PATTERN RECOGNITION is the act of making sense of complexity. Patterns enable us to anticipate what will happen next.

The human brain is the world's best pattern recognition machine. It identifies faces and voices. It spots familiar shapes among clouds and stars or in wallpaper designs and ceiling tiles. It can create new musical forms and artistic figures. It enjoys the patterns of jokes and dramas, especially the unexpected twists. It tries to interpret the logic of its own dreams or to see parallels between current events and historical ones. It can recognize winning patterns on the chessboard and in other games. With the help of computers, it can model trends in crime or the weather. It can diagnose diseases and try to find ways to prevent them. It can make money by recognizing a new investment or business trend.

Invention is commonly considered to be a product of an inexplicable leap of insight. When viewed more closely, though, great inspirations are often less mysterious than they might otherwise seem. New solutions often are found in the recognition of new patterns. Rather than being inhibited by prior knowledge, this thinking tool shows that past experience is often integral to the incubation of insights. We're often told that breakthrough innovators are the ones operating outside the box. On the contrary, inventors are the ones who learn to recognize boxes or other patterns in the first place. Inventors are constantly searching the world for patterns that can be reapplied and extended.

As Abbot Payton Usher suggests in a classic 1929 book, the history of invention is one of finding new patterns and then improving or completing them.[1] Building on that point is architect Christopher Alexander. In his 1977 book *A Pattern Language*, Alexander observes that "each pattern describes a problem which occurs over and over again in our environment."[2] But as with many important patterns that have been discovered, he notes, "no pattern is an isolated entity. Each pattern can exist only to the extent that it is supported by other patterns: the larger patterns in which it is embedded, and the smaller patterns which are embedded in it." New patterns describe "the core of new solutions."

In the world of biology, the double helix is a granddaddy of a pattern, solving a great mystery but also giving birth to thousands of new ones. "It was a scientist's dream," remarked one biologist, "simple, elegant, and universal for all organisms."[3] But it could very well have been found by someone other than James Watson and Francis Crick. The soon-to-be famous duo was in a race with other scientists. Like fifteenth-century mapmakers, they were using both theory and real-world observation to find a fundamental pattern, a new way of looking at the available knowledge. The already legendary chemist Linus Pauling was hot on the trail. Only a few months beforehand, he proposed a *triple-helix* model that seemed somehow faulty to Watson. Meanwhile, Rosalind Franklin was studying X-ray images of genetic material. Working across town from Watson and Crick's Cavendish Laboratory in Cambridge, England, she was only one tweak of a mental model away. "She had the data to do it," Watson noted years later. But as one of her future colleagues remarked, Franklin "needed to break the pattern of her thinking."

The double helix was obvious to virtually no one. Over the ensuing years and decades, it would become knowable to virtually everyone. As is typically the case with great scientific discoveries, this one would lead to great technological inventions. The discovery of this pattern wasn't an end, in other words, but rather was a new beginning. Entire generations of medical researchers and biotech inventors would spend their careers working with this elegant model fixed in their heads. But what could they do next? The double helix seemed perfect. How could you improve on it? The answer was to construct related patterns. Get inside the double helix. Unlock its secrets. Extend the pattern in new ways. Find new patterns that complement it. Use it as a tool of invention.

THINKING "WOW!"

Leroy "Lee" Hood has spent his entire career doing just that. Hood is a physically fit man of medium build who makes forceful hand motions whenever he launches into a scientific explanation. The Renaissance boy of his one hundred forty–student high school in Shelby, Montana, Hood starred on the football team; played the piano, clarinet, and oboe; acted in school plays; sang in the choir; joined the debate team; and edited the yearbook. In the summer, he rode horses and hiked mountains. In the parlance of cognitive science, his brain was becoming "well connected."

In his junior year, Hood submitted a geological mapping of a nearby oil incline to the national Westinghouse science fair, with the hope he'd become the first student from his state ever to be selected as a winner. He was indeed chosen. The long train ride to Washington, D.C., was the first time he had left Montana. As they said back then, Lee Hood was going places. But where?

One of Hood's most searing childhood memories takes him back to age nine, when his parents were having an argument. The conflict was over his one-year-old brother, Glen, who had been born with Down syndrome. "My mother wanted to keep Glenny in the family," Hood recalls. "My father felt it would be better for him and the family if he were placed in a state home. My father won the argument. It was very hard on my mother. At some point, I began thinking, 'What went wrong with Glenny?'"[4] Lee Hood didn't know it yet, but he would end up inventing instruments for finding new patterns in the wide-open field of biology, and his family's experience may have prompted him to choose a life of genomic rather than geological mapping.

His study of biology began with an opportunity. During his senior year, the chemistry teacher was called on to teach a new course in biology to sophomores. In need of some help, the teacher recruited Hood, clearly one of the school's brightest students. Hood began reading up on the subject to help prepare the lessons. The year was 1956. "I remember reading an article in *Scientific American* about Watson and Crick's discovery [three years earlier of the double-helix structure of the DNA molecule]," he says. "I thought, 'Wow!' I didn't begin to understand the implications. But I thought, 'Gee, this is incredible.' I understood it in the sense that this had to be the material that contained the genes that represented the instructions of life. My understanding was very simple compared to now. But it made me get very excited. I realized that there was something very concrete at the foundation of biology."

For Hood, that "Wow!" was a *cognitive snap*, a sudden realization. On one level, the now-famous Watson and Crick model—a twisty ladder with the base-pair rungs—was only a simple pattern. On another level, however, that pattern organized a mind-boggling array of data and concepts into a distinct, indelible image that would thereafter be imprinted on Hood's mind. He was among the first generation of kids to grow up in a world redefined by the double-helix pattern.

Unlocking Patterns

Hood wanted to experience more moments of pattern recognition. There were thousands of secrets hidden within the pattern of the double helix, and he was energized by the prospect of finding them. As a student at California Institute of Technology, he picked up patterns of thinking from some of the world's greatest scientific minds.

For freshman physics, he had Richard Feynman, only a few years before Feynman would win the Nobel Prize for his work on quantum electrodynamics. Feynman liked to play intellectual jokes on the students. "He made you leave class thinking you understood everything," Hood recalls, "and then you went home and tried to do your homework, and you realized you didn't." The lesson: If you didn't comprehend the underlying pattern that organized the information, bits of data that you thought you understood didn't lead to follow-on insights.

Feynman himself told a story of how he had learned "what patterns were like and how interesting they are."[5] At the age of three, he recalled, his father brought home bathroom tiles and demonstrated that they could be set up "in a more complicated way: two white tiles and a blue tile, two white tiles and a blue tile, and so on."

Hood also attended Linus Pauling's chemistry lectures. The winner of the Nobel Prize for his discovery of the nature of complex substances such as proteins and antibodies, Pauling often dispensed advice on creativity. "I am constantly asked by students how I get good ideas," Pauling said. "My answer is simple: First, have a lot of ideas. Then, throw away the bad ones." Knowing how to discriminate between the two, of course, is the trick.

Hood recalls being even more strongly influenced by the thinking patterns of other teachers and mentors, including his biology professor, George Beadle, who had won the Nobel Prize for medicine for his 1941 discovery that genes do their magic by controlling precise chemical events. Beadle confirmed that genes exist to execute a recipe for creating proteins, the building blocks of all living matter. Not only that, but Beadle also proved that genes could be manipulated. By shooting X-rays at certain cells, for example, the recipe could be altered, rewritten, artificially mutated. But how did it all happen? What use was all this knowledge? How exactly did genes create endless varieties of life? The race was on to crack the genetic code, to find the patterns by which genes construct proteins.

In the middle of his college career, Hood got hooked on this mind-set of unlocking biological patterns. A young French geneticist named Jerome Lejeune discovered the pattern deviation that caused Down syndrome. Reading Lejeune's 1959 paper, Hood learned that his brother Glen's condition was triggered by something called a "21 trisomy": an extra copy of chromosome number 21 on the double-helix ladder of 23 base pairs of chromosomes. Learning this gave Hood a deep appreciation for how, as he puts it, "such a little thing could have such a profound effect." He wanted to know more about human anatomy as well as human diseases and treatments, a topic not covered deeply at Caltech. "I was even more convinced than ever that I wanted to go into biology, but for reasons I never fully understood—perhaps in part due to my brother Glen," Hood later acknowledged. He enrolled in medical school at Johns Hopkins without any intention of becoming a doctor. "Most of the students wanted to become family doctors in small towns," he recalls.

Instead, Hood would go on to combine his knowledge of biology with the process of invention, cocreating a set of key instruments that would enable the eventual mapping of the entire human genome, humanity's ultimate pattern. He would play a large part in epochal breakthroughs, setting off an explosion of new patterns and pattern deviations that continue to reveal themselves to this day. His inventions would also sit at the core of the multibillion-dollar biotech industry, which didn't exist when Hood was in college and medical school.

SEEING SHAPES

But before we explore more precisely what Hood actually had a hand in inventing and how he did it, let's think back to simpler times, when breakthrough inventions involved things we could see more readily with the unaided eye. For a more mechanical model of how perceiving and applying patterns can work in practice, let's turn to a classic case.

The basic idea of the phonograph had been around for forty years before Thomas Edison reframed the problem. In 1857, inventor

Leon Scott, an American of French origin, realized that sound vibrations could be visualized. He fixed a bristle to a stretched piece of pigskin. When he spoke loudly into the diaphragm, the bristle vibrated and etched patterns onto a soot-coated piece of paper or glass. Scott called it a "phonautograph." Several inventors improved on the device, showing that visual patterns representing sound could be preserved for later study. Alexander Graham Bell was among those who built his own phonautograph from scratch.

To Edison, the problem wasn't in recording sound but rather in playing it back. Whereas Bell saw the phonautograph as a way of understanding sound, Edison looked for a new opportunity. Could one design a machine that spoke back sound? His mental model of the problem seemed to form in a unique way. Being largely deaf, he preferred to experience sound not through his ears but "by clenching his teeth around a metal plate attached to the sounding apparatus," according to Edison biographer Neil Baldwin.[6] "Vibrations were conveyed through his resonating jawbone—meaning, in effect, that *he virtually heard through his teeth*." By feeling the sound patterns reverberate through his jaw in this way, Edison hit on the question of whether one could record and play back the sound using the same machine.

For a solution, Edison turned to a pattern, a set of shapes and mechanical motions, that he was familiar with. "Any creative technologist," notes Reese Jenkins, another Edison biographer, "possesses a mental set of stock solutions from which he draws in addressing problems."[7] In Edison's case, one of his favorite stock solutions was the steel cylinder and the stylus. He had seen these simple but effective devices everywhere in his travels, and a pattern for creating new mechanical devices from these elements had already formed in his mind.

As a child, Edison sold newspapers on the Grand Trunk Railroad. By the age of fifteen, he was publishing his own small newspaper, the *Weekly Herald*, which contained gossip, advertisements for businesses along the rail line, and news about the railroad. Edison printed the newspaper in the baggage car of a train using a galley proof press. The machine was powered by a revolving, hand-cranked metal cylinder that pressed the sheets against a flat bed of movable type. The newspaper ceased publication after a chemical fire burned part of the baggage car, an accident that may have contributed to the loss of much of Edison's hearing when an angry conductor whacked him in the head afterward. (Other accounts blame a bout with scarlet fever, as in the case of Mabel Hubbard, Bell's future wife.)

Edison next became a roving telegraph operator, drifting from city to city in search of more interesting situations and higher pay. Most of the telegraph offices contained mechanical devices, such as relays and type-wheels, which were driven by rotating steel cylinders that transmitted electricity through a metal stylus. Was he beginning to recognize this pattern back then? We don't know exactly what he was thinking, but we do know that he soon made his first invention, a telegraph message playback device designed after this kind of rotating cylinder. That same year (1867), the twenty-year-old Edison found work in a telegraph machine shop operating a foot-powered lathe, which rotated materials as he cut them into cylindrical shapes using a styluslike tool.

Ten years later, when Edison first achieved fame for inventing the "talking machine" at Menlo Park, reporters wanted to know how the inventor came to his sudden flash of insight. The first sketch of Edison's phonograph, made in November 1877, shows a horizontal cylinder having grooves in its surface for encoding sound information. The drawing depicts a movable stylus that has an embossing point for making the grooves, which would be read for playback by another stylus. The pattern of oscillations was relayed electrically to a speaker. The sounds were to be preserved on paraffin and later on wax disks that wrapped around the steel cylinder.

Edison's conception seemed directly patterned after his earlier telegraph message recorder and on the machines he studied in his early travels. It employed the same shapes and motions and was aimed at the same sort of mechanical function. It may have been a new invention, in other words, but it was based on a recurring pattern.

Edison first envisioned his phonograph as being used primarily to record and play back messages from the telephone, which had been demonstrated and disclosed in a patent by his rival, Bell, only a year earlier. Edison didn't yet know of his lucky strike. He didn't see the applications that would give rise to the musical recording industry a quarter century later. Edison, who had previously come close to inventing the telephone, now inspired envy in Bell, who marveled at the talking machine. "It's a most astonishing thing to me," remarked Bell, "that I could possibly have let this invention slip through my fingers when I consider how my thoughts have been directed to this subject for so many years past."[8]

But it seems that Edison was able to arrive at the phonograph before Bell and all his other competitors because of the way Edison pinpointed the basic problem and then completed a pattern that no one else had seen in the same way. He recognized the versatility of a rotating, electromechanical cylinder. He kept seeing that shape repeatedly, drawing on the pattern in his mind. The printing press was based on a cylinder, as were many early telegraph relay devices and the machine shop lathe. Even the electromechanical printing wheels that Edison developed were cylindrical. The phonograph was considered Edison's breakthrough invention, but it really was a continuation of a pattern that he had recognized years earlier.

Ten years after he achieved fame for recording and playing back sound, Edison again invoked his favorite shape. By then, he had relocated his laboratory to West Orange, New Jersey. "I am experimenting upon an instrument which does for the eye what the phonograph does for the ear," Edison wrote in 1888, "which is the recording and reproduction of things in motion. The invention consists in photographing continuously a series of pictures occurring at intervals . . . at greater than eight per second . . . on a cylinder or plate in the same manner in which sound is recorded on the phonograph."[9]

This invention, which Edison called the kinetoscope, was housed in a cabinet that had a viewing peephole fitted with a microscope lens. His first sketches depicted a large cylinder for advancing the film. This shape was soon abandoned in favor of rollers that held coils of film, much like latter-day microfilm threaders. As the viewer looked through the peephole at the top of the cabinet and cranked a handle, the frames went by, giving the appearance of a moving image. There is some dispute as to whether Edison was truly the first to develop a commercial-quality motion picture machine, but there is no doubt that he again applied a familiar pattern in a new domain. His mind stored successful patterns, and he continuously searched for analogous situations in which his favorite shapes and structures could be used.

The key to recognizing patterns that lead to new solutions is to spot something that already works, learn why it works, and then reapply or complete the successful model. That is the thinking habit that Thomas Edison learned early in his career. He recognized recurring patterns in his environment that others were missing, and he practiced reapplying and completing those patterns.

Seeing Patterns in Data

For some inventors, the patterns that needs to be recognized are hidden in data that would seem meaningless to most people. This was the case with a computer scientist named Max Levchin. Levchin is thin, with short black hair, and he often seems reticent about what he's doing. As a child growing up in the Ukraine, Levchin drew pictures and took art classes, and these experiences may have helped him develop an appreciation of patterns. He also became obsessed with cryptography, the science of encoding information using secret patterns. Growing up under the old Soviet regime convinced him of the need to carry out communications in a way that would be undetectable by authorities.

In 1991 the teenaged Levchin immigrated with his family to Chicago. As a computer science student at the University of Illinois, he immersed himself in the mathematics of creating and breaking codes, not only making it the focus of his studies but also, he says, turning his pursuit into a "huge hobby" that consumed countless days and nights at the supercomputer center on the Urbana-Champaign campus.[10]

Dreaming that he would one day profit from his passion, Levchin aimed to start a company that would process financial transactions over the Internet, devising codes so unbreakable that hackers wouldn't be able to read the data even if they intercepted them. To make good on his goal, Levchin moved to Silicon Valley after graduating in 1998. With the emergence of eBay, he noticed that a growing number of people were buying and selling goods to strangers. It was the old Soviet black market, only legal.

Levchin created in his mind the opportunity to replace the predominant way online buyers paid for their order. More than 80 percent of them were sending paper checks through the mail, a ridiculous delay for a real-time marketplace. Millions of part-time hobbyists, collectors, and small-business owners needed a simple way to exchange money instantly without having to open expensive merchant accounts to accept and process credit cards. Along with Peter Thiel, a financial hedge fund manager Levchin met at a Stanford University lecture, Levchin cofounded PayPal, a Palo Alto, California, company that suddenly became the leading processor of person-to-person (P2P) payments over the Internet.

As designed by Levchin, PayPal was a simple way of allowing person A to send an e-mail payment to person B. The parties didn't have to know each other's name or location. The PayPal software authorized person B to take money from person A's bank account or to charge A's credit card. The software therefore had to police the transaction.

As it turned out, using advanced cryptography was only a small part of PayPal's success. Yes, financial data had to be stored and exchanged between computers using encrypted formats. But that technology had already been invented and built into standard Web browsers and databases. Millions of small businesses operating on eBay would adopt Levchin's invention only if it proved to be secure enough. So Levchin went to work searching for patterns within all those financial transactions.

What Levchin detected was patterns of crime. He didn't simply notice that there was a lot of fraud happening online. What he began to spot were specific tip-offs of online criminal behavior. People who sign up for PayPal provide certain information, such as name, postal address, e-mail address, bank account numbers, and so on. Levchin decided to look for correlations between the information PayPal had on each customer and the customer's behavior in using the system. If a user attempted to conduct several transactions at once, tried to make transfers of high dollar amounts, or tried to send payments to notorious locations overseas or to unverified addresses, Levchin wondered what this behavior might say about the probability that the transaction was fraudulent.

There was no doubt that the patterns of crime were there to be found. Whereas Visa and MasterCard report an overall fraud rate between 0.05 percent and 0.07 percent, a Gartner Group study of Web merchants indicated that the figure soared to 1.13 percent for online transactions. In other words, buyers and sellers online faced a twenty times greater risk of not being able to recover the money or merchandise due to them. In May 2000, officials from the Federal Bureau of Investigation revealed the results of Operation Cyber Loss, a sweep of stings that led to the arrests of ninety alleged con artists charged with defrauding fifty-six thousand citizens out of $117 million, mainly through online auction fraud, stolen credit card numbers traded and used over the Internet, and wholesale identity theft. "Subjects and victims involved in this operation were scattered throughout the world," Thomas T. Kubic, a deputy assistant director at the FBI, told a congressional hearing. "These cases reflect the nature of fraudsters to migrate from one fraudulent scheme to another, and [are] indicative of criminal behavior that would only continue to expand if left unaddressed."[11] Perhaps it would be more efficient to stop this kind of fraud before it happened rather than try to prosecute it after the fact.

Levchin invented financial surveillance software that closely monitored PayPal's customers and alerted the company to any suspicious account activity. The original requirement was that the crime recognition program show results on one screen that, like a police blotter, "could be parsed by a human in seconds," he says. As each transaction was placed, the screen would flash either the clear sign or a variety of red flags.

Levchin named his fraud detection program Igor, after a Russian hacker it apprehended early on, and PayPal filed for patents on Igor's ability to mine the data for clues. The patterns that this twenty-five-year-old had built into the software were so fascinating and useful that officials from the FBI, the U.S. Secret Service, and the U.S. Postal Service routinely drop by PayPal's offices to check cases against Igor's data to learn some of the crime patterns it reveals.

A typical online crime pattern works this way: The software spots an aggregation of fake accounts, stolen credit card numbers, and money withdrawals. The scam works as follows. A criminal steals a bunch of credit card numbers, opens many fake PayPal accounts at once under the stolen identities, and links the accounts to the stolen card numbers. Lots of money is then transferred from other accounts to one central account. Then the hacker attempts to purchase consumer electronics online or to withdraw the money in cash. When this kind of likely scam is spotted, accounts can be frozen instantly and transactions can be halted or delayed.

Some of the patterns that Levchin began looking for aren't obvious at all. Does the physical distance between buyer and seller have any correlation to fraud? If you opened your account in the middle of the night, does that increase the chance that you are a criminal? If buyer and seller are both transacting in the middle of the night in their respective time zones, does that increase the likelihood of fraud? If your password hint question happened to be "What is your favorite color?" and you said "Black," what does that say about your criminal intent? If you capitalize the first letter of your name in your e-mail address, does that decrease the chances you're a fraudster? "We looked at every little thing," Levchin says. In other words, he was creating perhaps the closest thing we have to the predictive human–machine technology depicted in the movie *Minority Report*.

As in the movie, a single scrap of information may not be important in and of itself, but combining everything into a model can result in a powerful predictor. Levchin calls Igor "suspect-generation technology." These small patterns could lead to big findings: funneling money to the Russian mob, say, or financing a small war in Asia.

PayPal is a system for transferring U.S. dollars among people in dozens of countries, so none of these possibilities is far-fetched.

Levchin was positing relationships that didn't previously exist and using new technology to do it. As a result, his invention was something that no one else had and that everyone seemed to want. The company raised more than $200 million in venture capital, with most of that coming after the dot-com collapse. Soon, PayPal was processing the payments for one in every four eBay transactions. With Levchin's Igor program, PayPal was able to claim an online fraud rate of about 0.3 percent, thus eliminating 75 percent of the risk of sending payments online. Citibank and Bank One, and even eBay itself, started rival online payment services, but no one has been able to catch PayPal. Bank One soon had to shut down its system after experiencing fraud rates as high as 25 percent.

"Humans are extremely good at pattern recognition," says Levchin. "Computers are only as good as programmed, which is a shame." The best solution, he says, is to have the computer crunch through millions and millions of pieces of data and instantly find the patterns it has been told to find. Then a human can review the results and assess the significance of the finding: Is this transaction normal and legitimate, or is it alarming and dangerous? Is this person exactly the kind of customer we want, or one of America's most wanted? Is this person a successful online merchant with a hot product, or an international rogue with only crime in mind? Among the other things Levchin recognized was a new pattern for getting computers and humans to work well together, a combination that is especially useful these days.

CHAPTER 4

Channeling Chance

What is hidden and unknown and cannot be discovered by scientific research will most likely be discovered by accident, if at all, by the one who is most observing of everything related thereto.

—CHARLES GOODYEAR

AN ACCIDENTAL INVENTION is a paradox of sorts. On one level, almost everything associated with the invention of something new seems to occur by happenstance. On another level, however, it seems that very little is accidental about accidental inventions. These mistakes tend to happen to the right people in the right place at the right time. We all know how important serendipity is for the success of almost everything, but we rarely explore this dual nature of chance.

Even the three princes of Serendip weren't merely lucky. According to the sixteenth-century Persian fairy tale that gave birth to the word *serendipity*, a three princes hailing from the fictional province of Serendip always found themselves riding their horses past things that they weren't seeking but that they ended up turning into brilliant insights. If you read between the lines, you'll notice that the princes were always traveling to interesting places and that they were always on the lookout for chance wisdom. "One sometimes finds what one is not looking for," said Alexander Fleming, who supposedly stumbled across some funny-looking bacteria-killing mold in his laboratory one day in 1929. It turned out to be penicillin, an antibiotic that changed the course of medicine and won Fleming a Nobel Prize. Disagreeing with such expressions of modesty was Louis Pasteur. "Did you ever observe to whom these accidents happen?" he said. Then he famously added, "Chance favors the prepared mind." [1]

DROPPING THE CHIP

The story of Bernie Meyerson is a case in point. Meyerson is a big bear of a man with a bulldog face, and he speaks in his New York accent about how he almost dropped out of college to become a cabinetmaker. Instead of showing up for his junior year, he went into business with his brother and some associates and opened The Cabinet Shop, which operated a factory just outside New York City in the mid-1970s. "We'd start with a tree and run it through an evil machine we called Oliver, which would eat the tree and turn it into boards," Meyerson recalls. [2] In contrast to goods for sale at Ikea and Home Depot, all the kitchen cabinets and bedroom furniture made at The Cabinet Shop were custom built and finished in exquisite detail. "We did some fine cabinetry, let me tell you," he says.

Then one day, Meyerson was walking down the street in upper Manhattan on his way to visit his girlfriend when he was lucky enough to run into his former City College physics professor. Bill Miller was a brilliant scientist who had once worked alongside Robert Oppenheimer, of Manhattan Project fame.

"What are you doing now?" Miller asked.

"I'm making cabinets."

"You're in the wrong line of work," said the professor.

Miller knew that Meyerson had been one of his brightest students, someone who seemed destined to become an engineer or a scientist. In fact, Meyerson had grown up surrounded by Radio Shack parts. As a child, he played pranks with radios and conducted electromagnetic experiments that he entered in science fairs, and he graduated from the Bronx School of Science, the city's prestigious magnet school. Now Meyerson was supposed to be taking a year off from college, trying to figure out what he wanted to do with his life. But Miller could tell that cabinetmaking was luring the student away. The professor convinced him to return to college the next fall. Meyerson again immersed himself in his studies, and he continued at City College for his graduate work in solid-state physics.

One day in 1979, while doing a lab experiment, Meyerson had what seemed to be a minor mishap. He was handling some one-inch-square silicon wafers. Following normal procedure, Meyerson put a wafer into a furnace to purify the material. Afterward, to clean it, he dipped it in hydrofluoric acid. The chip was then supposed to react with the oxygen in the air to form a microscopic layer of silicon dioxide, also known as silica or window glass. The thin glass surface would serve to protect the chip.

But as Meyerson was removing the wafer from the solution using a pair of tweezers, he accidentally dropped the chip onto a dirty metal hood, which had some "grunge" on its surface, he recalls.

When he rinsed the grungy chip with water, he noticed something odd. The chip didn't get wet. "It should have behaved like windshield glass," he says. Yet this substance didn't retain even a bead of moisture. Confused, he put the chip into a beaker of water for ten minutes, left the room, and then came back to remove it. To his surprise, it was still dry. He thought, "That's impossible." Needing to get back to his work, he "filed it away under scientific inconsistency," he says.

Perhaps his work as a cabinetmaker gave Meyerson an eye for fine detail that others might have missed. In any case, he knew that what he had just seen didn't make sense. He knew that it contradicted what he had read in physics textbooks. Nevertheless, Meyerson didn't immediately see what use his accidental discovery would be. "End of episode," he says.

Three years later, now working as a research scientist at IBM's Thomas J. Watson laboratories in Yorktown Heights, New York, Meyerson saw the happy accident come back into play. Like everyone else in the semiconductor industry, he was looking for ways to make faster and more powerful integrated circuits to drive the next generation of computing and communications devices. As always, that meant packing more circuits into less space on a fingernail-sized chip. And as always, accomplishing that would require some sort of breakthrough in the process of manipulating microscopic materials. The fact that the silicon chip remained dry in water had remained stuck in Meyerson's mind, and he set out to discover why that was so. He began thinking about how the answer might change the future of the technology.

Meyerson's chance encounter with his professor, along with his mishap in the laboratory, led to an opportunity. This accidental confluence of events would lead to a new kind of semiconductor that would result, twenty-five years later, in nearly $30 billion in annual revenue for IBM and other chipmakers.

"I can trace it all to dropping the silicon wafer as a grad student," Meyerson says. "It enabled this cascade of things to happen." But before we get into what the actual breakthrough idea was, we need to understand a few things about chance and how inventors throughout history have gone about channeling it.

Exploiting Serendipity

It isn't difficult to find examples to illustrate how serendipity can be exploited by inventors for commercial gain. History is replete with mishaps that led to great products, industries, and fortunes, especially when it comes to the accidental creation of new materials.

One day in 1876, for example, Swedish chemist Alfred Nobel badly cut his finger on a piece of glass in his laboratory. He applied collodion, a soothing ointment, to the wound, but the pain kept him awake that night. He began wondering about the properties of this gel and whether it might fill a special need in the lab. When he tested it, the results were impressive. It turns out that the combination of collodion and the volatile substance nitroglycerine formed the basis for his invention of gelatinous dynamite, one of several commercially successful explosives that made Nobel a millionaire. Nobel, of course, later donated much of his resulting fortune to establish an annual series of prizes in his name.

In another case, a DuPont research chemist named Roy J. Plunkett was experimenting with the refrigeration gas tetrafluroethylene, also known as Freon, one day in 1938. One of the pressurized cylinders of the substance seemed to malfunction. The gas failed to release even though a colleague had opened the valve. The two men set it aside to examine later. When Plunkett sawed open the cylinder, however, he found that the gas had somehow solidified into a mysterious white powder. Upon testing it, he found it to be more slippery than any other known polymer. DuPont later named it Teflon. First used to coat gaskets inside the first atomic bombs and then to line some of the first NASA spacesuits, the Space Age material was later applied to billions of dollars' worth of pots, pans, and muffin trays.[3]

In an even more famous case of accidental discovery, an early radar pioneer named Percy L. Spencer was walking through one of the laboratories at the Raytheon Company one day in 1946. He paused next to a magnetron tube, the heart of a radar system. According to legend, he suddenly noticed that a candy bar in his pocket was melting. Instead of throwing it away, washing his hands, and forgetting about it, Spencer took note. Pretty soon, he was aiming the tube's microwave radiation at a bag of unpopped corn kernels. Sure enough, according to his account, he quickly had fresh popcorn in his hands. The first industrial-sized microwave ovens, known as Radar Ranges, were on the market by 1953. They weighed hundreds of pounds, didn't cook food very well, and were widely ridiculed. But slimmed-down models eventually became standard equipment in homes and restaurants.

One day in the early 1950s, Swiss engineer George de Mestral came back from a walk in the woods and noticed that his jacket was covered in cockleburs: sticky round clusters of seedpods. Instead of being annoyed and throwing them away, he took a closer look. He noticed that the spikes on the burrs ended in tiny hooks. Eight years later, de Mestral succeeded in developing an artificial fastener crafted from nylon that mimicked the effect. Combining the words *velvet* and *crochet*, he came up with the name Velcro and formed a company to market his invention.

Dr. James Schlatter was a chemist developing a new anti-ulcer treatment at the drug company Searle. One day in 1965, as he was heating a mixture of chemicals, he accidentally knocked over the glass flask. Some of the powdery substance spilled onto the outside of the flask and stuck to his fingers. This mishap probably wouldn't have been of any consequence had Schlatter not licked his fingers a few minutes later before picking up a piece of paper. It was a lucky move. When he noticed the extremely sweet taste, he went back to sample more of the substance in the beaker. Tests confirmed that this powder, known as aspartame, was two hundred times as sweet as sugar, with none of the bitter aftertaste of saccharin and other artificial sweeteners. The resulting product, NutraSweet, made billions of dollars for the corporation before the patent ran out in 1998.

All five of these inventions seem to have come about by chance. But what is seldom noticed is that these kinds of happy accidents probably happen every day to an unknown number of people all over the world. In the vast majority of cases, these events would seem insignificant or would even elude observation. The inventors, however, did not let these situations slip by them. Could they have been waiting for such accidents to happen? In a sense, they were. Since history is filled with many accidental discoveries, inventors who know this tend to keep their eyes open for the unexpected.

This means that luck may come your way only if you are ready to welcome it when it does. "The first rule of discovery is to have brains and good luck," suggests mathematician George Polya. "The second rule of discovery is to sit tight and wait till you get a bright idea."[4] Harold "Doc" Edgerton, the MIT-based inventor of underwater cameras, stroboscopes, and sonar improvements, is more specific in his formulation of how to anticipate chance: "By combining hard work, careful awareness, perseverance, and unconventional thinking, a scientist could find himself or herself in the right place at the right time to experience serendipity."[5]

Successful inventors seem to make their own luck. They simply look much harder for clues. They stand ready to embrace the odd occurrences that may lead to something big. In other words, they learn to channel chance. They are on the lookout for random inputs that can generate a surprising new output. Harvard creativity scholar David Perkins puts it this way: "Chance is an engine of insight." Not always, of course. Most of the time, an accident or a random occurrence will turn out to be only that: something meaningless that offers no lessons.[6]

But when you realize that chance can be channeled, you can see that the examples we've just discussed weren't pure luck; rather, they were extraordinary opportunities in disguise. Alfred Nobel, in fact, had already invented dry dynamite sticks five years before he cut his finger. His brother and five other men had previously died in a nitroglycerine explosion—an accident of a more serious kind—and Nobel had since been on a constant search for new materials to combine with the unstable substance. His invention of gelatinous dynamite, which later evolved into what we know as plastic explosives, was the result of a minor accident that played into his existing search pattern. Incidentally, Nobel had noble intentions. Gelatinous dynamite was designed for civil engineering projects such as creating railroad tunnels in mountains, and not for use in weaponry.

The other accidental inventors deployed the same kind of deliberate reaction to random events. Roy Plunkett was working in a lab where the mission was to develop useful chemicals and materials. True, he could have ignored the mishap that led to Teflon, but he was observant enough to realize that when a known material behaves in a strange way, finding out why can lead to something new. Similarly, Percy Spencer was not a narrowly focused defense industry employee. Rather, he was a prolific inventor, with one hundred twenty patents to his name. He jumped on this new microwave application immediately. The morning after his serendipitous discovery, he was back in the lab using microwaves to blow up eggs. In the same way, George de Mestral didn't simply glance casually at the cockleburs on his coat; he immediately put them under a microscope to study their tiny hooks and their behavior in detail. Finally, James Schlatter's inadvertent success with aspartame wasn't a fluke. As it turns out, other artificial sweeteners, including saccharin about one hundred years earlier, were the result of remarkably similar industrial accidents.

STUMBLING INTO SUCCESS

Some inventors have no right to be successful. An inventor sometimes approaches the problem at hand with little or no theoretical knowledge and yet somehow hits upon a breakthrough anyway, confounding experts and expectations. But is it really sheer serendipity?

Consider the strange story of Charles Goodyear and his world-famous invention. Goodyear was born in 1800 in New Haven, Connecticut, and on his twenty-first birthday was named a partner in the family hardware store, A. Goodyear & Sons. By then, factories all around the world were producing rubber products, but their applications were severely limited because the material became too soft to use in the summer and too hard to use in the winter. Discovered in 1735 by French explorers who pillaged trees in Peru, rubber was given its name by famed scientist Joseph Priestley, who noticed that it could be used to "rub out" written errors. It was a substance born of plunder and blunder, and it seemed destined to be made popular by someone who made more than his fair share of mistakes.

Goodyear, who at a young age fancied himself an inventor, came across the rubber problem by chance. One day, he walked into a shop near his family's store to purchase a rubber life preserver. After taking a look at the air-intake valve on the tube, he told the shopkeeper he would be able to improve it. When he returned a few days later with an idea for how to do so, the shopkeeper told him he'd probably find it more lucrative to do something to improve the rubber itself, rather than the valve. Goodyear took the suggestion seriously.

In the 1830s, speculators were buying rubber harvested from India and promoting the "miracle product" as never before—for use in covering wagon wheels, for water-protective boots and trousers, for floatation devices, and for dozens of other things being dreamed up by American and European entrepreneurs. The excitement over this special India rubber set off an investment frenzy, with new rubber companies and retailers cropping up everywhere. But the India rubber boom came to an abrupt end in the hot summer of 1835. The industry melted down when everything made from rubber suddenly began turning into a gooey mush. The odor was so foul that the material had to be buried.

Some speculators thought that the heat of that summer caused a fluke occurrence, but the same thing happened the next year. So many investors lost their pants in the rubber bust that dozens of banks crashed along with the fledgling industry, and that in turn caused unrelated companies to go belly-up. The Goodyear family's hardware store was one of the thousands of businesses to go bankrupt around that time.[7]

In the heat of the frenzy, Charles Goodyear had dedicated himself to finding a way to "cure" rubber: to protect it from temperature swings and make it into the durable, versatile material he believed it was destined to be. "No one knew any more about rubber or the chemistry of rubber than he did, and he knew nothing," wrote author Wilson Mitchell.[8] Goodyear later suggested that he wouldn't have taken up the problem if he had known how difficult it would be: "I was blessed with ignorance of the obstacles I had subsequently to encounter," he wrote. If Goodyear was to find success in this field, he would have to stumble across it, because he truly didn't know what he was doing.

Goodyear first began to cure rubber by using things he found around the house. He tried mixing it with salt and pepper, and when that didn't work, he tried chicken soup. He experimented with witch hazel, cream cheese, and ink. When he tried magnesia, the results were so much better than anything else that he "laughed with joy," according to his journal. He made book covers, piano covers, shoes, and slacks using the mixture. He was briefly praised as the man who saved the rubber industry.

With his first profits, Goodyear bought a new house in the industrial town of Woburn, Massachusetts, and set up a laboratory there. But when the next summer came around, the new material began to melt on schedule. People wearing Goodyear's rubber shoes were sticking to the ground, and those wearing his rubber trousers had to carefully peel off their pants.

With the failure of his product, Goodyear lost all his money. Neighbors thought he was a pleasant but hapless madman. Perhaps he should have given up at this point. Instead, he tried to add quicklime to the magnesia-based formula but discovered that "the weakest acid, even apple juice, would destroy the product." He discarded the magnesia and used pure quicklime but found that it dissolved the rubber gum completely. He thought he had hit upon a happy accident when he buried in his backyard a sticky, smelly rubber shoe cured with the mysteriously named "aqua fortis." Goodyear didn't even know exactly what was in this chemical mixture, but when he later dug up the shoe, he found that the smell and stickiness had gone away. But he was unable to repeat the experiment with any success.

He then tried a product cured with nitric acid and sulfuric acid that he thought was good enough to sell in a newly opened store on Broadway in New York. The U.S. government was impressed enough with the "acid-cured" product to place an order for one hundred fifty rubber mailbags for postal workers. After collecting $5,000 for the sale, Goodyear left on a summer vacation. Once again, the product began melting, and again he lost everything he had. He sold his house, pawned his possessions, moved his family in with his brother, and rarely had enough money to buy food, but he continued to wear a rubber outfit whenever he was in public. If anyone was in need of some serendipity, it was Charles Goodyear. He had been at work on the problem around the clock for nearly a decade and had gotten nowhere.

Then one day, while working in his brother's kitchen, Goodyear inadvertently left a slab of rubber on top of the wood-burning stove. Because he knew well that heat melts rubber, he had never thought of doing this deliberately. But when the stove singed the outside of the substance, it produced a remarkable protective layer that prevented the rubber from melting further. It was a completely counterintuitive solution to the problem. "I was surprised," Goodyear wrote, "to find that a specimen, being carelessly brought into contact with a hot stove, charred like leather."[9]

Yet this was the accident that led to his patented vulcanization process. In his 1844 patent application, Goodyear gave the following description: "My principal improvement consists in the combining of sulfur and white lead with the india-rubber, and in the submitting of the compound thus formed to the action of heat at a regulated temperature, by which combination and exposure to heat it will be so far altered in its qualities as not to become softened by the action of the solar ray or of artificial heat.... [N]or will it be injuriously affected by exposure to cold."[10]

Goodyear acknowledged that his breakthrough wasn't exactly the result of theoretical knowledge. "I admit that this was not the result of scientific investigation," he wrote. But he was certainly practiced enough in observing variations in his favorite substance that he was able to recognize the breakthrough when it happened. The stove-singed layer that protected the rubber was only a few millimeters thick, but he saw how consequential that layer was. He may have known almost nothing about chemistry, but his powers of observation were excellent. He was keenly anticipating his lucky break, and when it arrived, he didn't let it pass him by.

Goodyear was flooded with orders for his new vulcanized rubber. He paid off all his debts and opened factories that eventually employed tens of thousands of workers. But he priced his product too low and spent lavishly on advertising and promotion, a business formula that put him back in debt. His great fortune and fame came after his death in 1860 at the age of sixty. The world-famous Goodyear Tire & Rubber Company was actually set up after the Civil War by the late inventor's associates, who eventually grew wealthy selling rubber bicycle tires, insulation for electrical wires, and later, automobile tires.

Was Goodyear lucky? Eventually he was. But he was also persistent in pursuing his good fortune and skilled enough to spot the breakthrough.

ENCOUNTERING THE ELEPHANT

Now let's return to the story of Bernie Meyerson. Like Goodyear, Meyerson was faced with a problem with his materials. Silicon, which is refined from ordinary beach sand, was found to be an ideal semiconductive material. Another element, germanium, was also found to have this core property. Semiconductors were so named because they were somewhat good and somewhat bad at conducting electricity. They are *semi*good, which was good enough to serve as the foundation for the first transistors when they were invented at Bell Telephone Laboratories in 1947 and 1948.

Silicon can conduct electrons one second and then block them in the next. This is critical because when you're integrating dozens, hundreds, thousands, or millions of electric circuits on a silicon chip, what you need is the ability to *control* each circuit independently.[11] If the electricity jumps between circuits across the chip—a defect known as tunneling—the entire invention is useless. The finer your control, the more powerful you can make the chips.

But silicon is also an excellent "garbage collector," in that the surface tends to react with things you don't want it to. To kill any junk on the surface, engineers would bake the silicon wafers in high-temperature ovens at about 1,000 degrees centigrade. Such temperatures prevented the use of more sensitive alloys; they might improve the performance of the chip but couldn't stand such heat. As it turns out, the main junk that engineers wanted to bake away was the native oxide layer, the same substance that Meyerson suspected did not exist. If it really was there, the chip he had dropped and rinsed three years earlier would have gotten wet. But if the oxide layer wasn't present, he thought, perhaps such high temperatures wouldn't be needed, and that might enable the use of more versatile, low-temperature alloys.

What Meyerson had in mind was combining, or "doping," silicon with another element into a material that would give much higher performance. Like Goodyear, Meyerson was focused on an ultrathin layer on the outside of the substance. But in contrast to Goodyear,

Meyerson had the opportunity to research the underlying science. "You can either stand on the shoulders of giants," he says, using Newton's famous phrase, "or you can try to be a giant on your own."[12] (In all fairness to Goodyear, there was then little published science in his chosen field.) Choosing the stand-on-shoulders approach, Meyerson studied how his predecessors had dealt with the problem. He read that physicists had already tried to grow an alloy of silicon combined with germanium.

One of them was Herbert Kroemer, a German-born physicist who was working at RCA Laboratories and later at Varian Semiconductor. In a 1954 paper, Kroemer proposed a silicon germanium alloy, calling it an example of a "heterojunction bipolar transistor." But he was never able to get these things to operate. "They didn't work at all," says Meyerson. "His physics was dead correct, but the materials were dreadful. I had to figure out *why* it didn't work."[13]

First, Meyerson needed to verify that the accident he had observed as a grad student was no accident. Not wanting to bias the experiment, he had someone else re-create it. He sent an IBM chemist named Reed McFeeley to Brookhaven National Laboratory with pure silicon wafers and a potion of what he told McFeeley was a "magic elixir." The elixir wasn't magic at all. It was ordinary water mixed with 10 percent hydrofluoric acid, the same stuff Meyerson had used in his accidental grad school experiment.

As per Meyerson's instructions, McFeeley baked the chip in an oven, dunked it in the elixir for 10 seconds, put it in a vacuum chamber, and then went to lunch. When he returned, he dropped the chip into a beaker of water and called Meyerson. After he pulled it out, he saw that it was indeed bone dry. "He thought I had done something magic to it," Meyerson says. But Meyerson swore that wasn't the case. Instead, he broke the news to McFeeley for the first time: "All the chemistry you've ever read in this field is wrong."

If there was no oxide on the surface, then what *was* on the surface of the chip? Meyerson suspected that it was a layer of hydrogen, produced by the reaction with the hydrofluoric acid. McFeeley tested it and confirmed that this was true. "This was not a small effect," says Meyerson. "This is like opening your closet and discovering there has been an elephant standing there for quite some time that you simply haven't noticed."

Of course, this could be an example of a corporate inventor tooting his own horn. But the results Meyerson was able to produce afterward serve as evidence of the fact that this was indeed a true breakthrough.

LUCKING INTO A PAYOFF

Attempting to keep his lucky streak alive, Meyerson took his fortunate finding and ran with it. He recruited a skunk works team of Watson Labs researchers that eventually grew to about two dozen people. They were able to produce silicon germanium chips baked at only 500 degrees centigrade, less than half the temperature previously thought possible. The low-temperature process for creating these new chips involved depositing the circuits on the silicon germanium using chemical vapors in an ultrahigh vacuum. By 1985, IBM had filed for the first patents on the breakthrough that put these devices at least ten years ahead of any known competition. In March 1990, the new technology received its first wide attention in a story published in the *New York Times*.[14] A couple years later, the company was able to produce 120-gigahertz microprocessors that yielded more than triple the theoretical maximum performance of any semiconductor technology then on the market.

Meyerson was especially lucky that organizational politics didn't kill his project. All along the way, he never had the full support of IBM's top brass. His team wasn't fully funded or even officially acknowledged, and most team members were juggling other projects deemed by management to be of higher priority. Even after the breakthrough was published, patented, documented, and announced, there was no plan at IBM to commercialize the technology. That's when Meyerson had the idea to take the technology outside the company, proposing it to other companies that might see a need to use it in their own products. This was something that IBM had not done in the past. But Meyerson was able to leap over layers of management and make his case directly to Lou Gerstner, IBM's new CEO. In carefully prepared demonstrations, Meyerson showed Gerstner how these new chips performed compared with pure silicon or other alloys such as gallium arsenide. "Data wins," Meyerson concludes from the experience.

As luck would have it, there was a ready market for these new chips in the exploding wireless telecommunications industry. Within a few years, IBM was making the new silicon germanium chips for Analog Devices, Alcatel, Tektronix, Hughes Electronics, National Semiconductor, Northern Telecom, and Harris Corporation. Everything from digital cell phones to network routers to cellular base stations was suddenly based on this new generation of chips made from silicon germanium, also known as siggy, after the chemical symbol SiGe. By 2000, siggy sales topped more than $1 billion per year in revenue for IBM, not including the millions in fees for the licensing of IBM's patents to other manufacturers and the billions more that IBM's partners were generating.

But for Meyerson, the crowning chance encounter came in 1999 when he was presenting a paper on the breakthrough at a conference in Japan. In his talk, he gave credit for the original idea of the heterojunction chip to Herbert Kroemer, a man whom he had read about and occasionally corresponded with but had never met in person. Meyerson didn't realize that Kroemer himself happened to be in the audience. Overjoyed to hear his work referenced in this way, Kroemer came forward to introduce himself afterward, and the two went out to lunch together. As often happens in the annals of science and invention, a technology that is first proposed by one individual is actually created by another person or group years later. Only in retrospect can one see clearly how the entire process of science and invention leads to revolutionary products. As Swedish philosopher Søren Kierkegaard once said, "Backwards understood be only can but forwards lived be must life."

Meyerson's work is exactly the sort of thing that the Nobel Prize committee looks for. Alfred Nobel launched the scientific prizes with the mission of awarding those who make discoveries that prove to have broad practical value. In a real sense, Meyerson demonstrated that one of Kroemer's theories did have that kind of impact. As fate would have it, Kroemer found himself in Stockholm a year later, in December 2000, accepting the Nobel Prize in physics for his discovery of the heterojunction bipolar transistor. He shared the prize with Russian physicist Zhores Alferov as well Jack Kilby, formerly of Texas Instruments, one of the inventors of the integrated circuit. Silicon Valley legend Robert Noyce, whose work at Fairchild Semiconductor coincided with Kilby's breakthrough, certainly would have also joined them on the stage had he not died in 1990. In his official Nobel interview, Kroemer acknowledged that he was forced by his corporate bosses at the time to abandon his work and leave the application of his theory to someone else. "I wasn't allowed to work on heterostructures," he said, "because I was told that it would never have any applications."[15]

In other words, Kroemer was leaving the completion of his effort to chance and fate, not knowing who would pick up on it or even whether someone would. "That's why I refuse to make predictions about the future," Kroemer said, "because I think the outcomes of science and technology are opportunistic rather than deterministic."

In retrospect, it seems a good bet that Kroemer's work would one day pay off. But who could have predicted that the payoff would begin with a former cabinetmaker trying to recover from a minor mishap in a grad school lab? If not for that fortunate mistake, coupled with Meyerson's persistence in channeling chance, this invention might never have come to be. Or, at the very least, it probably would have been completed by someone else at a different time and place.

CHANNELING THE FUTURE

If serendipity is bound to show its face sooner or later, how long should you wait for it? Should you go about your business as usual? Should you constantly be on the lookout for luck, always searching for the unanticipated occurrence that will yield a breakthrough insight? What if this behavior takes years, or the good part of a career, to pay off (as in the case of Charles Goodyear or Bernie Meyerson)?

It's clear that serendipity and chance, good luck and bad luck, accidents and coincidences are always going to come along at one time or another. The trick is to observe and leverage the more meaningful of these arbitrary occurrences into opportunities. That's how chance is channeled.

Meyerson could have spent his life crafting furniture rather than inventing things that generate billions of dollars of revenue for IBM. It's not that there is anything wrong with woodworking. But Meyerson's career change goes to show that chance encounters can change a life and that happy accidents can change an industry and the world.

These days, as the Watson laboratories' chief technologist responsible for worldwide telecommunications circuit design, Meyerson leaves plenty to chance. Soon, he says, human engineering of computers will reach a limit, and humans will have to create computers that design other computers with little or no human intervention. Circuits will have to know when to spontaneously generate new circuitry in a way similar to the way the human body grows new cells.

It's called intelligent design, and no one knows exactly how we'll get there. But the future inventors of this technology may be wandering the halls of Watson or another lab right now. Some of these researchers might specialize in cognitive science, others in nanotechnology, still others in micromechanics, and others in biotech. Perhaps one of these people will make a mistake and bump into someone at lunch who recognizes it as something more than just an accident.

CHAPTER **5**

Transcending Boundaries

All Fulton did was to locate an efficient new Watt engine in a warehouse and, in 1807, install it in a well-designed boat.

—JOHN LIENHARD, *The Engines of Our Ingenuity*

INVENTORS OFTEN NEED TO GO beyond the area of their training or past experience and extend themselves into new realms. They need to sense an opportunity to bridge two industries, two intellectual domains, or two different worlds. They need to combine conceptual models that have never been put together before. They need to cross or transcend boundaries.

In the realm of creativity, the bridging of two worlds is known by more precise terms. Sometimes it's called "boundary transgression." Other times it's called "bisociation." As defined by Arthur Koestler in his groundbreaking 1964 book *The Act of Creation*, the word *bisociation* means the combination of ideas from two seemingly separate spheres. Koestler writes that he coined this term "in order to make a distinction between the routine skills of thinking on a single 'plane', as it were, and the creative act, which always operates on more than one plane."[1]

Those planes could involve two cultures, two technologies, or any number of combinations that an inventor can imagine. As you've seen, discovery and invention often happen when we observe or experience something that inspires us to spot a new pattern, and often those patterns are formed at the intersection of disciplines. Jay Walker's combination of a slot machine and a medicine bottle is one such example. The DNA molecule itself was also found through bisociation. Watson was trained in biology, Crick in physics. The combination turned out to be a key to the breakthrough.

English military engineer Thomas Savery, blacksmith Thomas Newcomen, and Scottish instrument maker James Watt invented steam engines based on their observations of water pressure, evaporation, and condensation.[2] Each of them crossed a boundary. They were watching what happens to water at different temperatures, but they were also thinking about machinery and the potential uses of machines. With little or no formal scientific knowledge available to them, each man combined knowledge from the two domains.

This boundary crossing led to the hallmark invention of the industrial revolution. Indeed, this crossing happened so suddenly that the entire human race was mesmerized. For years, no one quite knew why the steam engine worked; they knew only that it did. Science and invention themselves were separated by boundaries. Only by studying Watt's engine was Frenchman Sadi Carnot able to begin to understand heat movement. His work and the work of others led to the second law of thermodynamics. (The total energy in the universe remains constant, whereas the entropy—the measure of disorder—of an isolated system is always increasing. That's why ice melts, why water evaporates, why houses get increasingly messy.) Then, some years later, scientists came up with the first law. (The internal energy of an isolated system can be harnessed only through mass change, heat change, or work. So stop trying to invent a perpetual motion machine, and clean your room.)

But there were even more boundaries to cross. For the first century of its life, the steam engine wasn't even called a steam engine. Instead, it was called a pump, according to Stanford University professor Nathan Rosenberg.[3] Some people called it the "miner's friend" because it was used to pump water out of flooded coal mines. Only after a "succession of improvements in the late eighteenth century" did it become a "source of power for the textile factories, iron mills, and an expanding array of industrial establishments," says Rosenberg.

Robert Fulton then became famous for doing something that may seem obvious now. He applied ideas from the world of steam-powered pumps to the new age of canal building. In 1807, he placed a Watt engine in a boat. Fulton's 150-foot-long *Clermont* steamed up the Hudson at an average speed of five miles per hour. Sails and oars were no longer the only way to travel by water. With this crossing of a boundary, Fulton became immortalized in newspapers and song, and the steam engine became the engine of transportation, a generalizable source of power not only for steamboats and oceangoing steamships but also for railroads. After the Civil War, adds Rosenberg, inventors crossed another boundary, and the steam engine became a "turbine," used to produce "a new and even more generalizable source of power, electricity." Concludes Rosenberg, "Thomas Newcomen and James Watt should surely be forgiven for having failed to foresee the far-flung applications of their ingenious inventive efforts."[4]

BRIDGING WORLDS

Similarly, Watson and Crick should be forgiven for not envisioning where their discovery would go. To apply their discovery, biology alone wasn't sufficient. What if the new knowledge of biology were taken into the domain of mechanical engineering? What if technology and biology were combined?

Leroy Hood began thinking on these two planes at once under a brilliant biologist named Bill Dreyer, whom Hood met during medical school while working part-time at the National Institutes of Health. A senior scientist at NIH, Dreyer had already coinvented an amino acid analyzer for Beckman Instruments. To Hood, Dreyer imparted two dicta: First, "Always practice biology at the leading edge." Second, "If you really want to change biology, invent a new technology."[5] It was a mandate for boundary transgression. Throughout history, the invention of new tools had often led to the discovery of new knowledge. It happened with the steam engine, and it had been happening with medicine. The stethoscope, the X-ray, and diagnostic ultrasound all resulted from the crossing of similar boundaries. In Hood's case, however, he and his colleagues saw the need for new technologies for delving deep into the cell-hosted world of biological material.

To live in both worlds at once, Dreyer had developed his own original thinking patterns. He had always struggled when he tried to read for more than a few minutes at a time, and some teachers thought he had trouble learning. Later diagnosed with dyslexia, Dreyer demonstrated powerful techniques for compensating. "He is brilliant at being able to think conceptually about problems in ways that are unrestrained," Hood says. "He would say, 'Here are the data. What are the different ways to think about it? And let's not worry about dogma.'" Dreyer saw three-dimensional shapes—chains of multicolored molecules—take form in his mind. "I have these hallucinations in my mind," says Dreyer, recalling more than a half century of thinking about biology this way. "I edit them like a film."

These kinds of image combinations are often the source of new ideas for inventions. At the time he met Dreyer, Lee Hood was consumed by one such image. He was becoming fascinated by the field of immunology, particularly the study of how blood produces antibodies to fend off viruses, bacteria, and other pathogens. The image was like a microscopic video game. In the war between antibodies and pathogens, Hood wanted to know, how did the two sides go about sizing each other up? Did they seek to destroy each other? Did they communicate? If so, how? Were the two sides negotiating in order to resolve the war for the sake of preserving the health of the body?

Dreyer, too, was intrigued by the antibody problem. But he said he was leaving NIH to accept a faculty position at Caltech. Would Hood like to come along? After graduating from medical school, Hood enrolled at Caltech for graduate school, following his mentor across the country. In 1963, Hood found himself back on the Caltech campus in Pasadena.

Dreyer set up the immunology study as a Saturday afternoon project so that the two could collaborate in their spare time. "I got there just in time to get into the incredible excitement of the whole field," Hood says.

At the time, biologists all over the world were studying Watson and Crick's double-helix model for clues on how to crack the genetic code, trying to determine just how the DNA molecule went about creating the proteins. Because antibodies are among the most interesting proteins, the issues Hood had homed in on were right at the center of the action. "This Saturday afternoon project became one of the most exciting areas in all of molecular biology," he says. "I picked it because I knew it was interesting. I had no idea that it would explode like it did and that it would drive my career for the next twenty years."

Hood and Dreyer began by isolating the simplest, most homogenous antibody molecule they could find. They chose a myeloma protein, which is secreted by a cancerous tumor. But to study this antibody closely enough, they needed to break it down into its molecular components, its sequential pattern of amino acids. This process is known as sequencing. They needed to invent something—a new technology, a new machine—that would improve their chance of making a scientific breakthrough. The existing tools weren't sensitive enough to see what needed to be seen. To get a close enough look at the composition of an antibody, Dreyer and Hood realized they needed to invent an automated protein sequencer. "Lee was doing protein sequencing by hand," Dreyer recalls. "I had to brainwash him into developing new tools."[6]

With the cracking of the genetic code in 1966, biologists became consumed by finding new protein patterns. Biologists had known that it was DNA's job to create proteins, but until then, they didn't know how it happened. The breakthrough finding was an astoundingly simple pattern: Three letters of the DNA language encode one letter of the protein language. Represented by strings of four nucleotide bases—C, G, A, and T—the DNA molecules contain genes in the same way that a book contains words and sentences. "The genes, the DNA, operate in one dimension," explains Hood, "whereas the proteins operate in three dimensions." Another popular analogy is that DNA letters are like notes on a piano, while proteins are like chords.

The proteins themselves act like Legos—simple building blocks. Proteins come in only twenty different amino acid varieties—represented by three-letter combinations such as GTA or CAT—but they can click together to make complex molecular machines. When proteins stick together, they form the skin, the nervous system, the immune system, and the organ systems of the body. If we could analyze the building blocks of these systems, cutting-edge biologists concluded, we could begin to troubleshoot these systems, understand how cancers and other diseases come about, and ultimately prevent many of those diseases.

Biologists alone couldn't solve the problem. Because biologists typically weren't engineers and engineers were seldom biologists, the two fields were isolated from each other. After receiving his Ph.D. and joining Caltech's faculty in 1970, Hood set about changing that. He was among the first to make the crossing.

He wanted his fledgling "molecular biotechnology" laboratory at Caltech to invent new instruments. To read a chain of proteins quickly, he and Dreyer worked in the lab to construct a desktop device in an airtight case. The case contained a large cup that would spin rapidly. "The proteins would be coated on the wall of the cup," Hood says, "and you could put in solutions and solvents to do the various washes. It looked like a little washing machine." The challenge was to construct plastic valves feeding in and out of the cup that could withstand the solvents. "A little spinning part could deliver the precise amount of agents and solvents to carry out the sequential steps, chopping the amino acids off the end of the protein chain, one at a time." Each individual protein was isolated and then delivered by the machine into a tube where it could be identified and analyzed. The result? "It meant we could look at all sorts of proteins that had been inaccessible before that time," Hood explains.

The protein sequencer provided key insights into Hood's original immunology question. This machine could also help decode other problems that were just as gnarly, including the study of how mutant genes, called oncogenes, created cancerous proteins.

Hood, Dreyer and their colleagues received several patents on their inventions, and eventually it led to a series of other discoveries in several fields of biology. By 1973, Hood and Dreyer had their protein sequencing machine working in the laboratory.

MOVING BEYOND BORDERS

But Hood was engaging in a type of bisociation that was considered taboo in his environment. The accomplishment of coinventing a protein sequencer earned Hood a stern warning from the chairman of Caltech's biology department. "The chairman sat me down," Hood recalls. "He was really concerned I was spending too much time on technology. His strong fatherly advice was to concentrate on biology and to give up on all these other things." Except for Dreyer, "all the other senior faculty members felt strongly that it was inappropriate to develop technology in a biology department, and if you wanted to do that, you should go to the engineering department."

Hood and Dreyer were becoming the outcasts of their own department. But they had hit upon a successful sequence: Find or create open scientific questions. See whether there is a need for new technologies to help scientists make their discoveries. Then go about inventing those new technologies. The new invention itself would create additional open questions, leading to the need for more new technologies, and the pattern would repeat. For example, Hood also coinvented a protein *synthesizer*, a machine that automatically manufactures protein samples from actual DNA. Hood insisted on pursuing this boundary transgression, so much so that he alienated Caltech's constrained culture. "Later, it all came home to roost, " Hood says, "and I ended up leaving Caltech over this very issue."

For Lee Hood, the traditional biology department itself was becoming a model that no longer worked. Others were transcending the same barriers at the same time. In 1973, the year he and Dreyer completed their automated protein sequencer, something big was brewing at two other California universities. Stanford's Stanley Cohen and Berkeley's Herbert Boyer spliced one gene from one cell culture to another. In artificially recombining two genes, they opened up a new field: genetic engineering. Two years later, Walter Gilbert and Allan Maxam of Harvard, and Frederick Sanger of Cambridge University (England), developed different methods for manually determining the sequence of the DNA bases—the exact G, A, T, C patterns—in a strand of genetic material.

All this suggested a new challenge to Hood. Just as Hood and Dreyer wanted a tool for automatically sequencing proteins, biologists all over the world would come to need a machine for doing the same for the underlying genes themselves. For this new field of mapping and engineering genes to take off, there had to be a way to automate the process. Hood already knew what should happen next. Just as he developed a protein sequencer, he immediately set out to invent a DNA sequencer, a "gene machine." He began with the same shapes and materials that had worked to form his earlier machine: the same tubes, the same cone, the same spinning mechanism, the same techniques for washing the genetic material with chemical solvents. But this project would prove to be much more difficult and would require much more time and funding.

Once again, he encountered stiff resistance from the higher-ups at Caltech, who felt that this was an engineering problem. The university wouldn't fund the project. A friend suggested to Hood that these new machines shouldn't be developed as nonprofit research tools but instead should be sold as commercial products to laboratories worldwide. Hood agreed. He could circumvent Caltech's biology department and place his inventions and his ideas in a major corporation that could successfully take these ideas to market.

"We went out and shopped it," he recalls. In 1979, Hood and Caltech colleague Michael Hunkapiller began visiting medical instrument companies, one by one. They received rejection after rejection. Eighteen of the nineteen companies Hood and Hunkapiller visited were not interested in manufacturing and commercializing his inventions. The nineteenth one, DuPont, seemed intrigued at first. But after considering it for a while, DuPont also rejected the idea.

As Hood saw it, the old models were broken. The academic biology department was no place to develop new technology, and the corporations that might make money on these instruments couldn't see this opportunity or weren't willing to take the risk. A new combination was needed.

This new pattern became the biotech industry. In 1980, the firm cofounded by Boyer and venture capitalist Robert Swanson, Genentech, launched a successful initial public offering, the first biotech company to do so. Their pioneering patent on gene splicing became a cornerstone of this emerging industry. Around that time, a venture capitalist named Bill Bowes approached Hood and offered to put $2 million behind Caltech's biotech inventions. They formed a team and started Applied Biosystems Inc., which would become one of the largest, most profitable, and most enduring of the new wave of biotech start-ups. Hood's Caltech colleague Michael Hunkapiller joined the R&D staff and is now the company's president.[7]

Putting Genes into Machines

Hood's bisociative behavior seemed to have found a home in the marketplace. The old model was in pieces, and Hood was picking them up and integrating the two worlds of biology and technology to form a new combination.

But such transcendence wasn't yet in vogue at Caltech. Hood proposed that the university create an entire molecular biotechnology department, which would draw professors and students from both biology and engineering into new research projects and degree programs. The president of the university liked the idea. So did the engineering professors. The biology professors, however, ended up vetoing it, perhaps because they felt threatened.

Meanwhile, Hood was having a hard time developing the DNA sequencer as he had imagined it. For three years, he worked on it without much to show for his efforts. The epiphany happened one day in 1982 at a gathering he attended of four colleagues from different backgrounds. The group included Hunkapiller, a chemist, and Lloyd M. Smith, a biochemist. "We sat around and came up with all the essential ideas in a matter of hours," he says. "You could separate the DNA fragments in a little tube. We could color the fragments one of four different colors corresponding to the bases." Fluorescent dyes of blue, green, red, and yellow could represent C, G, A, and T. "Then you'd need a laser detector. You could read out the colors, and that could be translated into the DNA sequences."

The group realized that more boundaries would need to be crossed. "We knew we'd have to integrate chemistry with engineering with computer science with biology," recalls Hood. The entire sequence of three billion letters of DNA would have to be fed into a computer database. "We needed really good people who could put all those things together. I came to appreciate how important the cross-disciplinary approach would be." What he would eventually discover is that invention isn't cross-disciplinary but *trans*disciplinary. It's an endeavor that doesn't just cut across subject domains but transcends all subjects.

The DNA sequencer, the gene machine, was an invention that would make it possible to launch what became known as the Human Genome Project, the massive effort to map more than thirty thousand genes in the human body. When the project was first proposed, at a scientific gathering in Santa Cruz, California, in 1985, Lee Hood was there to find out how his invention would fit in. But the meeting was followed by howls of protest against moving ahead. Politicians objected to the cost, projected at $3 billion. Some respected professors were categorically against "big science" and "megaprojects," arguing that they hogged funding. Many leading biologists felt that 98 percent of the data would be junk and "biologically meaningless," and therefore a waste of time. Nobel laureates from the world of biology called it a public relations stunt, and not real science. The debate over whether there should be a gene mapping project at all went on for five years.[8]

As the sequencing technology advanced and as the importance of doing the work became increasingly obvious, the project was at last approved, funded, and under way. At that time, Hood went searching for a new setting, a new place to form a cross-disciplinary laboratory. He landed at the University of Washington's School of Medicine. He introduced his multidisciplinary approach with a set of lectures that were attended by Microsoft's Bill Gates. Soon after, Hood and Gates went out for dinner and stayed for a four-hour conversation about the role of software in biology and related topics. Fascinated with the idea that human genes could be turned into massive amounts of computer data, Gates in 1991 donated $12 million to endow a a genuine department of molecular biotechnology, something that Hood had been trying to launch for twenty years.

With the boundaries finally erased, there was an outpouring of ideas and inventions. Two of the department's faculty members—John Yates and Ruedi Aebersold—founded a field known as proteomics, the mapping and study of all human proteins. The department also developed new ink-jet printers for analyzing amino acids, licensing the technology to a pair of corporations. New technology led to breakthrough studies of prostate cancer. Another pair of colleagues was doing things with computers that biologists would never have considered. "Ger van den Engh developed the world's most powerful fluorescent-activated cell-sorting machine," recalls Hood. "Phil Green pioneered the critical software programs for assembly and quality control in the Human Genome Project. The department was successful beyond my wildest expectations."[9]

CHAPTER **6**

Detecting Barriers

Blocked situations increase stress. . . . Where S represents the start-
ing point, and T represents the target, there are loops of trains of
thought all around S within the blocked matrix. Unfortunately,
T is located outside the plane of the matrix.

—Arthur Koestler, *The Act of Creation*

Inventors are often surrounded by hidden barriers. The
inventor may have created a fantastic opportunity or pinpointed a
question that urgently must be solved, but this doesn't mean that he
or she knows the right path to a solution or even whether such a
path exists. Many of us have had that feeling that we're running in
circles, banging our head against a wall, or hitting up against an obstacle that seems insurmountable.

Successful inventors tend to thrive on this kind of stress. They
know that the only way to work through the obstacle and the anxi-
ety it produces is identify the stumbling block in a way that others
who have approached the problem have yet to see. At some point, the
inventor will feel trapped in a vast maze, and the only way to escape
is to find a hidden passageway, discover a door in the floor, or realize
that the maze itself exists in three dimensions rather than two.

SEEING MICROSCOPIC BARRIERS

Kathryn Wilder Guarini faces just this kind of challenge. Guarini, a dark-haired woman with a calm, easygoing demeanor, is one of the younger members of the research staff at IBM's Watson Labs. Working on opening up a third dimension in the world of semiconductors, Guarini is up against a range of physical barriers. In accordance with Moore's Law, the famous principle set down by Intel founder Gordon Moore, the number of transistors we can pack into a square inch of microchip has been doubling roughly every eighteen months for more than three decades. Thanks to breakthroughs by hundreds of researchers and inventors in dozens of companies, we can now fit more than 200 million circuits onto a fingernail-sized chip that can process more data more quickly than could the room-sized computers of yesteryear. But we need a way to transcend that matrix. "We're going to need some new kinds of breakthroughs," says Gerald Marcyk, director of components research at Intel. "The single-dimension path of the past thirty-five years is now limited."[1]

Guarini's approach is to add another dimension. "With current microchips, there is only a single layer of active devices," she says.[2] Whereas others are plunging into new areas of scientific discovery—attempting to build "molecular computers" by lining up individual atoms or to design "optical computers" by arranging photons of light—Guarini is working with conventional technology. But instead of trying to pack more transistors onto the same surface, she is asking the question, "Can you have more than one layer of transistors?" she says. "It's like making a layer cake. We need to build or grow a new layer on top of the first one." It sounds simple enough. The only problem is that it has never been done successfully, and no one knows whether it's possible.

Guarini thrives on the challenge of detecting and working through these kinds of barriers. Growing up in Connecticut in the 1970s and 1980s, she enjoyed puzzles, mind games, and math problems. In high school, she was inspired by an enthusiastic physics teacher who would leap on top of a desk and declare, "Physics is life!" Guarini went on to major in applied physics at Yale and received her Ph.D. in the same field from Stanford, where she studied under the coinventor of the atomic force microscope. She worked as an intern at Hewlett-Packard before joining IBM at the age of twenty-six in 1997.

As Guarini sees it, the stumbling block to creating 3-D chips must lie somewhere in the manufacturing process, in microscopic construction techniques. As you try to add a new layer to a chip, "you can damage or degrade the layers below." She has made real progress in addressing that barrier using scanning probe lithography, a method of manipulating nanoscale transistors. At an international conference in December 2002, she presented a newly patented technique for adding a new layer of circuits without destroying what lies beneath.

Given that her employer receives more patents than any other corporation in the world, it's no surprise that Guarini is listed as coinventor on several interesting patents such as this one. But none of those patents represents the smashing of a really big barrier. "I don't think that we have had an epiphany or a breakthrough yet," she says. "We try to outline what the major roadblocks are, and we will try to mow them down one by one. We might know whether this or that is a potential challenge or a potential roadblock. Only then can we come up with an innovative solution."

Like a chef baking layer cakes, Guarini dons a white hat and uniform for her daily duties. Hers, however, is a bright white bunny suit that covers every inch of her head, hands, body, feet, and clothing. She takes a visitor into the "cleanroom" where she conducts her 3-D semiconductor experiments, checking on crystals that are growing in vacuum chambers and peeking at silicon wafers that are baking in ovens that typically crank up to 900 degrees centigrade. Guarini works with robotic arms to manipulate acid bath tanks, spin dryers, and electron microscopes. "We look for microscopic bumps," she says. "We spend a lot of time on the art of measurement: How do we see what we made?"

Only by detecting what is happening at the nanoscale level will she be able to overcome what she now sees as the next set of barriers: the process of connecting the circuits between the two layers so that they work as one microchip. "The goal is to make the layers work together," she says. "That hasn't been done yet."

Detecting barriers can be frustrating work. By looking around at her colleagues wandering the halls of the crescent-shaped Watson Labs headquarters in Yorktown Heights, New York, Guarini can see what the stakes are. The danger here isn't losing your job; there aren't very many applied physicists on the unemployment line. Instead, the danger is falling into obscurity. Some researchers work their entire careers in a single problem area without making a significant break-through. Others, such as Guarini's colleague Bernie Meyerson, de-tect and overcome a significant barrier and go on to become labo ratory superstars who are promoted to the top of the organization.

"I have an opportunity to make a mark," Guarini says. "But this is the nature of corporate research. Breakthroughs are rare. You have to study what others are doing and try something a little differently."

DETOURING AROUND AN INDUSTRY

Sometimes it takes only one person to detect a barrier that is hold-ing up an entire bureaucracy. By trying to do something a little dif-ferently, a young inventor named Isaac Berzin thinks he may have found such an obstacle. Berzin, who has lively dark eyes, a quick laugh, and a slight Israeli accent, works in a basement laboratory just off the campus of MIT, where he's attempting to invent what he believes will be the cheapest form of commercial power and the cleanest-burning fuel known. If what he is doing works as planned, Berzin's renewable biofuel will leap ahead of wind power, photovoltaic cells, and hydrogen fuel cells to become the leading contender to replace coal, oil, and nuclear power in the world's electrical power plants. That's a big claim, but Berzin knows he will have to overcome an even larger series of hidden barriers to realize this possibility.

Berzin is growing a specially modified form of algae and turning it into what he calls GreenFuel. He's talking about the stuff that clings to the walls of fish tanks—the stuff that requires only water and photosynthesis to breed right before your eyes. "Photosynthesis,"

Berzin says. "That's how all of nature survives. The division time of algae cells is measured in hours. It's very tolerant of everything. You can find it in the Charles River, in sewage, in boiling water, in ice, in Antarctica, in fresh water, in the Dead Sea."[3] By infusing algae with carbon, the key source of the energy locked inside coal, Berzin believes he may be able to turn this plentiful, naturally growing plant into a source of power.

Researchers at the U.S. Department of Energy (DOE) have known about this carbon-algae possibility for years. The department's experiments, however, involved growing algae in an open pond and pumping carbon-based gases into the pond's water. As it turns out, this is an inefficient and ineffective way to grow the algae. Only the top of the pond receives sunlight, and it receives too much. This means that the pond must be churned by heavy machinery, itself a process that requires energy. And harvesting the carbon-infused algae from the pond is itself an expensive process. As a result, Berzin says, the pond-based approach isn't scalable or cost-effective. It simply isn't worth doing, and any new form of energy must be cost-effective to be successful. There needs to be a cheap and highly controlled way to grow and harvest massive amounts of algae. This was the barrier that Isaac Berzin detected while reading reports of these past experiments.

The son of an inventor, Berzin grew up in Israel and received his Ph.D. in chemical engineering from an Israeli university. In 2001, he began his postdoc work in the MIT laboratory of Robert Langer, a prolific biomedical inventor whom the *Boston Globe* recently called "the smartest man in Boston."[4] When Langer saw what Berzin was proposing, he helped set up the GreenFuel project in the offices of Payload Systems, a 10-year-old NASA contractor that has been developing a process to cultivate and harvest hydroponically grown plants in atmospheres other than that of Earth. Langer has long been MIT's faculty adviser to Payload.

Near the bottom of the creaky wooden staircase in Payload's basement, Berzin constructed a set of three biofuel reactors. He has filed for patents on the basic approach. Each reactor is built around a long Lucite tube filled with water, and the tubes sit under a series of full-spectrum lightbulbs. The other inputs to the reactors sit in tall pressurized tanks. One tank is filled with carbon dioxide, and the other is filled with nitrogen oxide. Both are well known as pollutants given off by power plants. Anyone who can recycle these gases can receive "credits" under set of DOE regulations devised to reduce greenhouse gases. In the world of energy, these credits are as good as cash. As a result, any cost of producing GreenFuel can be offset by these pollution credits, and this is one reason it promises to be cheap.

The chemical reaction is simple. The artificial sunlight hits the water and produces algae. At the same time, the CO_2 reacts with the N_2O in the algae-filled water. As a by-product of this reaction, oxygen is released into the room, and pure nitrogen is piped out of the building through an exhaust system, where it mixes with the outside air. (Nitrogen is harmful when it is part of a compound with oxygen; that compound is the main ingredient of smog. But releasing pure nitrogen into the outside air isn't harmful. It gets absorbed by plants. Nitrogen itself is the main ingredient of fertilizer.)

The key here is the carbon; it gets trapped in the algae. Berzin's reactor pushes the carbon-infused algae to one end of the plastic tube. This mixture is then harvested and pumped to another room by means of desktop-sized machines that Payload built for NASA in cooperation with MIT's spaceflight program. These miniature automated bio-reactor systems (MARS) essentially convert the green watery sludge into a dry crystalline powder. The result is a green chunky substance that consists mostly of carbon. When it burns, the substance produces 90 percent of the energy of carbon-based coal.

Unlike coal, however, GreenFuel yields energy without any harmful emissions. In fact, the process of making it actually consumes harmful emissions, so much so that coal plants become the perfect place to create and burn GreenFuel. The substance can even be sprinkled in with coal, and they can burn together. Needless to say, the coal industry will probably be highly skeptical. "I'd like to find a way to work with them," Berzin jokes, "or else they will kill me."

By detecting a barrier in the process of producing and harvesting carbon-infused sludge, he seems to have achieved a breakthrough that had escaped the attention of an entire bureaucracy and all the corporations that do business with it. Berzin believes that his cheap GreenFuel process is infinitely scalable. Whether he is right is a huge question. To prove the idea, he must build more reactors and place them side by side. At first, the process was being conducted in a basement under artificial light. But Berzin is planning to launch his first pilot project out in the open, with the sun as the source of the photosynthesis.

Berzin has found some early believers in his initial breakthrough. His business plan for GreenFuel won $10,000 as the runner-up in the MIT $50K Entrepreneurship Competition, an annual contest for student-led start-ups. That recognition helped Berzin land a round of venture capital investment in 2004 and move his company, GreenFuel Technologies Corporation, into a larger office space in Cambridge. With those funds, Berzin plans to conduct pilot projects at several steam and power plants.

Berzin may have detected and overcome one major barrier, but he'll know for sure whether he is on the right path only if he is able to detect others. "I'm like a little duck learning to swim," he says. "Maybe I'm starting to fly a little." But he realizes he can't go it alone. Scaling up his system is going to be an enormous task. Eventually, Berzin wants to grow GreenFuel in the sun-drenched Great Plains of the United States. "I'm going to need to connect with people in ten different fields to get this out into the world," he says.

FINDING THE WRIGHT BARRIER

Orville and Wilbur Wright may be history's most remarkable example of having what it takes to detect the right barrier at the right time. In the most simplified understanding of what the Wright brothers accomplished, there is the tendency to ascribe to them the very idea of the airplane. Nothing could be further from the truth. Birds have served as mental models for future flying machines since the days of Leonardo da Vinci. "The wind may serve as a wedge to raise them up," he wrote. In 1738, Daniel Bernoulli gave future inventors an equation for understanding the relation between pressure, velocity, and elevation. But applying Bernoulli's principle wasn't enough for inventors to achieve the proper liftoff. Something else, some other lack of understanding, was standing in the way of the invention of the airplane as we've come to know it.[5]

The Wrights are often portrayed as garage tinkerers—bicycle repairmen—who empirically tried various approaches to solve the problem of powered flight, learning only from trial and error. This, too, is misleading. The Wright brothers studied the theory of flight and pondered why others had failed. They constructed a wind tunnel and performed sophisticated simulations before trying to take flight themselves. But they achieved what they did for a key reason: They detected the exact barrier that had eluded other aeronautical pioneers and then focused intensely on overcoming it.

Rubber band–powered toy helicopters made of cork, bamboo, and paper had already been around in various forms for at least a century when Dayton, Ohio, minister Milton Wright presented the toy to two of his young sons. The year was 1878. Wilbur was nine, Orville seven. The brothers noticed the remarkable stability of this toy's flight pattern. But when they built their own model helicopters, they were surprised to learn that that the bigger they made them, the more unstable they became.

As young men, the Wright brothers were interested in all sorts of things, including developing their own photographs and editing and printing their own newspaper. Those other interests faded after Orville borrowed three dollars from his older brother to buy his first bicycle, the kind with an oversized front wheel and a high saddle. Soon after, they each bought new, more expensive "safety" bicycles, in which the two wheels were of the same size. The innovations in bicycle design—including sprocket chains replacing direct pedaling, air-filled rubber tires, and comfortable seats—triggered a national craze in the 1890s. In anticipation of a continued surge in demand, in 1892 the brothers opened a shop for bicycle assembly and repair.[6]

They continued to read occasional articles about others who were tackling the problem of manned flight, mainly from the point of view of amateur enthusiasts. One story in August 1896 especially struck them. German flight pioneer Otto Lilienthal, who had built eighteen variations of his hang glider over six years, was hit with a sudden gust of wind while in flight. He thrust his body to compensate, but he wasn't able to avoid a sideslip, and he plunged to his death.

This was the same year the first horseless carriages came to Dayton. But the Wrights weren't impressed by the automobile or interested in its early limitations. They were fascinated by bicycles and by the perplexing problem of flight.

Because neither of the brothers went to college, one might assume that they knew little of the science behind the problem. But they studied their chosen challenge even more voraciously than a typical academic. Both had equal parts intelligence and mechanical skills, and both worked as closely as two people had ever worked, applying what has been called their "dual gift" to their objective. Assembling and repairing bikes by day, in their spare time they searched for books on the subject of flight. In the summer of 1899, they wrote the Smithsonian Institution for references to available flight literature. (No, they weren't referred to airline magazines.) In the letter, Wilbur stated, "I am an enthusiast, but not a crank." Until then, the Wrights had been reading mainly about ornithology, the study of birds. Now, with the references provided by the Smithsonian, they learned about the aviation experiments of those who had come before them.

They read the works of Lilienthal and those of Octave Chanute, author of *Progress in Flying Machines*. They also read about Alexander Graham Bell's experiments with multidimensional kites and about Hiram Stevens Maxim, who had invented the machine gun before taking up this new problem. They also read a translation of Louis-Pierre Mouillard's *L'Empire de l'Air*, which Wilbur called "inspiring."

The Wrights were not interested in gliding but rather in powered flight, and they were not interested in balloons, only in "heavier-than-air" flight. The literature developing around the problem as they saw it wasn't voluminous, but the Wrights investigated everything of importance, searching for holes in theories and for assumptions that might be incorrect, much as a modern-day inventor will scan patent filings and peruse technical journals for similar gaps and gaffes.

Probably the most daring of the experimenters was Samuel Pierpont Langley, the secretary of the Smithsonian. To Langley, the barrier was in powering the plane. In 1896, Langley launched a dualwing, twin-propeller plane, powered by a steam engine, from a bluff by a bank of the Potomac River. He called his craft an aerodrome, and he improved on his design by adding an ingenious lightweight engine. Bell, by then famous, was on hand to take photographs of Langley's first flights. Of course, Langley's early aerodromes were unmanned, so his achievements don't rival what the Wrights later accomplished. But at the time, Langley was the man who had proved wrong the professors and experts who claimed to have scientific proof that heavier-than-air flight was impossible.

In reading about Langley, however, the Wrights concluded he was heading in the wrong direction. They were surprised by how little attention was being paid to the problem of controlling the aircraft. Who cared about the engine? Langley had no way to steer the plane. They observed how birds controlled direction and steering, whereas others had focused on how birds achieved lift and aerodynamic glide. The airplane, the Wrights imagined, would have more in common with the bicycle, which requires delicate, constant steering, rather than the automobile, in which the breakthrough was in the engine. In their reading, they took note of Chanute's call for "a better way to maintain equilibrium than by thrashing the legs and torso about—gyrations made necessary by wind fluctuations that caused the center of pressure on a wing to move back and forth."[7] To the Wrights, the term *powered flight* was misleading. Powering the aircraft would be relatively simple. The engine could come later. What use is an engine if you can't control the aircraft?

That was the barrier they detected: one of maintaining control and balance. "We at once set to work to devise a more efficient means of maintaining the equilibrium," wrote Orville.[8] That was the stumbling block that had foiled previous inventors, although they didn't realize it until they saw the Wrights redefine the problem.

The result was a discovery known as "wing warping," a technique for stabilizing the plane by controlling the position of the wings. The idea of twisting the wings became the basis for the most valuable and contentious patent in the history of aviation. Orville had the inspiration one day while fiddling with an empty bicycle tire tube box, twisting each end in the opposite direction. The brothers then applied this analogy to their latest flier, and in December 1903, the Wrights made history with their breakthrough flight at Kitty Hawk. But they never would have had anything to break through if they hadn't detected the critical barrier in the first place.

CONVERGING ON THE BARRIER

Within established industries, lots of inventors often converge on the same barrier at roughly the same time, and it takes a little extra juice to be the individual or team to be the first to break through. Carl Crawford has got it. He was one of a handful of inventors to discover a critical boundary at the core of the medical equipment business, and he is constantly searching for new ones. Crawford is slightly built with thinning light brown hair, and he acknowledges that he's "somewhat weird, like most inventors I know." A bicycle enthusiast who likes to get up early to go for a ride every morning, he sometimes becomes so preoccupied with technical problems in his mind that he forgets where he is or how he got there. Growing up in Milwaukee in the 1960s, Crawford recalls spending hours ripping apart and repairing transistor radios.[9] He also remembers his family's shock upon getting his SAT results: a 200 on the verbal portion, the lowest possible score, and a near perfect 790 on the math portion. "I couldn't communicate," he says. That has since changed, but Crawford still points to these scores as evidence of his quirkiness and his reliance on having his inventions speak for him.

While Crawford was studying electrical engineering at Purdue, a professor interested Crawford in computed tomography, or CT. At first, Crawford says, "I couldn't spell CT." Not long after receiving his Ph.D. from the same institution, he took a job in his hometown of Milwaukee as a staff engineer with GE Medical Systems. At GE, he was struck by the limitations of commercial CT scanners (sometimes called CAT, or computer-assisted tomography, scanners). The technology was already a mainstay of the conglomerate's medical equipment business. A vast improvement over the film-based X-ray machine, which took only a two-dimensional snapshot, CT provided superlative three-dimensional images of the body's interiors. If something important, such as a tumor, was blocked by bones or other organs, the X-ray machine would often miss it. With CT, though, doctors could finally see everything in graphic detail.[10]

The technology had revolutionized medical diagnostics to such an extent that its inventor, Allan Cormack, and the engineer who commercialized it, Godfrey Houndsfield, shared the Nobel Prize in medicine in 1979. By then, these SUV-sized machines had been installed in hospitals all over the developed world, at a cost of about $1 million each. A patient, lying on a conveyer, was carried through the contraption much as a piece of paper is fed through a fax machine, except that the scanning occurred in three dimensions. The scanner acquired cross-sectional images of the head and body and then reassembled the slices and rendered them as images for study by doctors. Indeed, the Latin root *tomo* means "slices." Typically, the slices would be only ten millimeters thick, so the machine had to acquire hundreds of them.

But these machines had a drawback: It often took several minutes to scan an entire body. Each thin slice had to be rendered as perfectly as possible. The slightest movement by the patient, including something as simple as breathing, would cause blurring or streaking in the images. As a patient moved through the scanner, technicians had to pause each time the scanner arrived at a new section of the body. To get a proper scan, patients had to hold their breaths during each scan to prevent artifacts and gaps. "How long can a person hold their breath?" remarks Crawford. "For twenty seconds, maybe thirty or forty, if you're really healthy." Between scans, the patient was typically allowed to breathe for only six to eight seconds.

Inventors around the world had been working to improve the machines for years, trying to detect barriers and work through them. First-generation scanners were based on a single X-ray detector that rotated and translated around the cross sections. This process often took more than an hour, and it required such stillness from patients that early CT scanning was limited to the head. Later scanners employed an array of detectors. Now each slice could be

acquired in several seconds. This improvement opened up new applications for scanning not only the head but also the neck, chest,
abdomen, pelvis, legs, and feet. But most hospitals had only begun
buying these machines when they started to come equipped with
hundreds of detectors. This reduced scan time even further per
body section, but the problem remained of patients having to hold
their breaths, notes Crawford, and many of the images still ended
up with some blurring and had to be redone.

After joining GE, Crawford spent large chunks of time reviewing the technical literature, a habit he continues to this day. To detect
a new barrier, and therefore a new opportunity, he searches for
flaws. They often present themselves as holes in logic. "I look for assumptions that might be wrong," he says. "I also look for adjectives
and adverbs. They often hide the fact that the writers don't understand fully what they are writing about."[11] In articles about CT
scanners, he found an interesting logic gap. Previous inventors had
believed that the solution was to incorporate increasing numbers of
X-ray detectors into these machines or to rotate them faster around
the body.

Crawford, however, hit up against a different obstacle. "History
said the patient had to be completely stationary," he says. "That was
impractical." He believed that the ultimate CT scanner should scan
sections of the body in less than one second. In this way, the patient
wouldn't have to worry at all about blurring due to moving or
breathing.

Others hadn't seen it that way. Back in the mid-1980s, the barrier to instantaneous scanning was thought to be the time it took for
the X-ray tubes to cool or by limitations on data bandwidth. "We
made the assumption that data acquisition was not limited by those
factors," he says.

Crawford and a fellow engineer named Kevin King were especially focused on the problem. Like the Wright brothers, Crawford
and King were not far apart in age, and they developed an effective
way of working together. When one got burned out thinking about
something for too long, the other would pick up where the first one
left off. By bouncing ideas off of each other, they discovered a previously unseen opportunity: Why not find a way to acquire the image

data continuously, rather than in discrete slices and intervals? Why not find a way to scan sections of the body in a single breath hold so that blurring is no longer an issue? Why not reduce the time between scans to zero? These were radical questions at the time. "We had to cross this threshold," Crawford says. In heading down this new path, Crawford and King reinvented the challenge. They set out to create a new machine that would scan the body in a new way.

To solve the problem, they homed in on the scanning pattern itself. If the patient was moving, they thought, the X-ray detectors would no longer be able to capture a perfectly cut slice of the body. Instead, it would be like winding a string around a slowly moving cylinder. The detectors would actually be acquiring a continuous spiral pattern. The scanning pattern would resemble a Slinky toy rather than slices of salami. Along with the new pattern, there needed to be a new mathematics for translating data taken from a moving patient in this way.

The two engineers had detected the roadblock, but they didn't yet know how they were going to get around it. "That was the barrier," Crawford says. "We created our own necessity just by looking at the problem in a different way." They were determined to come up with a new method of scanning and not a better way to conduct the old method. They viewed the existing scan pattern, fixed for the preceding twenty years, as obsolete.

HITTING THE NEXT BARRIER

In an internal GE paper in 1987, Crawford and King first described their resulting solution, based on a breakthrough interpolation algorithm. They called their invention "helical extrapolative scanning." Also known as spiral CT scanning, the technology was first introduced to the industry in 1989 and then perfected in the early 1990s, when it would lead to what Stanford University radiologist Sandy Napel called a "virtual renaissance in CT, improving its capabilities in existing applications and creating new ones."[12] By the mid-1990s, virtually all CT scanners would be spiral scanners.

But Crawford and King weren't the only ones who detected the same barrier. As is typically the case, they were simply *among* the

first. Simultaneous invention was happening all over the world. That
is the nature of barrier detection. Inventive minds tend to converge
on good ideas. In the days of the Wright brothers, the pace of invention was far more rapid than it had been in all of history. But at
least the Wrights had a few years to work through their barrier before others caught up with them.

Crawford and King had no time at all. Other inventors and corporate researchers were on the road toward a similar result. In their
patent search, conducted along with GE attorneys, they came across
a 1989 University of Illinois patent by inventors headed down a
convergent path. They also discovered a 1986 patent, filed in the
United States by a Toshiba engineer, that referred to helical scanning. But the biggest source of competition came just as Crawford
and King were getting ready to file their own patent applications
and as they were preparing a paper for submission in the journal
Medical Physics.

In June 1989, Crawford went to Berlin to attend an industry
conference. It was there that he met his counterpart at the medical
systems division of Siemens, the German industrial giant. Electrical
engineer Willi Kalender was part of a Siemens team readying its
own patent applications, as well as a paper on spiral CT scanning, for
the journal *Thoracic Radiology*. The two groups knew of each other
but didn't know exactly what the other was working on. One late
night, Crawford and Kalender met and went out for a drink. The
most convenient bar happened to be located in a nearby brothel. It
was there, over beers in that less than reputable establishment, that
Crawford said something like, "I am working on the best thing,
something that will revolutionize CT, but I can't tell you what it is."
Hearing that, Kalender replied with something like, "So am I!" They
sidestepped their secrets for the rest of the evening, beer after beer,
trying to talk about other things.

In the subsequent months both teams filed for patents and submitted papers.[13] By the end of 1990, the patents and papers of both
teams had been published, and their work was no longer secret.
At that year's radiology conference in Chicago, each team summa-
rized its work and discussed the results back to back, in the same
room, on a Sunday morning. First, Kalender, from the Siemens

team, spoke about spiral scanning. King, from the GE team, followed with his presentation on helical scanning, a minor difference in terminology that continues to be argued about.

With both teams detecting the same barrier and announcing similar breakthroughs, one might think that the race to market would have been intense, but that wasn't the case. Instead of supporting the findings of their own engineers, the management of GE Medical Systems went on the attack against this new method of scanning. GE denounced the approach taken by Siemens as well as the approach taken by Crawford and King. "GE was scared about cannibalizing" its existing market, Crawford recalls. At the time the world leader in selling the current million-dollar machines, the GE division was led by managers and marketing executives who figured that word of a revolutionary new approach could kill their current pipeline of product sales, significantly impacting near-term revenue. They assigned other GE executives to write papers claiming that this new form of CT scanning wouldn't work, according to Crawford.

Siemens took the opposite approach, rushing a new-generation product to market in early 1991. The Siemens product started capturing some market share, at the expense of GE. But according to Crawford, Siemens had released its machine prematurely because it incorporated the wrong algorithm for interpolating the spiral scan data. Kalender seemed to encounter a significant new barrier. The Siemens engineer was unable to correct for a mathematical effect of the spiral scanning process, and this led to a doubling of the scan time. That defect slowed Siemens from further penetrating the market, as Kalender and his team tried to figure out how to overcome this more specific problem.

Crawford and King, meanwhile, hit this new barrier hard. What was this more specific barrier? As it turns out, helical scanning until then was based on collecting data in half-scans of approximately 180 degrees. One set of X-ray detectors scanned the top half of the body, and a second set scanned the bottom half. With the spiral scan pattern, the body moved too fast to get this approach to work without producing image artifacts. Crawford and King, in a separate patent filed only two weeks after their first one, disclosed something new: a method of having all the X-ray detectors acquire data in full, 360-degree scans around the body, thereby obtaining *two* measurements of everything. The double measurements were used to cancel out the image artifacts and retain the time goals. "Our invention was in doing it without doubling the scan time," Crawford says.

This was the breakthrough that eventually caused a massive changeover in a rich market. Within two years, the results from these new spiral scanners were proven to be so superior that everyone became convinced. Even those within GE protecting the status quo had to acknowledge that the new spiral CT technology was here to stay. Within ten years, everything had been replaced. By now, virtually all the CT scanners in use worldwide are helical, or spiral, scanners. According to the National Electrical Manufacturers Association, some twenty thousand of these machines were sold in the 1990s. At about $1 million each, that's $20 billion in revenues.[14]

The machines opened up new applications, such as virtual colonoscopies, in which a patient's colon seems to become the setting of the latest Pixar movie. Entrepreneurs began buying the machines to circumvent the existing healthcare system, opening CT scanning centers in malls and storefronts, typically charging about $1,000 for a full body scan that can detect tumors as small as three millimeters wide in any organ. A recent study in the *New England Journal of Medicine* showed that CT scanners can now display such precise renderings in detecting colon cancer that they can serve as accurate replacements for invasive and expensive colonoscopy procedures.[15]

As these case studies show, the barrier that is blocking a new invention is often more complex than it may seem at first. Finding the obstruction that is holding back a valuable improvement can set off a backlash inside a corporation or an industry before the new invention ever gets a chance to disrupt the market. As such, detecting barriers can be considered dangerous, even subversive, behavior. Once that obstacle is out of the way, however, inventors can see their way more clearly.

CHAPTER 7

Applying Analogies

The inventor has a logical mind that sees analogies.

—THOMAS EDISON

ANYONE WHO HAS TAKEN a standardized aptitude test is familiar with the trick of completing analogies. Pipe is to water as wire is to what? If you are smart or lucky enough to eliminate the silly choices from a given list of options and end up with "electricity" as your answer, you get one point on the test. Inventors, however, must extend this ability to analogize by a couple of giant steps. Instead of simply completing analogies, they must create new ones and then apply them to the problems they are trying to solve.

Inventors are fueled by the analogies that they spot all around them. Applying an analogy is a process of spotting knowledge in one context that can be abstracted and transferred to another context. Inventors are particularly skilled at this kind of context shifting, but virtually anyone can do it once he or she recognizes the pattern. Typically, analogies shift from the world of the familiar, which is called the knowledge "base," to the new picture of a new invention, which is called the invention "target." Analogies, in other words, suggest solutions.

Woody Norris was searching for an analogy to help him slay an elusive problem. In 1988, he was running American Technology Corporation, his San Diego invention shop. He was brainstorming a way to eliminate speakers from audio systems when he realized that what he needed above all else was an apt comparison to the problem he had created in his mind. "By this time in my life, I had figured out how you invent things," he says. "Here is the key: You invent by analogy. Nature, science, chemistry, pick your field. Almost everything in those fields has an analogy to something else."[1]

Before he could spot an accurate correlation, Norris had to pare the problem to its essence. "There were two parts to the hi-fi systems that were still crude and mechanical," he says. "One was the mechanical needle in the groove of a record, which has since been replaced. The other was the speaker, which is this mechanical piston vibrating back and forth and bumping air molecules to make sound." Even the best speakers are subject to distortion, he says. "It's the weak link. Everything else is electronic."

He asked himself a radical question: Can I eliminate the speaker? "Why don't I figure out how to make the sound in the air? Then I'd have theoretically perfect sound." Making sound in the air? What's analogous to that? "I started picking my brain," he recalls. "What I was looking for is something that is done in one area that might help me solve a problem in another."

By now, Norris was invoking analogies to understand almost everything he knew about electronics. "I'll give you an easy one," he says. Most people don't understand how electricity is made. But when shown the proper analogy, they finally see what Michael Faraday accomplished in 1831. Picture a giant spring suspended from the ceiling, with a weight attached to the lower end. "The spring will vibrate with a certain resonance," Norris says. That reverberation is energy, pure and simple. "If you know something of the nature of the spring and the weight, you can have a simple formula for how it will resonate. In electronics, the coil is called an inductor, and the capacitor is like the weight. The same circuit that works for electricity also works for mechanical resonance. That's the analogy."

STEALING FROM ART

To conceive of his invention in the hi-fi realm, Norris lifted an analogy from the world of art. "When an artist takes a palette with six or eight colors on it, she can mix new colors," he says. He realized that this mixing metaphor could be applied to the problem: "To create sound in the air, I'd have to mix together different frequencies to create new ones."

A similar analogy had already been demonstrated in the world of video. A color television set, for example, can produce only three primary color frequencies: those of red, green, and blue. But the electronic mixer inside the set can blend these three colors to create the millions of combinations that we see on the TV screen. Applying the same analogy, Norris figured that "there ought to be a way to mix sound frequencies in the air and get new ones. I knew mixing worked in electronic circuitry, and I knew it worked optically. Why wouldn't it work sonically? That was the inspiration. I began to see mixers everywhere."

From his earlier invention, Norris already understood ultrasound, the electromagnetic waves that beat at more than 20,000 cycles per second (hertz), too frequent for the human ear to hear. What if you mixed different frequencies of ultrasound waves? "If I mixed 100,000 cycles with 101,000 cycles, could I get the 1,000-cycle difference?" Such a frequency can indeed be processed by the human ear, which can decode sound in the ranges of 20 to 20,000 cycles per second. (Dogs have a slightly higher range, explaining the "silent" dog whistle.)

Following the logic of his analogy, Norris's question became this: Could you mix sounds that you *couldn't* hear to produce sounds that you *could* hear? The answer, as Norris puts it: "Absolutely! Unequivocally! Yes!" Instead of mechanically vibrating air molecules, Norris believed that he could produce sound in midair by using mathematical combinations of ultrasonic waves.

When he first tested his analogy, however, nothing worked. He pointed a pair of ultrasound emitters in such a way that the beams crossed paths. He tried all kinds of combinations of frequencies. Instead of producing sound, this arrangement produced only silence. Eventually, he was able to produce faint sounds in this way, but his theory wasn't proving itself very useful in practice.

Still, Norris was so confident in his analogy that he persisted. Giant companies, among them Sony, Motorola, and AT&T's Bell Laboratories, had already been down a similar path, and when they failed to harness ultrasound for this purpose, they gave up—something Norris found out years after his own attempt began. "Not that I'm smarter than them," Norris says. "They gave up, in part because of the lack of appropriate materials at the time, but mainly because they didn't know for sure during the process that it could be done. Often, if you don't know something can be done, it doesn't take a lot to get you to quit." Norris even persisted when his own engineering staff expressed doubts that his invention would ever produce sound that was as loud as that produced by traditional speakers.

To get his system to work, Norris increased the amplitude of his ultrasonic waves to levels that others had not tried, and he tinkered with various sound combinations and audio-processing techniques. "It took me seven years to simplify it, pull all the distortion out of it, and bring up the efficiency," he says. "But I had no doubt that it would work." Total investment in developing and patenting the invention has so far exceeded $40 million.

The resulting product, the HyperSonic Sound (HSS) system, is a set of electronic components that converts sound from a CD player or other audio source into patterns of ultrasonic waves. The waveforms are fed through an electronic mixer, acting as a painter's palette, which in turn sends the waves through an ultrasonic amplifier that powers a set of emitters. The emitters are thin silvery films, typically made from aluminum, that send the silent, high-frequency waves into the air. When two or more of these silent waves interact and interfere with one another, they produce new sounds, in much the same way that a cacophony of voices in a noisy restaurant mix together, augment one another, or cancel one another out. "If you know how the air itself affects the sound waves," Norris explains, "you can predict what new frequencies will be added into the sound wave by the air."

Once again, an inventor was invoking the work of Hermann von Helmholtz, the German physicist who inspired Alexander Graham Bell. When playing two notes very loudly on a pipe organ, von Helmholtz noticed faint third and fourth tones resonating in the air—one at a higher frequency than the original notes, and the second at a lower frequency. He proved that the resistance of the air itself was producing this distortion effect. In doing so, he was well on the way toward invoking one of the greatest analogies of all time: that all matter is like all other matter. The air is like water. Water is like flesh. Flesh is like rock. Rock is like the moon. The moon is like the stars. The stars are like air. All are made of molecules that experience resonance in different ways.

For his part, Woody Norris knew that if he worked his sonic mixing palette just right, he could resonate the air so that it would produce these new frequencies. As a result, his HSS system has no speaker cones, no tweeters, no midrange diaphragms, and no woofers; instead, it has only a pair of thin films that serve as the ultrasound emitters.

Norris knew it would take him years to perfect his invention, but he also knew that his analogy was rock solid. "You can take great comfort if you are confident your analogy is valid," he says.

As you'll see later in this chapter, Norris applied an entirely different analogy to understand and define the dozens of unexpected applications for HyperSonic Sound. But before we get to that, let's take a look at other recent and classic cases in which inventors achieved breakthroughs by applying analogies.

MIMICKING BIOLOGY

Like many thinking strategies, the spotting of useful analogies is an inventive behavior that typically reaches back into childhood. James McLurkin developed a knack for analogizing while growing up on Long Island. McLurkin is an articulate, young African American inventor, with closely cropped hair and a thin mustache. As a kid, he was bored by school and was constantly told he was not working up to his potential. Instead of focusing on his schoolwork, he spent much of his time constructing imaginary worlds. He went from Legos and erector sets to model train sets to radio-controlled car kits to designing his own computer video games. He also spent hours with his family watching science, nature, and animal TV shows, and that led him to make connections between the natural world and his own world of physical materials.

As a student at MIT in the late 1990s, McLurkin began building hand-sized robots, known as "swarm robots," that simulated behaviors found in the occupants of ant colonies and beehives. Using sensors to detect one another, actuators to control motion, and infrared beams to coordinate communication, the robots performed functions by picking up signs from their teammates and their surroundings. He was getting in on the ground floor of the new field of "biomimetics," the science of designing technology that draws analogies from the natural world. "Nature is the best engineer we know about," McLurkin says.[2]

McLurkin shares credit for his invention with mentors who are also steeped in biological analogies. Foremost among them is Rodney Brooks, the director of the MIT Computer Science and Artificial Intelligence Laboratory. Brooks has changed the field of robotics and artificial intelligence (AI) by replacing the "top-down" approach with a "bottom-up" philosophy. Instead of trying to build human knowledge and rules of reasoning into software, he has pioneered the idea that the perception of intelligence can emerge from lots of relatively dumb components interacting with one another. Ant colonies and bee swarms are just two examples.[3] To put some of his ideas into action, Brooks cofounded iRobot, a Somerville, Massachusetts, developer of consumer robot devices such as the Roomba, an autonomous vacuum cleaner. Brooks encouraged McLurkin to study other natural systems and apply the resulting analogies to McLurkin's own set of robots. This central idea—that complex behavior can emerge from the interaction of simple beings—became one of the core analogies put into practice at iRobot.

While completing his Ph.D. at MIT, McLurkin became the lead scientist on the Swarm Robotics Project at the company. Soon, McLurkin's intelligent swarm grew to more than one hundred robots. The inventor equips his robots with food sensors, trail sensors, and cameras. Future applications range from locating land mines to patrolling chemical plants and other sensitive security zones to exploring terrain on other planets. It's all part of what McLurkin calls his "biologically inspired mind-set."

When McLurkin accepted the Lemelson-MIT Student Prize for Inventiveness in 2003, which came with a $30,000 grant, he brought his robot swarm to the Boston Museum of Science for a demonstration. Each of the microrobots looked like a Nintendo game cube with set of red, green, and yellow lights mounted on top. Individually, the robots couldn't do very much. But McLurkin commanded them with a remote control to exhibit collective behaviors. For example, the "orbit" command had the robots moving in a circle, a behavior that could be used to help secure a large perimeter in a war zone. The "dispersion" command had the robots spreading out in different directions, a behavior that can be used for exploring a mine field or a lunar surface. When he commanded the lead robot to "cluster" his friends, the followers gathered tightly in a small space. McLurkin was also able to get the robots to perform synchronized dance routines. As the demonstration wore on, groups of kids on field trips kept gathering around the railings that overlooked the stage, watching in wonder.

McLurkin's swarm of robots is but one example of biomimicry. Nature is not only an engineer, in the Darwinian sense, but also a source of ideas for a diverse range of industries, especially the medical field. A case in point is the work of Jay Vacanti, a doctor and research scientist at the Harvard Medical School. While on vacation one summer, Vacanti came across a simple analogy for a complex concept. He had been thinking about the possibility of simulating human skin in the laboratory. Like other medical researchers, he saw the need to grow skin for grafting, for medical testing, and for creating new anticancer treatments.

The solution came to Vacanti in the summer of 1986 while he was relaxing on a beach in Cape Cod. He was watching seaweed float in the surf when he thought to get up and take a closer look at it. When he observed the intricate branch structure in the flesh of the seaweed, it struck him that mimicking such a structure in lab-grown skin would be the perfect way to bring oxygen and other nutrients to the skin culture as it grew. He ran the idea by Robert Langer, a colleague and a renowned inventor from MIT's bioengineering division. Langer happened to be looking for a similar solution. The two agreed to collaborate. They ended up pioneering the field of human tissue engineering, which is now a multibillion-dollar market with dozens of cutting-edge medical applications. Thus, seaweed ended up providing the clue needed to create artificial tissues and organs.[4]

Reaching into History

This behavior—of moving from base to target and sometimes back and forth repeatedly—reaches far back into history. Leonardo da Vinci, for example, observed that birds, when they spread their wings, used the air as a "wedge to raise them up." He used the mechanical concept of a wedge as the base to understand behavior in the natural world. In turn, he used the flight of birds as the base to conceive of his target: a flying machine. Brainstorming an example of a rotating wedge, da Vinci conceived of a mechanical analogy: that of a screw boring into wood, lifting material out of the way as it turns. From that observation, he conceived of an "air screw." His famous sketches of a helicopter-like apparatus feature screw-like rungs lifting a cone-shaped basket into the air. "If this instrument made with a screw . . . [is] turned swiftly," he wrote, "the said screw will make its spiral in the air and it will rise high."[5]

Da Vinci's conception of an air screw as a flying machine was unworkable, but it was a breakthrough analogy nonetheless. It would be left to future inventors to conceive of an even better analogy, that of a rotary wing, a concept that led to the development of the propeller.

Johannes Gutenberg, by contrast, was able to put his analogy into practice. Gutenberg, a fifteenth-century German metalworker, was searching for a system for mass-producing the Bible. At that time, monks hand-carved wooden plates for each page they wanted to print. They inked the plate, laid a piece of paper on it, and rubbed it until an impression was made. It beat copying manuscripts by hand, but it wasn't an efficient way to reproduce books. Although the Chinese are known to have invented movable type earlier, Gutenberg didn't know about it. He set out to reinvent aspects of printing, as often happens in the world of invention.

In his revolutionary creation of a printing press, Gutenberg applied two analogies. He took the first one from the stamps and wax seals used for embossing emblems or characters on paper. He saw that if he were to line up many of these stamps in rows, he'd be able to rearrange and reuse them. When he miniaturized the characters and fashioned them out of metal that could be positioned in rows, he became the first European known to create movable type.

What remained was to replace hand rubbing with a way of rapidly printing page after page from the same plate. Gutenberg stumbled into this more interesting analogy at a wine festival. There, amid the drunken revelry, he saw a hand-cranked winepress that was used to extract juice from flat beds of grapes. That was the inspiration for creating a hand-cranked machine that rapidly pressed blank pages against a flat bed of easily arranged characters.[6] Nearly six centuries later, we use that analogy every time we refer to the media as "the press."

Gutenberg's isn't the only media invention that originated from analogies that recall the world of agriculture. Before the days of radio, for example, *broadcasting* was a farm term that referred to scattering seeds in all directions at once in an effort to cover as much area as possible and yield a rich crop.

Television as we know it is also based on a farming analogy. Philo T. Farnsworth lived with his family on an Idaho potato farm. In 1921, as a fourteen-year-old, he read in science magazines about radio and about predictions that someday it would be possible to send images through the airwaves. No one had been able to do it, and Farnsworth set out to find a solution.

Others had tried to create mechanical television systems, but Farnsworth, reading about Einstein's Nobel Prize–winning photoelectric theory, was inspired to seek a solution based on the relationship between electricity and light. One day, while plowing the potato field, he glanced back at the parallel furrows and envisioned a process of using electrons to scan and reassemble moving images line by line. Keeping this analogy alive in his mind, Farnsworth built and patented the world's first electronic television system six years later.[7] In other words, the potato field led to the couch potato.

Analogies and metaphors often form the basis of scientific understandings that lead directly to invention. Benjamin Franklin, for example, saw the mysterious force of electricity as directly analogous to lightning. The analogy that aided the conception of the artificial heart was to see the heart as a specialized kind of pump. Molecular biologists such as Leroy Hood view proteins as building blocks that can form a huge variety of structures. Analogies between the mind and the computer have long pervaded both computer science and cognitive science.

Analogy is also at the heart of patent number 4,490,728, which was filed by an inventor named John Vaught and assigned to his employer, Hewlett-Packard.[8] Vaught knew well the limitations of the available inkjet printers, which worked by vibrating toner out of a cartridge and onto the paper. Although the output quality was low, inkjets cost about the same as high-end laser printers. One morning in 1979, Vaught was making coffee when he began taking a close look at the coffee machine. He noticed how quickly and efficiently the machine employed heat to percolate the water, and he wondered whether he could use heat to do the same with printer ink. Perhaps a printer could be built like a coffee machine. The analogy led to one of the most valuable patents in the modern history of computers.[9]

At about the same time, a rival engineer at Canon in Japan came across the same technique by accident. He dropped a soldering iron onto an ink cartridge and thought of the same thing when the heat of the iron began acting on the ink. The Canon engineer also filed a patent on the idea. But instead of competing with each other, H-P and Canon included the new heat-activated, "thermal" inkjet technology in their already formidable alliance. The two companies cornered the market on low-cost computer printers for the next twenty years.

In one of the all-time most brilliant shifts from base to target, Niels Bohr applied the Copernican understanding of the solar system to a model of the atom. The nucleus is analogous to the sun, Bohr said. The orbiting electrons, in turn, are analogous to the planets.

Although this analogy remains vivid and useful, other analogies have refined and in some ways refuted Bohr's model. Max Planck wondered why electrons sometimes seemed to jump to different orbits. Such jumps produced energy, which were measured in photons, or "quanta," of light. In his conception of quantum theory, Planck compared electron orbits to waves. Louis de Broglie, a violinist, took this analogy even further. He compared the orbits of electrons to strings that resonated, much like the strings of a violin. When physicists invented instruments that were able to listen to and measure this atomic resonance, de Broglie's "string theory" was confirmed.[10] As a result, he joined Bohr and Plank as a winner of the Nobel Prize in physics.

This concept—that energy can be used to produce resonance in all types of matter—has led to numerous inventions. Foremost among them is MRI (magnetic resonance imaging), a method of vibrating the matter inside the body to create precise image maps of internal organs.

SHINING THE FLASHLIGHT

Conveniently, the violin analogy leads us back to the story of Woody Norris and his invention of HyperSonic Sound. His analogy of using ultrasound energy to resonate air molecules is essentially the same one that led to the invention of the MRI. "Everything has a resonance," says Norris.[11]

But Norris also applied a second analogy from the domain of light to the sphere of sound. The analogy was a beam of light, such as a beam from a flashlight or from a laser gun. When you are in a dark room and shine a flashlight at a wall, the beam illuminates the dust particles in the air and creates a spot on the wall, but the area outside the beam remains dark. This is the simple principle behind a spotlight. The more intense the light, the more focused the beam. Norris had learned that ultrasound waves work in the same way. The higher the frequency of the ultrasound waves, the more "directional" the waves become. Whereas sound from a speaker will scatter to the far corners of a room, ultrasound waves are like laser beams of sound.

In other words, ultrasonic energy is highly directional. These high-frequency sound emissions form a column of sound in front of the emitter, much like light from a laser. The electromagnetic energy exists only inside that column and doesn't spread in all directions. As Norris puts it, it's "locked tightly inside."

Applying this insight, Norris postulated that the sounds he would be mixing in the air might be heard only by ears located within the beam. If you were outside the beam, you'd hear nothing. The sound beam would also be able to travel much greater distances than traditional sound waves, and it could be redirected by bouncing it off of solid surfaces, just as a flashlight beam in a dark room will bounce off the wall. "You can hear the spot of sound," explains Norris. "And with two channels, one for the left and one for the right, you get stereo sound." Norris isn't the only inventor who has been driven by this analogy between focusing light and focusing sound. F. Joseph Pompei, a graduate student who led a research project on directional sound at the MIT Media Laboratory, has applied the same analogy to come up with a remarkably similar invention that he calls the Audio Spotlight. While completing his Ph.D., Pompei started Holosonic Research Labs in Watertown, Massachusetts. The two inventors are now locked in a head-to-head battle for what they both believe is a billion-dollar market.[12]

The analogy to the flashlight, spotlight, or laser beam suggested an endless array of applications to both inventors. Sound from a computer could be directed only at the user without disturbing coworkers in an office. Museum exhibits could talk only to those who stand in front of a painting. Those in the front seat of a car could listen to one type of music while those in the backseat would listen to another, without the need for headphones. Conference speeches could be translated into different languages, and audience members could sit in the section whose beam generates the speech in their native tongue. Vending machines could speak to people passing by, perhaps making special sales pitches. Fast-food restaurant displays, department store clothing racks, grocery store products, and trade show booths could do the same thing. The sound would feel as if it were inside your head, and a person only a few feet away wouldn't hear it.

With home entertainment systems, you could deflect sound off walls rather than wire the speakers throughout a large room. Being able to control the sound dispersion area could also change concert-hall acoustics by eliminating the dreaded problem of feedback from amplifiers into live microphones, and it could vastly improve the sound at outdoor concerts. Instead of allowing the sound to disperse into the surrounding atmosphere, you could direct it at audience members hundreds of yards away from the stage. Music can travel from an emitter at ranges up to five hundred feet, with the intensity of the sound remaining virtually the same every step of the way.

Thinking of HyperSonic Sound as a laser beam also led Norris to imagine security applications. Law enforcement officials, for example, could use HSS for policing crowds. Instead of speaking through a megaphone to an entire group, an officer could direct a vocal warning—"Drop your weapon!"—to one person in a crowd, and only that person would hear it. "It allows for individual communications in public spaces," Norris says. Ambulance sirens could be directed only at cars directly in the emergency route rather than throughout an entire neighborhood. "In'dat cool?" Norris asks.

The first companies to express interest in HSS and the Audio Spotlight represented a wide range of industries. Sony is selling directional sound systems for use in department stores and museums in Europe. Disney has evaluated it for its theme parks. The U.S. Army and Navy are using it to hail troops and warn enemies. Retailers have been testing it for in-store sale pitches, with products and displays talking to one customer at a time. Vending machine companies have expressed interest, and DaimlerChrysler is evaluating it for car audio. Both Norris and Pompei are contesting one another to win these industrial and military customers before going after the general consumer market. Replacing the millions of mechanical speakers that are sold annually remains the long-term goal. Before they reach mass acceptance, though, both inventors will have to overcome early performance kinks, such as an inability to produce low bass tones.

According to Norris and other inventors, the great news about analogizing is that it's one of many thinking strategies that anyone can learn to do with practice. Analogizing is one of the higher-order cognitive tools that separates us from other animals. Once you see the pattern of how analogies work and how this strategy can generate many useful ideas, you may be able to practice it regularly.

When you're moving from base to target, your analogies can stick closely to one domain. For example, a transistor works like a vacuum tube. But some of the most evocative analogies leap across domains: A flying machine might be like a bird. But that doesn't mean an automobile should be like a horse. "When man wanted to make a machine that would walk," goes a French proverb, "he created the wheel, which does not resemble a leg." Those who invented and reinvented the wheel in isolated civilizations thousands of years ago probably saw something—a rock, an acorn, the moon, a person tumbling downhill—that triggered analogies. Like children, grown-up inventors are constantly scanning the world, looking at objects and processes, and asking, "What does this remind me of?" Sometimes, analogies are so powerful that they do much of the work of invention for you. Often, what's left is simply a matter of ironing out the wrinkles.

CHAPTER **8**

Visualizing Results

We've got a prefrontal cortex that works
as an experience simulator.

—DANIEL GILBERT[1]

PERHAPS NONE OF OUR mental capacities is as underutilized as our power of visualization. Einstein spoke of the "gift of fantasy" that virtually every child develops, saying that "imagination is more important than knowledge." Immanuel Kant said that "thinking in pictures precedes thinking in words."

We can make movies in our minds and construct three-dimensional models of things that do not exist. Yet we don't use this built-in experience simulator as much as we should and could. We dream at night, but we usually can remember only random bits of footage. While we're awake, we are constantly overexposed to so many images—on television, in movie theaters, on computer screens, in video games—that we seem to consume the imagery of others as a surrogate for making our own. To invent, you often need to close your eyes, block out everything external, and project original visuals onto your prefrontal cortex.

Stephen Jacobsen would be nowhere without tapping into this ability. Jacobsen makes robots. Sarcos Research, his tightly run company in Salt Lake City, is what Jacobsen calls "a skunk works for hire."[2] It's an invention shop built on Jacobsen's reputation among inventors for creating things straight out of science fiction novels: an android that can learn to juggle after watching humans do it; a mechanical replacement arm for amputees that is controlled by the brain; a lightweight, robotic "exoskeleton" for soldiers to wear into combat; an eighty-thousand-pound dinosaur that walks, writhes, and serves as the feature attraction at a famous amusement park. The initial drawing boards for all these things, and hundreds of other inventions, are inside Jacobsen's head.

Visual representations preoccupy Jacobsen so much that one of the first things one notices as he talks about his past creations is that he has virtually no recollection of nonvisual data, such as dates. It's not that he forgets what month or year something happened; he can't even place events in the correct decade. Whether he has worked on a project in 1983 or 1967 or 1975 or 1996 is something Jacobsen often can't recall. "What I see is the geometry," he says. He visualizes the progression of the hundreds of projects he has worked on in terms of how their intricate shapes were formed and assembled over time, and yet he can seldom recall time itself. Just as a digital photo or movie often requires more computer storage space than a book's worth of text, Jacobsen's visual images seem to have crowded out the other things in his mind.

Jacobsen's laboratory is a visual feast. His fifty-employee company is perhaps the closest thing to a pure invention playhouse. Nestled in the Wasatch Mountain valley, at the end of Utah's Pioneer Trail, Sarcos is housed in a low-lying brick building in a research park just east of the University of Utah, where Jacobsen has long been an engineering professor. A visitor to Sarcos is issued a name badge adorned with pictures of a bird and a dinosaur and then is greeted in a conference room by handcrafted heads of various creatures peering out from wooden shelves. There's a space alien, a green gladiator, a rubber gargoyle, a menacing-looking man in need of a shave, a metallic circuit board with eyes and teeth, and various humanoids fashioned from blue plastic, white foam, and metal fixtures.

Jacobsen himself has bright white hair and blue eyes, and he speaks softly. He has an easygoing disposition, but when the conversation turns to his favorite topics—robotics, microelectronics, and artificial biological organs—he begins painting word pictures in rapid-fire succession that illustrate how his creations work. He is the kind of man who wouldn't seem out of place zipped up in a silver jumpsuit as the scientific captain on a space station orbiting the galaxy.

Clearly, Jacobsen has an ability that is in great demand. The holder of more than one hundred patents, the creator of a constellation of high-tech spin-off companies, Sarcos has a long list of corporate clients notable for its range—it includes healthcare concerns such as Merck, Pfizer, Baxter, and Johnson & Johnson; legendary technology outfits such as Bell Laboratories and the Xerox Palo Alto Research Center (PARC); aerospace leaders such as Boeing, McDonnell Douglass, and Lockheed Martin; automakers such as Ford and Honda; entertainment powerhouses such as Mirage Hotels, Madame Tussaud's Wax Museum, Universal Studios, and Walt Disney Imagineering; and divisions of government such as the U.S. Department of Defense.

Jacobsen's visual way of inventing and processing information leaps out at every turn as he leads an informal tour of the Sarcos lab. Like many of his peers, Jacobsen collects inventions from the past. In his case, especially, these props serve as inspirations for thinking visually. In one hallway, he points to a colorful graphic rendered by Benoit Mandelbrot, the Polish mathematician who developed the fractal theory of geometry in the 1970s before coming to the United States and joining the research staff at IBM. "People looked at mathematics for centuries," Jacobsen says. "Then all of a sudden some guy takes a stupid little equation and generates the fractal," which explains the constantly recurring patterns in nature. Jacobsen is awestruck at the paradox inherent in Mandelbrot's equation. Like

Einstein's E=mc², it's humble and yet profound. "How can a simple equation like that generate such complex patterns?" he asks. "You can go infinitely close to [a fractal pattern] or infinitely far back, and it looks the same." A tiny section of a beach, for instance, can mirror the shape of a vast stretch of coastline.

Jacobsen's office is cluttered with souvenir inventions from the past as well as half-assembled projects from the future. There's a century-old crystal ball that measures the sun's illumination, a glass-encased radiometer for keeping tabs on electromagnetic waves, a Watt fly ball for controlling the speed of a steam engine, and an encoding device for triggering a hydrogen bomb. Down the stairs from his office Jacobsen keeps a second-stage *Saturn* rocket engine, circa 1968, capable of expelling two hundred thousand pounds of thrust. "Some people collect this stuff just for the sake of owning it," he says, "but I collect it because I'm interested in the thinking that went into it." Also on display is a piece of the famous O-ring from the ill-fated *Challenger* space shuttle as well as a twisted section of molten metal from the World Trade Center, which he possesses "not as a morbid thing," he says, "but to show how violent things get" when things go horribly wrong.

Jacobsen wants to peer into the visualization process of both invention and destruction to understand not only how things work but also how they sometimes fail. This is even more essential now that most of the things he and others build are constructed from microchips and software. Modern technology is superior because you can program computing devices to do whatever you want, and yet something is lost. "With mechanical inventions, you can see what was going on," Jacobsen says. "You can use these things to teach." He calls such devices "*is* machines." He explains, "The *is* machine is the machine that *is*. The behavior is due to the physics of the device."

With many of the things Jacobsen invents, however, almost nothing is apparent to the unaided eye. "You can't see much with a microprocessor," he says. "A digital chip is emulating a behavior you want. But to do the software-based things, you still have to understand the principle." Jacobsen does that by enlarging microscopic devices in his mind, building mental models of physical devices. Inside his head, these virtual machines work in the same way that his collectibles work. After he visualizes a physical machine in his mind, he can go about constructing robots from chips and software. The materials are different, but the thinking strategy is the same.

It's the same kind of visualization that existed in the minds of the people Jacobsen spends his time studying. Among his favorite visual thinkers are Leonardo da Vinci, Isaac Newton, Michael Faraday, James Clerk Maxwell, James Watt, Alexander Graham Bell, Albert Einstein, Thomas Edison, John von Neumann, Leo Szilard, Richard Feynman, and Benoit Mandelbrot. Jacobsen's bookshelves are overflowing with biographies that show how brilliant scientists and inventors got that way, as if he is trying to discern the patterns common to technological and scientific breakthroughs. And the one thread that he has picked up on, above all others, is how these great minds learned to visualize.

LEARNING TO VISUALIZE

Jacobsen's drive to visualize grew out of daydreaming and distraction. Descended from Presbyterian pioneers who came to Utah around the same time as the Mormons, Jacobsen seems to have inherited a restless spirit. His mother was a teacher, and his father was a commercial artist, and ideas were always discussed vigorously in the household. "I was hyperactive," Jacobsen recalls. "As a kid, I was always building things and taking them apart. Everything I could get my hands on. But I could never remember names and dates and places. I was a lot of trouble in school. Teachers would say, 'Little Stevie can do it, but he just doesn't.'"

John Warnock, a friend of Jacobsen's since childhood, recalls that both he and Jacobsen responded poorly to authority and refused to accept the way most of their teachers taught. "We were not your normal, sedate students," says Warnock, who went on to cofound Adobe Systems, among the all-time most successful Silicon Valley software start-ups.[3] He adds, "We didn't even think much about school." Actually, he says, they were part of a group of drinking buddies who spent much of their time partying. Warnock flunked ninth-grade algebra, and Jacobsen's grades were equally dismal. "I hated school," Jacobsen recalls. "Teachers would get up at the front of the room and the clock would stop."

But the two buddies ended up graduating and attending the University of Utah, where they thrived in a culture that emphasized experimentation instead of letters on a transcript. Other troublesome, rebellious students converged on the place, or emerged from the place, at around the same time, inspired by campus luminaries such as computer graphics pioneers Dave Evans and Ivan Sutherland, who originated head-positioned display devices. Classmates also included Alan Kay, who would go on to create the software for the original Apple Macintosh; Jim Clark, who would start Silicon Graphics and Netscape; Nolan Bushnell, who dropped out to form Atari Games; and Ed Catmull, the future cofounder and president of Pixar Animation Studios.

Jacobsen's learning style meshed well when it came to working in campus research labs, and yet he was so distracted from schoolwork that at one point he found himself on the verge of receiving straight D's. Briefly kicked out of the university, he was reinstated only when he promised the dean of students that he'd never let his grade point average slip below 3.5. Jacobsen put his mind to adapting quickly, drawing on his ability to compensate for his poor ability to memorize facts by using a visual approach he calls "playing games with ideas" that he still uses. Jacobsen received straight A's for the remainder of his college career and through his Ph.D. at the Massachusetts Institute of Technology.

Warnock went through a similar transformation when he had trouble concentrating on his class work. For an entire year, Warnock hyperfocused almost exclusively on trying to solve an open question in the world of mathematics. It was an esoteric conundrum posed by a professor ten years earlier, involving a field known as ring theory. Warnock spent almost all his time visualizing three-dimensional mathematical structures. When he came up with the proof, his life turned around. "It's amazing when you solve an open question in mathematics how differently people start perceiving you," he says.[4]

Later, while working at the storied Xerox Palo Alto Research Center in the 1970s, Warnock used his visual thinking skills to attack the gnarly problem of getting printers to produce the exact image seen on a computer screen. Although it's hard to believe now, the problem was then thought to be unsolvable. For a novel approach, Warnock went into deep visualization mode. "I think graphically," he says. "I see images in my mind, as opposed to formulas." He left PARC to form Adobe and market his resulting invention, PostScript, a program that describes endless variations of fonts and graphics to printers. Warnock's visual language became a standard for the Apple Macintosh and later for IBM PCs running Windows. Along with his friend Steve Jobs, Warnock launched the desktop publishing revolution. As a result, the multibillion-dollar PostScript became the first building block of the Adobe software house.

Time and again, Jacobsen has seen this visual approach fuel the ability to invent among friends and colleagues. The reason? Visualization fosters originality. You need to understand something in a concrete way in order to picture it in your mind and make changes to it. Memorizing facts, figures, and formulas—the central task in much of the educational system—simply doesn't lead to this kind of thinking. "I can tell you a story of a guy with best memory I've ever seen." Jacobsen says. "He can read books and know everything on every page. I read nothing—well, I read general things. I read biographies. I only read technical things after working in those areas. That sounds arrogant, but when you learn something in a certain way, it freezes in the way you approach it. Your brain is not magic. It's a visual imaging machine."[5] In other words, learning someone else's way of thinking about something can cause you to fall into someone else's patterns and ruts. Jacobsen is more interested in perceiving problems and quandaries firsthand—unburdened by the knowledge of prior approaches—and then visualizing a new idea on his own.

His favorite historical example of how others have done it is the story of Michael Faraday, an apprentice bookbinder who had no scientific training. One day, at the age of twenty-one, Faraday attended a scientific lecture given by Humphry Davy, head of Great

Britain's esteemed Royal Society. After showing the scientist his notes and colorful diagrams, Faraday was hired as an assistant. Later, while playing around with batteries, wires, and pieces of iron, Faraday came to understand firsthand the principle of electromagnetism, which had only recently been discovered by Hans Christian Oersted, a Danish physicist. Faraday experimented with turning pieces of metal into magnets, in much the same way that modern science students will attach batteries to wires, wrap those wires around nails, and discover they can attract paper clips. But Faraday did something new. He visualized the lines of force emanating from these electromagnets. He saw these invisible force fields so clearly in his mind that he was able to draw pictures that showed how strong they were in each direction.

These lines of force became so concrete in Faraday's mind that he began to visualize an experiment. Yes, electricity causes magnetism. But what about the reverse? Could a magnet cause electricity? The idea of moving a magnetic field past a wire was an image that popped into Faraday's head. He was able to conjure that image because he actually saw magnetic fields as concrete things. That is how Faraday, in 1831, became the first to "induce" electricity. He invented the generator, perhaps the greatest electrical discovery of all time. Chemical batteries were expensive and weak. Electric generators were cheap and strong. Faraday did it by visualizing those imaginary lines of force in his mind. In 1867, James Clerk Maxwell formalized Faraday's discovery with a series of universal field equations.

But equations can kill a child's curiosity, according to Jacobsen. "Teachers start out teaching you the formalism [of Maxwell's equations] because it's easy to teach, and they can get some points for it, and then students can go out and do tricks like some monkey. But you don't know the essence," he says. "The equations are a manifestation of the reality. They aren't reality itself." When Jacobsen teaches engineering, he has his students learn about force fields by playing around with electromagnets, as Faraday did. They can begin to "see" these force fields firsthand, in their mind's eye. Only then can they really know how Maxwell came up with the equations in the first place.

To be able to visualize, then, is to be able to understand. For another example of how to learn this thinking strategy, Jacobsen cites an anecdote about Richard Feynman. The Nobel Prize–winning physicist remembered the tale decades after it happened. "Say, pop, I noticed something," began the young Feynman. "When I pull the wagon, the ball [inside it] rolls to the back of the wagon, and then I'm pulling it along and I suddenly stop, and the ball rolls to the front of the wagon. Why is that?"

Feynman's father could simply have said, "This is called inertia" or "This is called Newton's first law of motion." Instead, the elder Feynman focused on what his son was seeing. "Nobody knows why," he said. "The general principle is that things that are moving try to keep moving, and things that are standing still tend to stand still unless you push on them hard."

"Now that's a deep understanding," explained Richard Feynman. "He doesn't give me a name. He knew the difference between *knowing the name of something* and *knowing something*, which I learned very early."[6]

Feynman developed a deep understanding of matter at the molecular level, and he called on it to imagine things that might be invented in the future. He was able to predict the coming miniaturization of physical devices because he saw it all in his mind. In a 1959 talk at Caltech, Feynman challenged physicists to make a working motor that was "no more than $\frac{1}{64}$ of an inch on all sides." He wondered how you'd go about building a machine by rearranging individual atoms, how you would lubricate a machine the size of the period at the end of this sentence, and how you would store an entire set of encyclopedias on something the size of the head of a pin. It's because of these thought experiments that Feynman later became known as the "father of nanotechnology."

Steve Jacobsen is one of those who took Feynman's challenges seriously. Jacobsen named his company, Sarcos, after *sarcoplasm*, the medical term for muscle fiber. His vision was to simulate the functions of living creatures, "to use miniaturized stuff to solve new problems," to create "information-based machines that moved."[7] Jacobsen came up with a new term, *micro electro mechanical systems*, or

MEMS, that was soon adopted by other researchers, spawning a new subindustry. Jacobsen started building motors that were five hundred microns thick and testing them by doing things such as drilling holes in hair. "These machines are really simple and cheap, and they run forever," he says, "but we didn't know what to use them for." He began searching for ways to match these new technological capabilities with real-world applications, visualizing a new world populated by micromachines doing thousands of tasks.

Playing Mind Games

But to imagine how things work on such a small scale, or even on a large scale, you need to conduct thought experiments and play mind games. Sometimes, the simplest of these mind games can yield the most remarkable results.

Albert Einstein was a master of this kind of simple visualization. Legend has it that it all began with something concrete. Presented with a gift compass at the age of six, Einstein began to wonder why it worked. Such a question naturally led to basic visualizations of phenomena such as magnetism and polarity. He hated like poison the rote methods of his grade school in Germany, but he embraced his later school experiences in Switzerland for enabling open-ended inquiry.

Early in his career, while working as an examiner for the Swiss patent office, Einstein would daydream in his spare time. He pictured himself as a painter falling off a roof. Wouldn't it seem as if the ground were rushing at him rather than him falling to the ground? He wondered what it would be like to fall through the ground to the center of the Earth. Would he know which direction he was moving at any given moment? Wouldn't he feel weightless? What if gravity as we know it were not a universal force, as Newton said? What if it were only an artifact in our particular corner of the universe, only a warp in space-time?

Einstein imagined what it would be like to ride a beam of light. How long would it take to travel from the Earth to the moon this way? How long would it take if you were traveling on a train going fifty miles per hour? What if you turned on the train's headlights? Would the light move any faster if the train was moving? What if you were riding on the light beam and checked your watch? How could you measure the speed of the train? Wouldn't your watch on the light beam seem to run slower than the clock on the train? What if time weren't constant, as Newton said? What if time were relative? Do moving clocks run slow?

The visualizations seem simple now, but the results were so profound that people refused to believe them. The *Times* of London called Einstein's special theory of relativity "an affront to common sense." In 1914, Einstein famously predicted that the eclipse of the sun would show that the sun's rays bending around the planet Mercury would warp in different ways depending on where on Earth you observed the phenomenon. Even when that prediction turned out to be correct, when he had the data to back up his theory, many Newtonian scientists refused to believe it.[8]

Steve Jacobsen performs these sorts of visual mind games all the time. So does Woody Norris. "Einstein is always getting challenged," Norris says, "but he usually emerges closer than anyone else. I think we'll find that he was the most brilliant guy who ever lived. But he was still a child. We've got collective brains now. We have communication and instruments he never had. We have data he never had. Yet most of what he came up with, which was amazing, was based on these little thought experiments."[9]

Norris invents using his own visual experiments. "What if I could speed off just fast enough to get beyond the edge of the expanding universe and go off into empty space?" he says. "I did this for a couple days. Every time I would get five minutes, I sat down, closed my eyes, and picked up from where I was. I zoomed off, and I found another universe that had its own big bang and was expanding into space at a rate near the speed of light. I thought, 'Wow, that is cool.' Those guys are over there, and we're over here. And there are probably others. You don't bump into a wall. There is no end. The big bang isn't pushing the wall out of the way, it's pushing into emptiness. Whatever mechanism caused the big bang can't be unique. I was just zooming around watching all this. Then, a few weeks later, while reading *Scientific American*, I read about the 'multi-verse.'[10] I said, 'What's the deal here? That's my idea!'"

Norris's inventions are fueled by this process of pure imagination. "What's so cool about the human brain is that you have the ability to go anywhere. You can stand on the moon right now. You can see all the little rocks. You can look out the slit in the eyes of the Statue of Liberty. You can visualize it. You can picture a polar bear in a car speeding down the freeway. You can walk around it, get above it. You don't need a ladder. You can float up above it and look down from the top, or pick it up and tilt it around with your hand. It doesn't matter what it weighs. Weight, size, shape, gravity—nothing matters. Some people think this a useless skill. But if you work at that process and apply it to creativity, it can be very productive."

This is how Norris came to invent what he calls the AirScooter. "I have a private pilot's license," he says. "Every time I fly I complain that this is like being in a soapbox derby. These things are so dang rickety, so noisy. The floor is only a quarter-inch thick. They're just a tin can. I don't like to be going one hundred miles an hour just to stay in the air. They're a death trap."

Norris tried to imagine his ultimate flying machine. "Here is what I'd like if I had my druthers," he says. "Number one, I don't want to have to go one hundred miles an hour. I want to lift up one foot and hang there. Number two, I don't want to go to the airport. Number three, I don't want to have a license. That can cost $50,000. Number four, I don't want a helicopter. Helicopters are nonintuitive. The blades want to spin the body around. They crash too easily. Every hour of flight requires an hour of maintenance. I want this to be safe and affordable."

With these goals in mind, Norris went into an empty room, dimmed the lights, and built his AirScooter in his mind. "I can fully construct anything I can think of," he says. "I can look at it from every angle. I can see it screwing together. I do this all the time. I think it's an ability we all have. It's like learning to jump rope or dive. We all have a lot of skills we don't tap. I wasn't very good at it at first. But anyone can do this with practice, and I mean that honestly."

In his visualizations, Norris found that there were many barriers to inventing his ultimate flying machine. He used mental simulations to attack each of these barriers. He pictured controlling his new aircraft with a bicycle-like handlebar that moves it in any direction. He visualized ways to eliminate complex linkages that would cause high maintenance. He pictured it as a single-passenger machine. That gets rid of liability lawsuits. Before you can start the engine, you push a button to sign an electronic contract and accept the risk. Norris pictured his machine as lightweight. (If it weighs less than 254 pounds, it would be classified as an ultralight hobby aircraft, the least-regulated category of aircraft governed by the Federal Aviation Administration.) Norris wanted to be able to take off and land vertically. He wanted there to be no tail rotor to destabilize the aircraft. He pictured a pair of helicopter-like blades mounted on the top, rotating in opposite directions, to provide balance. He also envisioned the device moving like a humming-bird, with the user having the ability to constantly adjust speed going sideways, forward, backward, up, or down, or to hover in midair.

The biggest barrier that Norris saw was the engine. "The only lightweight ones out there are two-stroke engines," he notes. Two-stroke engines mix oil with the gas, and that eliminates many of the valves that are required by four-stroke engines. The problem is that two-stroke engines are highly polluting because they operate at six thousand revolutions per minute. "I couldn't see putting my life in the hands of a two-stroke engine screaming at me and scaring me to death." Such high-rev engines are prone to seize up, and there would be no way to glide to a safe landing.

Norris searched online for a company making a lightweight, four-stroke "Otto" engine that operates at lower revs. He found one made by a New Zealand company now called AeroTwin Motors Corporation. These aluminum and titanium engines weigh only 78 pounds and operate at 65 horsepower. Norris was so impressed that he acquired the company outright and opened a factory in Texas to begin producing them.

Meanwhile, he opened an AirScooter plant in rural Nevada to begin building the same personal aircraft he had pictured in his dreams. More than anything else, Norris's AirScooter looks like a catamaran. The aircraft sits on a pair of bright red rubber pontoons, with a red stabilization tail sticking out the back. The open-air cockpit has minimal instrumentation dominated by a handlebar-like control stick. The pair of rotor blades sits on top of a cage. The gas tank holds five gallons, and the machine can fly seventy-five miles per hour for about two hours before needing to be refueled. The whole thing is shorter than a midsized sedan. The target price is $25,000, depending on whether Norris can integrate the new engine cheaply enough. Norris claims that anyone can learn to fly an AirScooter in one afternoon.

Are these tall claims? Yes. Have dozens of other inventors over the past fifty years also promised the ultimate personal aircraft? Anyone who reads *Popular Science* knows the answer to that one. Will the AirScooter become the first "flying car" to succeed? No one knows yet. Is Norris crazy? That's a relative term. Has he tapped into his power of visualization? No question. "You can do it, too," he insists. "I'm not that smart. If you don't believe me, ask my wife."

ENVISIONING THE HUMAN BODY

Stephen Jacobsen's early career was spent visualizing the organs of the human body and picturing ways to create machines to replace all of its parts, or at least most of them. In 1968, while working on his master's degree at the University of Utah, he got caught up in this behavior when he became the first student to sign up as an assistant in the newly opened campus laboratory of Dr. Willem Kolff. As a physician working for the Dutch resistance during World War II, Kolff imagined a way to create an artificial kidney. "Meeting Kolff was a big, big moment for me," Jacobsen recalls. He remembers being in awe of "this tall, aristocratic Dutchman."[11]

Jacobsen had heard all the stories. He had heard how Kolff crafted the first artificial kidney using sausage skin as a semiporous membrane. Portions of a patient's blood would be extracted and funneled through the membrane; it would retain the red and white blood cells, which are too big to pass through, while allowing urea and other harmful elements from the blood to be funneled into a container. Jacobsen had heard how Kolff used fruit juice cans for the containers in which the remaining portions of the blood would be cleansed with dialyzing solution before being recombined with the red and white cells and pumped back into the body. In 1945, Kolff revived his first patient using this handcrafted contraption. A comatose fifty-seven-year-old woman suffering from acute renal failure suddenly sat up in her hospital bed and blurted, "I am going to divorce my husband!" She went on to do just that and then lived another seven years.

In 1950, Kolff came to America. He never patented his invention, and while working for the Cleveland Clinic, he donated his intellectual property to Baxter Healthcare, which manufactured Kolff's kidney dialysis machine and installed the devices in treatment centers all over the world, eventually saving millions of lives. "That was still the time when doctors did not take out patents," recalls Kolff, now in his nineties.[12] "The AMA [American Medical Association] considered it unethical to do so." That started changing by the late 1960s, but Kolff remains ambivalent about medical patents. "People ask me all the time whether I'm worried about someone stealing my work. I tell them, 'If it will benefit mankind, they can have it.'"

Kolff arrived at the University of Utah in 1968 to set up his artificial organ laboratory, which he ran for three decades. A young Steve Jacobsen enlisted in the first project: an effort to visualize an improved artificial kidney, again made with odd parts. At first, Kolff and Jacobsen used the drum from a Maytag washing machine; then they turned to a nose cone from a rocket. The project yielded Jacobsen's first patent, held jointly with Kolff. The student was becoming an inventor.

Later, as a grad student at MIT, Jacobsen began searching for new artificial body parts to model in his mind. While pursuing his Ph.D. and working at the university's famed Artificial Intelligence Laboratory, Jacobsen came across an early artificial arm called the Boston Arm. "It was crummy," he says. "It was heavy and noisy and didn't have fine motor control. You could tell it was artificial from a hundred feet away."[13] Jacobsen became obsessed with visualizing a far superior artificial arm.

"I got interested in the idea of grace," he recalls. "I got intrigued by how groups of muscles got orchestrated by your brain. They really are like a symphony. Grace is a beautiful thing. It's about your brain and your body making a deal." He says he doesn't buy the "dominant brain" theory, which suggests that the brain is in complete control of the rest of the body. "The intelligence in your body is distributed," he says. "You're a model-based controller. You have a one-hundred-millisecond time delay in your legs. If you're walking down the stairs, you're planning that the next stair is going to be there, and if it's not, you have a catastrophe. You can't stop yourself in time." Jacobsen began seeing clear pictures of how the entire human body was a machine with parts that could be replicated by technology.

After MIT, he returned to Kolff's laboratory in Salt Lake City to begin work on his own artificial arm. Jacobsen set out to visualize an arm that was stronger, lighter, and far easier to control than the Boston Arm. He also wanted one that was mass producible so that it could be sold to the thousands of people who needed one. "Steve was the main person" behind what became known as the Utah Arm, Kolff confirms.[14] The arm was equipped with bioelectrical sensors that detected the signals sent by the brain and relayed by the shoulder muscles when they expanded and contracted. "This arm moved before the owner of arm even knew it," says Kolff. "It knew enough to go slowly near your mouth so it wouldn't crack your teeth, but it was strong enough to crack a nut, and gentle enough to peel an orange." As Jacobsen explains it, the Utah Arm is "electrically powered but body commanded."[15] With production spun off into an independent company, now called Motion Control, Inc., also based in Salt Lake City, the Utah Arm remains the leading artificial arm in the world.

Kolff was assembling a group of extraordinary medical inventors who visualized ways of recreating the basic functions of almost every major body part. A researcher named William Dobelle spearheaded an effort to create an artificial eye, an implantable visual processing machine that would literally connect to the optic nerve and map into the brain's visual cortex. "We wanted to make a map of the brain's visual cortex," Kolff recalls. "Once you have that, you can begin to program visualization. The simplest thing to program is Braille. A blind person can read it three times faster when we stimulate the brain."[16] But Kolff couldn't get the project funded. "The resistance has been enormous," he says. Dobelle later went to Columbia University to continue his experiments. Today, nearly thirty years later, the Dobelle eye is reportedly working in a small group of test patients, literally connecting camera-like equipment with fiber-optic wires to the brains of blind people. Kolff claims that he will enable blind people to drive cars.

Kolff began imagining designs for artificial hearts when he was at the Cleveland Clinic in the late 1950s, and he even designed fist-sized pumps and implanted them in monkeys and dogs. A former medical student named Robert Jarvik heard about Kolff's work and visited the lab. Jarvik had first learned about heart transplants years earlier when his own father had undergone open-heart surgery. Kolff hired Jarvik and raised funds to support an artificial heart team that grew to 147 researchers and scientists. Various researchers worked on various aspects of many different designs, with Steve Jacobsen pitching in to model the fluid flow of the blood inside the chambers.

What happened next gave Jacobsen enormous confidence in the power of imagination. He was a firsthand witness and a participant in one of the biggest medical spectacles of the century. As a way of identifying the different models of artificial hearts in the lab, Kolff assigned different researchers' names to different models. One model, for example, was called the Jarvik-7. In 1982, Kolff's team implanted the Jarvik-7 inside the chest of a dying patient named Barney Clark. "Nobody cared about the name Jarvik until Barney Clark," Kolff recalls. The media responded to the news of the first human to receive an artificial heart with such swiftness and force that half of Kolff's lab was suddenly filled with reporters and television cameras around the clock. The Jarvik heart was featured on the covers of *Time* and *Newsweek*. The public wanted to see how long Barney Clark would live. The suspense fed a media frenzy. Clark ended up living for 111 days, with newspaper and TV crews documenting his experience every step of the way.

Jacobsen keeps a Teflon-coated Jarvik heart on one of the shelves in his office. The invention represents many things to him.[17] Among the lessons he learned is how circumstantial and disproportionate it can be when the media is in charge of assigning credit for a momentous lab breakthrough. Why do people remember Jarvik but not Kolff? But what Jacobsen remembers most is how exciting it was to be there when the big moment happened. He calls the first successful artificial heart "an immortal result." Just being part of it gave him enough confidence and curiosity to visualize dozens of other immortal results that could be achieved.

Jacobsen decided to strike out on his own. He retained his professorship at the University of Utah and formed a separate company, Sarcos, to focus on building the most spectacular robots the world had ever seen—not toys but robots that mimicked human functions at a very basic level.

All the visualizations he had ever had would come into play. "When you were a little kid, didn't you know there would be robots?" he asks. "Some would wash your car, some would perform medical functions, some would be your house servants, some would be entertainers." Jacobsen cannot recall the exact year he started Sarcos to launch this massive new invention effort, but records show it was 1983.

CHAPTER 9

Embracing Failure

*Success consists of going from failure to failure
without loss of enthusiasm.*

—WINSTON CHURCHILL

FAILURE IS THE RULE rather than the exception, and every failure
contains information. One of the most misleading lessons imparted
by those who have reached their goal is that the ones who win are
the ones who persevere. Not always. If you keep trying without
learning why you failed, you'll probably fail again and again. Perseverance must be accompanied by the embrace of failure. Failure is
what moves you forward. Listen to failure.

But there are different kinds of failure. Sometimes, failure tells you
to give up and do something else entirely. Other times, it tells you to
try a different approach, a new route to the top of the mountain. Or
it may tell you to make a detour. Sometimes, it tells you that you
need help. Sometimes, it doesn't seem to tell you anything.

Linda Stone, a former executive at both Apple Computer and
Microsoft, recalls a conversation she participated in with Steve Wozniak and Dean Kamen, perhaps the two best-known living inventors.

"I'll never forget it," Stone says. "They just were talking about all their failures, and how they both felt like failures."[1] They were almost bragging about various laboratory fiascoes and catastrophes. Given their success, this seemed extraordinary. According to Stone, the conversation occurred just before an awards ceremony. "They were both being celebrated," she says. So Wozniak and Kamen clearly weren't talking about their failures as a way of feeling sorry for themselves. Rather, they were identifying with a thinking strategy they both had in common. "Every failure is a learning experience," concludes Stone, "and it should be seen as part of progress, rather than seeing it as the enemy."

TRYING THIS, THIS, AND THIS

You wouldn't normally associate Steve Wozniak with failure. His early career has often been described as a rocket ride. Born in San Jose, California, in 1950, the son of a teacher and a Lockheed engineer, Woz played with surplus transistors that his father brought home from work, making his own walkie-talkies and intercoms. Woz was operating ham radios by age eleven and designing computers by age thirteen, but mostly on paper. A habitual prankster, in high school he built "blue boxes": devices that patched into phone company switches, enabling the user to make free calls and redirect other people's lines.[2] As he was creating these things, Woz learned about tinkering—trying something, learning why it doesn't work, recovering from that small misdirection, and then using the resulting knowledge to try something else. "I'd scrap things together—try this, try this, try this," Woz has said.[3] He was embracing *failure iteration*. "Another way of looking at failure is learning the ability to iterate," says Linda Stone.

Through a common friend at Homestead High School in Santa Clara, Woz was introduced to Steve Jobs, an ambitious hippie and fellow prankster who later ended up getting a gig as a technician at Atari Inc., maker of computer games. "He could persuade people to do things that normally couldn't get done," Woz recalls. After graduating from college in Boulder, Colorado, Woz worked as an engineer with Hewlett-Packard, designing handheld calculators. There, he learned from the failures of others. He recalls being able to walk around to various workbenches and quickly tell when his colleagues were crafting designs that wouldn't pan out. He enjoyed the job, but Woz has repeatedly speculated that if he had tried to create a personal computer at H-P, it would have failed. "We probably would have made the wrong decisions technically and built the wrong product," he has said. With the future demand for individual desktop computers clear to both of them (but not to their bosses at Atari and H-P), the two Steves went into business together in 1976, setting up shop in Jobs's garage.

Many times, Woz would induce his own failures by reviewing work he had already done. "I once laid out the whole board, and then I got an idea to save one feed-through [circuit]," he recalled in an interview some ten years later. "So I took the board apart, I trashed maybe a week's worth of work, and then I started over."[4] The Apple I computer featured eight kilobytes of random access memory. While Woz did the inventing and the engineering, Jobs typically was out making sales pitches and raising money. The Steves built 200 machines and sold 175 of them to hobbyists over ten months.

With the modest success of the Apple I under their belts, Jobs convinced Woz to quit H-P and form Apple Computer, with $3 million in backing from local venture capitalists. Wozniak then created the Apple II, the last personal computer to be designed entirely by a single human being. It contained dozens of innovations, including support for color graphics, word processing, and games, and it, too, was the product of rapid failure iteration. For example, in creating the disk drive Woz began with a design based on fifty chips. In a frantic engineering zigzag that featured dozens of false starts, he managed to reduce the number of chips to three. The result of all this iterative failure, the Apple II, was so clearly superior to any other personal computer then on the market that it dominated the field for three years. By 1980, Apple Computer was a public company, with revenues exceeding $100 million. The Apple II architecture managed to hold on to a small piece of the personal computer market even after IBM introduced its famed PC in 1981 and Apple unveiled the Macintosh in 1984.

But looking back on his career, Woz remembers far more failure than success. He didn't cope well at Apple as the company grew. He felt that the talent-rich Macintosh team needed him less and less. He resisted being a manager or a businessperson. He was distracted by his wealth. After he became successful, he has said, "I wound up trapped by the world."[5] He left Apple in 1985 and immediately went searching for something new to invent, hoping to duplicate his earlier success.

Instead, Woz made new mistakes. His next company, Cloud Nine, was a failure in many respects. He pinpointed a problem: that the average consumer had too many poorly designed remote controls. But Woz's invention, a programmable remote control designed to work with any TV or other consumer electronics device, didn't work well with some equipment, and it was not embraced by manufacturers or consumers. His failure was so complete that he felt as if his artist-like ability to connect different ideas in his head was gone. He felt that he couldn't program software anymore. "It gets to the point where you can't tell where the inventiveness was lost," he said not long after the Cloud Nine dream died. He lost most of his Apple fortune, and he became disillusioned by the entire industry.

Faced with failure, Woz seemed to give up. He became one of the world's most famous teachers, holding classes in computer graphics for elementary school kids in his own garage. His former partner, Steve Jobs, soon moved on to learn a fantastic set of lessons from his own "failure," Next Computer Inc. But Woz seemed content to sit on the sidelines. "He's uniquely undriven," said industry pundit Stuart Alsop.[6]

But maybe Woz was just responding to failure in his own way. His style of inventing complex electronics all by himself was no longer applicable in a world made infinitely more complex by his own invention. He decided to specialize, to immerse himself in the one component of the computer that was most prone to failure, the only part he still found interesting: the user, particularly the young user, the kid in school. He was taking a giant detour. While dabbling in philanthropy, he delved into the practice of teaching and the study of learning, more specifically how children use computers to learn. He did this for nearly fifteen years, during which time more of his fortune evaporated.

Then, in January 2001, gathering all he had learned, Wozniak got back into the game of invention. Now in his early fifties, he started a company called WOZ (for Wheels of Zeus) and secretly began building prototypes and showing them to potential investors. He called WOZ "a new wireless products company to help everyday people do everyday things." He was inspired by his dog outsmarting and escaping the electric fence in the yard one too many times. He raised $6 million in venture capital, to back his prototype of developing a set of cheap radio-frequency chips that communicated with Global Positioning System satellites, so people could keep tabs on the whereabouts of their kids, pets, or other valuables. He called the network that would send location data to end users wOzNet. "The goal is doing something neat and fun," he said.[7] Was Woz about to capitalize on his past failures? Or was he going to make a new set of mistakes? Knowing the history of Woz, he was about to do both, and that's the way it should be.

FAILING FASTER AND FASTER

Dean Kamen has probably failed more consistently and more often than his friend Steve Wozniak. That's because Kamen has never let up from the process of invention and never intends to. Along the way, Kamen has become the ultimate just-do-it inventor and a master at failure iteration. As with Wozniak, Kamen's mother was also a teacher. His father carved out a career as a highly successful comic book illustrator and portrait artist. Growing up in Rockville Center, Long Island, Kamen, a year younger than Wozniak, loved to learn but was impatient with the structure of school. "My hobby was thinking, and watching people," he says.[8] His father advised him, "If it's not a big deal, don't complain. If it is, do something about it."[9]

Kamen created his first profitable invention one summer during high school. In his basement, he experimented with connecting a box of multicolored lights to a stereo system and coordinating a light show to the patterns of music. (Hey, it was the 1960s.) One day, his boss, a cabinetmaker, took Kamen on a business call to the Hayden Planetarium, part of the New York Museum of Natural History. The sixteen-year-old Kamen decided he would build a version of his sound-and-light show box for the museum, and he persisted in bringing his improved box back to the museum and installing it himself for a demo. As soon as he plugged it in, boom! All the circuits in a wing of the building blew. "I almost set the place on fire," he recalls. From this failure, he learned about a thing called a three-phase power system, and he accommodated his next version to that system. The museum ended up ordering five units for $10,000. News of Kamen's sound-and-light show invention made the *New York Times,* and he was flooded with orders. Pretty soon, his basement "looked like the inside of a transistor radio."

For Kamen, the prospect of failure sometimes served as a motivator in and of itself. William P. Murphy Jr., the founder of Cordis Corp. and the inventor of many medical devices, heard about the museum's sound-and-light show and hired Kamen to design an audiovisual presentation for the unveiling of his company's latest invention, a physiologic pacemaker. But when Cordis engineers installed Kamen's equipment at a big trade show in California, something went haywire and the power supply melted only a day before the big presentation. Kamen flew out to the show, crawled under the stage, and diagnosed the problem as backward wiring. Then he flew back on the red-eye to his basement lab, worked all day to rebuild a new power board, caught another flight back to California that evening, reinstalled the equipment, and got it to work just in time. Murphy, the son of a Nobel Prize–winning doctor, recognized in Kamen a kindred spirit, someone who had the same compulsion to create. Murphy was so impressed that he became a mentor to Kamen.[10]

Inspired by his association with Murphy and by the stories told by his older brother, Bart, a Harvard Medical School student, Kamen turned to inventing new medical devices. But he recognized that he wouldn't be able to invent these sophisticated instruments unless he was able to make a lot of mistakes very rapidly. He needed a way to do failure iteration. In particular, he needed a lathe, a three-thousand-pound device that can sculpt intricate parts. So he had one delivered and installed in his parents' basement.

Kamen called his company Independent Prototype, and he ran the shop for four years. All through his college years at Worcester Polytechnic Institute, he drove back and forth between his lab and his dorm room, doing a lot of inventing but not very much school-work. In the shop, he created a miniature syringe that automatically delivered precise doses of medicine. The drug-infusion device led to a story in the *New England Journal of Medicine*. After reading it, offi-cials at the National Institutes of Health ordered one hundred of Kamen's syringes at $2,000 each. Large research hospitals became clients of Kamen's company, which he renamed Auto Syringe Inc. By now, Kamen no longer found much use for the charade of going to college, so he dropped out and became a full-time inventor.

To keep up with the demand for his devices, he needed to ex-pand his operation and acquire the means to iterate a wider range of ideas and concepts. "I wanted a full machine shop," Kamen recalls. "And I saw all that wasted space in my parent's backyard." So, with his parents away on a ten-day cruise, Kamen ordered in a crane and a bulldozer. The construction crew lifted the entire house off its foundation and dug an eight-foot hole in the backyard to expand the basement. Town officials came by, screaming that he didn't have a permit. "Pieces of sidewalk were popping up," says Kamen. "It was worse than I thought it would be." When his parents came home and surveyed the full scope of what their son had done to their home, his father turned to his mother and said, "Okay, now what's for dinner?"

Kamen was clearly oblivious to the consequences of trying new things, and perhaps his parents knew they couldn't and probably shouldn't stop him. Most of his ideas flopped, but he was having so many of them, and he was able to test them so quickly, that a small portion of his ideas turned out to be good ones. In addition to the Auto Syringe, Kamen developed a portable insulin pump for dia-betics that found strong demand in the market. The product led to a six-figure income by the time he was in his early twenties.

One day Kamen spotted a license plate with the motto "Live Free or Die." He had never been to New Hampshire, but he decided that the motto sounded pretty good. He needed to be closer to his medical clients in Boston, he needed cheap and abundant laboratory and manufacturing space, and he liked the idea of not paying personal income taxes. He had his lab gear and machine shop loaded into four Ryder trucks, formed a convoy with twenty of his employees, and headed north.

Upon his arrival in Manchester, Kamen rented a set of buildings "for next to nothing" and proceeded to embark on a string of ill-fated projects that once in a while led to a big payoff. Taking the first two letters of his first and last names, he soon renamed his company DEKA Research. "It's always been a continual series of failures," says John Morrell, one of DEKA's top engineers. "But it's punctuated by an occasional success."[11] Under this business model, those few successes pay for all the failures, and learning from the failures often leads to a success. In 1982, for example, Auto Syringe was considered such a success that Kamen was able to sell the product to the healthcare giant Baxter International for $30 million. Baxter came back a few years later and asked Kamen to fix a problem with the valves in its kidney dialysis machine, used in hospitals worldwide, but Kamen rejected the premise of the assignment. He instead built a portable, compact machine that for the first time enabled patients to filter their blood in their own homes.

With the cash from the sale and the continual flow of royalties from Baxter's new HomeChoice dialysis machines, Kamen bought an airplane, a helicopter, and his own small island, called North Dumpling, in Long Island Sound. He famously seceded from the United States to form his own tiny country. "The only 100 percent science-literate society," goes Kamen's credo. "America can learn a lot from its neighbor." For his provisional government, he named Ben Cohen and Jerry Greenfield, originators of Ben & Jerry's ice cream products, as the Joint Ministers of Ice Cream.[12]

But Kamen has little time to relax on his island. More often, you can find him tooling about among a cluster of old red-brick mill buildings on the banks of the Merrimack River. Containing a half million square feet and featuring eighteen-foot ceilings, the Manchester mill complex was at one point the world's largest textile plant. But it had stood empty for fifty years when Kamen bought it and established DEKA there. "It was in tough, tough shape," Kamen recalls. He proceeded to invest more than $10 million to transform the place into the ultimate inventor's playground, installing a football-field-sized machine shop on the fourth floor so that he could iterate new ideas and learn from failure faster than anyone else in the world.

KISSING FROGS

Often, inventors will tell you that they would never have embarked on a particular project if they had known ahead of time how much trial and error and disappointment and money they would have to invest to make it a success. You might think that Dean Kamen's IBOT project would belong in that category, but only if you didn't know Dean Kamen.

One day in 1990, Kamen became fascinated while witnessing a wheelchair-bound man trying to get over a curb en route to a shopping center in Manchester. Kamen followed the man into an ice cream parlor and saw him struggle to reach the counter and grab his ice cream cone. As a lover of ice cream, Kamen was outraged. As an inventor, he was inspired. He thought it was ridiculous that a wheelchair couldn't climb a curb—or stairs, for that matter—and he thought it must be debilitating for wheelchair-bound people when they couldn't rise up to interact with someone else eye to eye.

For the next two years Kamen pondered the problem, but neither he nor his team of engineers could think of a reasonable solution. One day, when Kamen slipped on a wet bathroom floor, the solution came to him. Balance. That was the problem. The technique of catching yourself before falling—that was what needed to be simulated in a new kind of wheelchair.

What followed was ten years of nearly constant frustration, with only an occasional eureka. Soon after pinpointing the problem, the team Kamen assembled homed in on the enabling technology: a set of electronic gyroscopes that could provide the IBOT with its automatic balance. "We didn't invent the gyroscopes, the microprocessor, the sensors, and the other components," Kamen says. "We find the best-in-breed components and integrate them. Twenty years ago, gyroscopes used to be big, mechanical objects with spinning masts. Ten years ago, they had smaller rings. Five years ago, they went solid state. These days, they're building gyroscopes at the size and scale of the microchip."[13]

Kamen was talking about these electronic gyroscopes on a hot July morning while giving a private tour of his vast laboratory. In the IBOT development area, a visitor could catch only a glimpse of the kind of failure and pressure that has gone on here. A sign on the wall read, "God said: Let there be light. Dean says: Let's make it lighter." The joke was in reference to Kamen's challenge "to put the IBOT on a diet," reducing its one-time weight of 300 pounds to something closer to 200 pounds. It had to be done without reducing reliability and functionality and without increasing the costs. At the time of this visit, the 225-pound IBOT was functioning beautifully—climbing stairs, providing the rider with the ability to stand up while retaining perfect balance, and so forth. The system had passed a set of clinical trials, and was going through a laborious process of gaining FDA approval so that it could be sold by Johnson & Johnson, the company that had purchased the sales and marketing rights. (The final approval came a few months later.)

The IBOT, of course, inspired Kamen's most famous invention. "We built an IBOT, and once the balancing systems worked perfectly, we realized that they could be used in other places," he says. He generalized the technology so that it could apply to everyone. "When you're a baby, you stick your butt out or head out and you fall on it. You move your center of gravity in front of your feet, and then you start to fall and you put a foot out in front. You go into a controlled fall, but you catch yourself on the ball of your foot." That's the basic principle behind the Segway, Kamen's two-wheeled personal electronic vehicle. "The Segway becomes an extension of yourself," he says, "because it is acting in response to your own basic understanding of balance."

The Segway is yet another invention built upon failure after failure. "People think engineering is a nice, neat, clean, linear process," says Doug Field, Segway's vice president of product development.

He joined DEKA in 1996, after twenty years with the Ford Motor Company. "But there's never an obvious solution," Field continues. "There's so much complication. It's a messy, dirty, frustrating process."[14]

To get through this process, DEKA's culture doesn't merely tolerate the occasional mistake; it provides incentive for creative failure. "Most companies penalize failure," Field says. "[But] failure is important. Don't punish it. Don't make it difficult to try something. You can fail without letting down the team." To encourage his engineers to fail in the most dramatic fashion possible, Kamen instituted a peer-nominated award known as the Frog. As the saying goes, "You've got to kiss a lot of frogs before you find a prince."

The objective is to prompt a lot of frog-kissing—to elicit as many ideas as possible, test them as rapidly as possible, throw away the bad ones as soon as possible, and end up with what survives. The best ideas become part of finished products, but the most fantastically bad ideas are also rewarded—with the Frog. Winning it is a badge of honor. "We want people to put their heart and soul into it," says Field. To win the Frog, "we want a beautiful implementation that is fundamentally flawed." Distinguishing the perfect product from the frog is never obvious. As Field puts it, "You never know the quality of the idea until the end of the kiss."

The handlebar system for the Segway was one of the areas in which the team produced and kissed many frogs. Forty engineers and designers focused some of their keenest attention on the handlebar's user interface and steering mechanism. They began by constructing prototypes on screens, using computer-aided design (CAD) software. But Kamen prefers to see physical objects made in his machine shop so that you can hold them your hands and test them in actual machines. "Everybody talks about rapid prototyping and all that CAD activity, but there is nothing like real parts," he says.[15]

One early prototype—a straight aluminum handlebar with a radio-button-like dial for controlling the steering—proved too difficult for riders to learn. "It required a surgeon's touch," says Field. Frog. In a subsequent design, engineers developed a plastic sleeve so that users could control the steering with the whole hand and wrist, as opposed to the fingertips, and that design proved successful. But it featured steering handles at right angles to the main bar, and these handles kept getting caught in riders' belts and shirts. Frog. A more rounded, M-shaped version included more electronics and was crafted from hard plastic. That proved to be much easier to manu-facture, but its many buttons and features, Field says, caused confu-sion and distraction. Frog.[16]

In the end, it came down to a design emphasizing simplicity and aesthetics. "This is a beautiful form," marvels DEKA engineer Mor-rell, pointing to the product they decided was just right. "It looks like a bird flying, right?"[17] Yet the team still keeps the rejected frogs around the lab as a way of embracing failure and learning from it.

CHASING RAINBOWS

Dean Kamen and Stephen Jacobsen, the Utah-based robotics in-ventor introduced in Chapter 8, are rivals in some areas, but they are also peers who spend time talking about the process of invention, admiring each other's skills, and they've developed a certain form of mutual respect. They have a common set of acquaintances. Bill Murphy has served as a mentor and key business contact for both Jacobsen and Kamen. Woodie Flowers—a legendary MIT engineer professor who works with Kamen on running the annual FIRST robotics competition for students—was Jacobsen's roommate as a grad student at MIT. In addition, both Jacobsen and Kamen have done projects for a common set of clients, including Baxter and Johnson & Johnson.

But Kamen has become famous, whereas Jacobsen hasn't. To see why, consider a few examples of how Jacobsen invented successfully but still failed to make an impact or get the credit he deserved. For instance, he recognized the limitations of Baxter's kidney dialysis machines fifteen years before Dean Kamen reinvented the same de-vice. Jacobsen collaborated with Willem Kolff, the original inventor of the Baxter technology, and received a string of patents on a new machine that was many times better than the one Baxter was mar-keting worldwide. But Baxter wasn't yet ready for these ideas, and so the company repeatedly rejected Jacobsen's product. "Timing is everything in the world of invention," says Jacobsen. "If you're too early or too late, you're screwed."[18]

Overall, you'd have to say that Stephen Jacobsen's career has been a stunning success. After he started Sarcos Research in 1983, his reputation for inventing "information-based machines that move" grew and grew. Demand for his services became so great that he was able to pick and choose which invention projects to undertake for some of the world's biggest and best-known corporations. He calls Sarcos a "skunk works for hire." At any given time, his laboratory is working on dozens of different projects, under contracts ranging from $50,000 to $30 million. He expands and shrinks the size of his invention team from between thirty and two hundred people depending on what kind of medical devices, robots, and miniature electronics products he has agreed to invent and develop.

But visit Jacobsen at his Salt Lake City laboratory on any given day, and you'll encounter a jumble of half-assembled robot heads, motors, and circuit boards. He admits that most of the things he does simply fail. "People come in here and see all these prototypes and they say, 'Gee, you have a lot of failures,'" says Jacobsen. He replies with a quotation from Thomas Edison: "These aren't *failures*. They're *experiments*." Edison also proudly declared, "I have discovered a thousand different ways *not* to make a light bulb." Jacobsen, too, spends much of his time learning how not to do something that's never been done before. "We try to make mistakes as fast as we can," he says, echoing Kamen and almost all other successful inventors.

For years, Jacobsen has pursued a somewhat secret goal. After he watched Robert Jarvik get all the credit for the artificial heart at the University of Utah in 1981, he thought he too could one day achieve an immortal result. "I'd love to invent something that gets remembered, something like the phonograph," he says. Yet however great his achievements, wider recognition has eluded him. When he invented the Utah Arm, it probably should have been seen as a breakthrough, something that captured the imagination of the general public. But it came at a time when *The Six Million Dollar Man* and *The Bionic Woman* were hot on prime-time television, so the advanced technology embodied in Jacobsen's invention didn't come as a surprise to a public accustomed to bionic and robotic special effects in their living rooms. Later, Jacobsen invented a whole new field, MEMS, the forerunner to today's nanotechnology boom. What did that get him? A position on the editorial board of the *Journal of Microelectromechanical Systems.*

In recent years, he has contributed to some of the key micromechanical sensors inside Honda's famous ASIMO, a sophisticated toy robot. But as an inventor for hire, Jacobsen rarely gets any credit. Instead, he is almost completely focused on where such robots fail rather than on what they can already do. When he demonstrates the robots he has created, people naturally get excited. Perhaps his most spectacular demo product is a robot that can juggle three balls. You can watch the robot calibrate its actions and get better over time. It seems to be learning before your eyes. "You show people these juggling robots, and people think it's one step away from doing a lot more," he says, "but these are actually very primitive learning programs."

Failure is what drives the development of these robots. Jacobsen spends his time working out theories of what a real robot would be like. He's trying to develop robots that aren't just programmed but rather act on their own and don't need to be refueled or recharged. "Robots are very hard to do," he says. "Honda, Toyota, Sony—they all believe that the time has come for robots. What would really be nice is autonomous robots. Take it out of the box, teach it, then it goes and does things. It would learn and see and perceive. They need intellectual independence. But that's just part of it. There has to be energy independence and sensory independence, too."

When it comes to learning from failure, Jacobsen has collected a pile of lessons the hard way. At one point in the late 1980s, he decided that the real hot spot for robots would be in the entertainment industry. Hollywood. Las Vegas. Disney. That's where the money and recognition really are, he thought. Jacobsen was engaging in a behavior to which many inventors succumb: He began chasing rainbows. For a Disney theme park exhibition, Jacobsen built a lifelike Joe Cocker robot that sang "Feeling Alright" with many of the singer's body gyrations and facial expressions. He built sword-fighting robots that mesmerized audiences. He made a John Wayne robot that drew big laughs whenever it said, "Round 'em up, partner." But he doesn't make much money on these projects. "They beat you up on the price," he says, "and under these sponsored contracts, you have to sign these big documents that tell you to keep your mouth shut."

In the course of making mistakes on these projects, Jacobsen became one of the world's best developers of animatronics, lifelike robots that put on a computer-coordinated show. Larry Miller, owner of the Utah Jazz basketball team, hired Sarcos to produce one of these animatronics spectacles for a new theme restaurant called The Mayan. Jacobsen created a flock of pelicans, toucans, iguanas, and other colorful birds and lizards that banter with one another and sing songs such as "Women" by Mungo Jerry ("In the summertime, when the weather is hot ..."). Creating each robot cost $100,000. But the restaurant didn't do as well as expected, and the entire exhibit was soon relocated to the basement at the Sarcos lab. "Every time I'm in a crummy mood, I just come down here and watch and listen to this," he says "This makes you feel good, doesn't it?"

For the Bellaggio, the world-famous $1.3 billion hotel and casino complex in Las Vegas, developer Steve Wynn hired Jacobsen to create robotically controlled wave fountains that would put on a spectacular water, music, and light show for guests twice per day. Over the course of two years, Jacobsen and his team designed and constructed a set of ten-foot-tall underwater wave machines that form beautiful water patterns that travel a quarter of a mile in the Bellaggio's man-made lake. "This had to be done on time, or they'd cut your legs off," Jacobsen recalls. When the project was completed, there was a black-tie dinner scheduled for thousands of press and VIPs. When Jacobsen and his team arrived, they were led into the hotel's basement. "They actually made us eat dinner in black tie in the basement, in this shitty storage room," he recalls. "We were then led upstairs and put behind a fence so that we could never be where the big people were. They didn't want us to be known. They never mentioned us."

The failure to gain recognition was even more painful after Jacobsen completed a project for the Universal Studios theme park. For the Jurassic Park exhibit, Universal hired Sarcos to create the centerpiece attraction, a giant robotic dinosaur, to be as lifelike and scary as possible. Jacobsen developed an eighty-thousand-pound tyrannosaurus rex robot called the Ultrasaur. The neck alone was forty feet long. The project took two years, and there were so many pieces that Sarcos had to subcontract some of the components to dozens of design shops all over the western United States. But when it came to unveiling the Ultrasaur to the press and the public, Jacobsen wasn't invited or mentioned. "Management saw us as an outside vendor," he says, "as someone to provide services at a minimum price."

Jacobsen has learned a lot from these failures to receive credit for his work. Achieving a spectacular success doesn't necessarily get you anywhere. If Jacobsen had secretly programmed the Ultrasaur to start attacking tourists, perhaps that would have made him famous. Maybe that would have gotten the public's attention.

From all these episodes, Jacobsen learned an overarching lesson: Don't let disappointment lead to disillusionment. Surprisingly, after all these letdowns, Jacobsen has kept the faith. "I tell students this all the time," he says. "The most important thing you can have is the ability to believe. Believing is a controllable aspect of people. You can let it be beaten out of you by bad events. You can become cynics, and a cynic does nothing. If you are going to invent or create, you have to put a lot of effort into something strictly on the idea of belief, because you can never know enough to justify doing it otherwise. It's pretty much the same way in anything you do. The venture guys bitch and moan and fail about 60 percent of the time. I bitch and moan, and I fail about 60 percent of the time. You've got to roll the dice. It's easy to be let it be stomped out of you. But failure can teach you to keep the faith."

BUILDING BIG MUSCLES

These days, inventors rarely get the chance to become identified with their own inventions. Steve Jacobsen is proof of that. If you are working at a corporation or if you're a contractor for hire, someone else will receive the credit. Perhaps this explains why there are so few famous inventors these days. Perhaps it also explains why Dean

Kamen decided to market the Segway on his own even though the chance of failure was high.

There is no doubt that the Segway is an engineering marvel. Steve Jobs, for one, was so impressed by early demonstrations that he apparently felt he was witnessing another Woz-like creation in the making. Jobs reportedly offered the buy the invention outright and then negotiated to purchase a minority share. The deal ended up falling apart, but not for lack of excitement. Other investors stepped in and eagerly ponied up $100 million for a small stake in the company, Segway LLC, making it one of the most highly valued start-ups ever.[19]

Why such excitement? Does the Segway solve a huge problem or fill a huge need? As defined by Kamen, the Segway is the answer to the urban transportation problem. "Cars are so good that we've paved entire continents to accommodate them," he says. "But no one enjoys traffic in cities. It causes congestion and pollution, and your speed is one-tenth of a mile per hour. Think of the fuel used in traffic. Forty-three percent of the world's gas is used by cars. Nineteen point six percent of people's disposable income goes to car payments and gas. In New York City, people will spend six hundred dollars per month just to park their car. Sixty-five percent of the land area in cities is parked cars. Every city in world! Three point two billion people live in cities—half of the world's population."[20]

Backed by all these statistics, Kamen is convinced that what people really want is a vehicle that can move four times as fast as walking but takes up only a little more space than a pedestrian. He pegs the market for the Segway at a few billion people. He doesn't see it as an expensive toy for rich people or gadget freaks. "I didn't spend thirty years in the medical business to come up with a new toy," he says. It all sounds compelling, and there is no doubt that Kamen's invention and his argument have made Segway into the most talked-about invention in a very long time. In a way, Segway has revived the very notion of invention itself as something important and fascinating.

What's unusual here is the way the inventor has put himself on the line. We rarely see the inventors. They are the men and women behind the curtain. Even Kamen typically licenses or sells his best inventions to giant corporations, makes a lot of money, and then moves on to invent the next thing. Friends and colleagues told him that this would have been the wise course of action here as well. "I tried to talk him out of it," says Nathan Myhrvold, the former Microsoft research chief, who learned from Kamen how to fly helicopters.[21]

Myhrvold says that a great inventor like Kamen should be back in the lab creating something new rather than out being a "social crusader," promoting and marketing. "Inventors sometimes go on a crusade to get the world to accept their idea," Myhrvold says. "Inventors are often seduced by their own ideas. They fall in love—like with their kids—often irrationally so. It's a pitfall. It's a dangerous path to be on." The easier route, adds Myhrvold, would have been to look at the market for the Segway like the market for snowmobiles. The snowmobile is a terrific invention. It's fun, it's useful, and making and selling snowmobiles is a profitable business. But it's not an especially large business. Not everyone wants or needs a snow-mobile. Myhrvold says that Kamen should have outsourced everything. "In ten years, who can make the Segway more cheaply—Dean Kamen or Honda?" Because Kamen is doing everything himself, says Myhrvold, "there is a huge risk of failure for things that have nothing to do with the invention itself."

Maybe that's the point—maybe Kamen doesn't particularly mind if the Segway is perceived as a spectacular failure in the short term. That would explain its hefty initial price tag of $5,000 and Kamen's decision not to do any advertising so that he could fine-tune his message in the face of great hype and expectation. With reported first-year sales of less than fifty thousand units, no one could argue that initial sales have set the world ablaze. For Kamen, though, it might be about something more than the Segway itself. It might be about reviving the Edisonian ideal of the inventor as the hero.

That is certainly one of the main driving forces behind Kamen's nonprofit organization, FIRST (For the Inspiration of Science and Technology), which funds an annual robot-making competition as a way of getting high school students as excited about creating technology as they are about playing and watching sports. The annual finals are typically held in a giant football stadium. Kamen is so passionate about FIRST that he deflects almost every question about his own ambitions into a speech about FIRST. Perhaps this explains Kamen's decision to cast himself as the front man. Wherever he goes, he's riding the Segway and wearing his trademark uniform: workboots, blue jeans, denim shirt. Perhaps he's doing all this for a reason. Perhaps it's important to him to project his image as a blue-collar engineer who is at work full time changing the world. Perhaps he sees himself as a new-kind-of-old-kind-of role model.

Linda Stone, who counts Kamen as a friend, says that Kamen perceives failure and success much differently from what is considered normal. Among the common traits Stone has observed in many inventors is their ability to delay gratification, a characteristic that she feels is discouraged in our instant gratification society. "Culturally, we behave in a way that weeds out, or that selects out, an ability to really develop a sense of delayed gratification," Stone says. "When I look at Dean Kamen, his IBOT wheelchair took ten years to develop. All of these things have taken at least ten years. The Internet was thirty years in the making before it found that place where technology met human needs and desires. So I'm both concerned and disturbed about the degree to which the ability to handle delayed gratification is not rewarded, and we are so aggressively looking for immediate gratification and we have such a compromised sense of time horizons today."[22]

As with any new invention, no one can tell what the Segway will look like in ten years, who will be using it, and for what purpose. Kamen has already offered his own guesses. First, he suspects that it may make a bigger splash in China than anywhere else. "The percentage of people living on farms there is getting smaller every year," he says. "China will have to move 800 million people into cities over the next twenty years." It may be physically impossible for all those people to be driving cars, even if they could afford them. He sees the Segway as revolutionizing the Chinese city of the future.[23]

The most promising way to improve the technology may lie in replacing the current rechargeable battery with a Stirling engine. Talk about learning from failure. In 1816, Scottish inventor Robert

Stirling came up with the concept for a single- or double-piston engine in which simple differentials between hot and cold chambers generated energy. An "external" combustion engine, the Stirling can run on anything from cow dung to leaves to propane. In principle and in practice, the Stirling works. But it doesn't work well enough. Kamen and his team have studied nearly two centuries' worth of experiments. They are trying to boost the power and efficiency enough so that such an engine can keep the crankshaft turning on the Segway, and Kamen has formed a separate company, New Power Ventures, to develop the engine technology. He sees a reinvented Stirling as a long-term replacement for the ubiquitous internal-combustion engine and our dependence on oil.

On the day of my visit, he's working on the Stirling in his machine shop. "This would be part of a ball bearing assembly to hold one of the rotating components," Kamen says, picking up a heavy metal gasket crafted by a large machine. He explains that the engine's mechanisms must withstand extreme heat and pressure. "You can't buy standard bearings that can do that. Nobody here planned to invent new ball bearings, but in order to make this engine practical, we have to eliminate some problems, and so unfortunately we have to develop a bearing technology that doesn't exist."

This work might not pay off for five years or more—if at all. In the short run, all Kamen can do is feed information from his failures back into his development projects. That goes for marketing as well as engineering. By spearheading everything himself, he's learning not only about engineering and manufacturing but also about public relations, about negotiating new uses and markets for his invention, about convincing national and state governments to alter their laws and their urban planning to allow Segways on sidewalks, and so on. We're talking about a man who learns so much from failure that this experience could make him virtually unstoppable.

Just because Kamen's Segway hasn't yet transformed life on Earth, that by no means rules out his potential to do so in the future. "Everybody knows that in order to build big muscles, you have to work against the heaviest weights until you fail," says Linda Stone.[24] In this way, every failure that doesn't kill inventors will make them stronger.

CHAPTER 10

Multiplying Insights

Invention breeds invention.

—RALPH WALDO EMERSON

SOLVING ONE PROBLEM creates new ones. Every invention, then, presents an opportunity for the inventor to build on its ideas or to solve the unanticipated problems that it may have produced. One good insight is almost never enough to achieve a breakthrough or trigger a transformation. But whoever comes up with one insight is the most likely person to generate another idea that makes the original one far more valuable. The inventor may also bounce the initial idea off of someone else, who then adds to it or implements it in an unexpected way. When ideas and inventions accumulate in this way, there is a powerful multiplying effect. A series of brainstorms may yield an idea that rates a solid eight on a scale of ten. But if you can build on it with a follow-on insight that also rates an eight, suddenly you have a sixty-four. If you keep at it, layering insight on top of insight, you can build something worth a million.

More significant than the seminal idea is the inventive process that follows—the explosion of eurekas that leads to the complex end result that the world recognizes as a complete invention. "Discovery is almost never a single idea," wrote Hungarian mathematician George Pólya. "Always look for new, related problems after solving the initial one."[1] If the original idea is elegant enough, it should by its own virtue lead to an exponentially more valuable cluster of insights.

Ronald A. Katz has been multiplying insights in this way for more than forty years. Katz didn't set out to be an inventor, and yet he unleashed this thinking strategy so methodically that he has quietly become the most financially successful inventor in history. He has never studied engineering or computer science, and yet he was the first to sketch out a critical set of new information technologies that the world would want and need, an achievement that has put many major corporations on the defensive. He has never worked in a corporate research lab, and yet he has created sophisticated new business models that enable him to be compensated for his ideas. He didn't even consider himself an inventor until more than ten years into his career, when the company he cofounded was struggling to survive and he resorted to licensing his patents as a way of keeping the business afloat. His inventions have made him extremely wealthy, and yet he has received remarkably little recognition.

These days, Ron Katz works in a six-room suite in a low-rise office building just off Sunset Boulevard in Beverly Hills. The small staff of Ronald A. Katz Technology Licensing, L.P., consists of attorneys and administrators who draw up contracts, resolve disputes, and process an avalanche of improbably fat checks sent in by dozens of famous corporations. A visitor sees no clutter, no gadgets, no machine tools, and no engineers at graphical workstations. Except for the fact that the walls of Katz's conference room are lined with plaques displaying his portfolio of patents, the place bears no resemblance to what one would expect of an inventor's lair. But what happens here is only the end result of an epic process of layering one insight upon another.

Katz grew up in an inventive family. Born in Cleveland in 1936, he moved with his family to Los Angeles when he was eight years old. He traces his ingenuity to his father, Mickey Katz, a Borscht Belt musician, composer, lyricist, and comedian. The elder Katz gained fame for Jewish self-parody songs such as "Duvid Crockett,"

"How Much Is That Pickle in the Window?" and "Knish Doctor" on albums with titles such as "Comin' Round the Katzskills" and "Greatest Shticks." A clarinet and saxophone player in the Spike Jones band and later the leader of his own touring troupe called The Borscht Capades, Mickey Katz was a practitioner of what his son calls a "genius form of klezmer," the wildly spirited and improvisational genre of Jewish jazz.

Ron Katz's older brother, Joel, went into the family business. After touring with their father's stage show as a teenager and moving to New York City, Joel changed his last name to Grey. Some years later, he originated the role of the outrageous master of ceremonies who shared the stage with Liza Minnelli in *Cabaret*, winning a Tony for his performance in the 1996 musical and then an Oscar for best supporting actor in the 1972 film adaptation.

Instead of following his father and only sibling into the world of entertainment, Ron Katz has made a career of proving that plenty of good can come from sitting alone in your room. Building on insights that he had in the 1960s and 1970s, he developed his most valuable inventions in the mid-1980s working by himself in his home office. Joel Grey has always been wowed by his younger brother's persistence. "Even as a kid, he was always out hustling and selling his ideas," says Grey. "He is a phenomenal brain. He's tenacious about what he believes in. I've seen him struggle. But he's always stayed with it. He never lets it go."[2]

The seed of Ron Katz's thicket of insights was planted more than forty years ago. After graduating from UCLA with a business degree in 1958, Katz took a job as an accountant at a large dam-building project three hundred miles north of Los Angeles, living in a one-bedroom trailer with his wife and young son. Like almost everyone else, Katz took his paycheck directly to the grocery store. That simple experience led to an initial set of ideas. Years before the advent of credit cards, credit reports, automatic credit authorization, and the marriage of computers and telephones, Katz began thinking about all these things.

"I was fascinated by the inefficient way that checks were approved," Katz recalls. "You'd go to the grocery store with your personal check or paycheck to get your food and some cash back. The grocers were the check cashers, and they still are in many cases. At the very most, they took your driver's license number, and they may have looked at a typed list, by last name, of people who had cashed bad checks. This didn't seem to make sense. It was a system that led to bad behavior because people recognized that the system was so limited."[3]

A year later, Katz moved with his family back to Los Angeles to take a job as an administrative assistant at the computer division of industrial giant Bendix Corp. As he learned about the versatility of computers, he began to imagine a new application: a computerized service for authorizing checks. "What you really needed was a list of everyone's IDs, and something that was dynamic, something that could verify a check in real time. You needed to look at the history and the patterns of the proffered IDs—not just the cashing of bad checks but the patterns and the number of checks they cashed." He ran the idea by Robert Goldman, an older colleague and friend. An electrical engineering graduate of Cornell, Goldman was then the director of technical information at Bendix. Based on their excitement about this new idea, the two men quit their jobs and started their own company. Instead of calling it Goldman Katz, the pair came up with the name Telecredit, which opened for business in a one-room office above a shopping center in Brentwood, California, in 1961.

Over the next several months, Goldman wrote a special program for a modified early IBM mainframe based on his and Katz's concepts; meanwhile, Katz obtained the numbering system for the state's 8.5 million driver's licenses from the Department of Motor Vehicles, along with a current list of bad check writers from the Los Angeles police department. The LAPD cooperated because Telecredit promised to help solve the department's overflow of cases. Whenever a merchant received a bad, stolen, or forged check, the evidence was turned over to law enforcement for investigation and prosecution. Nationally, the FBI had pegged check fraud as a $1 billion sinkhole for banks and merchants, and J. Edgar Hoover was cursing "fountain-pen bandits."

Early subscribers to the Telecredit service, including the Ralph's chain of supermarkets and the Sears, Montgomery Ward, and May department stores, typically paid twenty cents per call to verify checks over the phone. Operators at Telecredit did two things: They typed the license numbers into the system to see whether the customer had a history of writing bad checks, and they asked for eye color and date of birth to guard against fake licenses, entering that data into the system as well. "This data never before existed on computer," Katz says. "This was as high tech as you could imagine for 1961."[4]

As the service gained critical mass, people began to take notice. IBM sent a film crew to document the Telecredit application for its sales force and customers. In early 1963, *Time* magazine featured the company in a short piece, under the headline "Checking the Bouncers." Almost as an afterthought, Katz hired a young and talented patent attorney he had worked with at Bendix and filed for a patent on the basic system of "real-time, online, credit authorization," just to protect the company's basic idea.

Turning Chaos into Creativity

Success led to a certain sort of chaos. "People began to depend on us," Katz says. Telecredit grew to hundreds of employees taking up three floors in a building in Century City, California, and the LAPD insisted on installing a special hotline there. Whenever a bad check writer was uncovered—something that happened two thousand times in 1964 alone—an off-duty police officer working at Telecredit phoned the LAPD dispatch center, which sent a patrol car to the scene. An officer would say something like, "We have a bad check writer at the Ralph's on 420 Fulton."

Often, check kiters were involved in more serious crimes, and sometimes they had guns. Occasionally, shootouts erupted as police and security officers chased an alleged criminal from a store to a getaway car. Telecredit was becoming like a branch of the LAPD. Anyone who has seen the movie *Catch Me If You Can*, based on a true story and starring Leonardo DiCaprio and Tom Hanks, has a sense of what it was like to stop check kiting in the 1960s. "This was going on twenty-four hours a day," Katz says. "It was an exciting but very wild time."

The business model was a little bit wild, too. Telecredit was charging twenty cents per call, and it was costing the company forty cents per call to operate the service. Katz spotted a newspaper ad touting the practice of going public as a way to raise money, and that led to his and Goldman's decision to sell 155,000 shares in the company for $1 each. Telecredit was now a public company in constant need of cash, and it took on hundreds of thousands of dollars in debt. The company didn't have a single profitable month during the 1960s.

But Katz and Goldman had invented what later would be recognized as the first computer-automated call center providing online real-time credit authorization—and they continued to innovate. "It was like a laboratory," Katz says. "The creative stimulus was seeing how things work and thinking how they could work better." The two men didn't yet consider themselves inventors, only entrepreneurs who had new ideas as a by-product of growing the business. To improve the economics of approving checks, they developed a real-time credit-authorization terminal that eliminated the human operator. When store clerks punched in an account number, the terminal consulted a remote database and spit back a verdict. The terminal had three lights: green if there was nothing negative on the check writer's record, red if there was a negative history, and yellow if the customer was trying to cash a second check in the same day. Telecredit was successful in selling to a number of banks what were the first point-of-sale real-time credit-authorization terminals that accessed and updated a central database.

To protect their ideas, Katz and Goldman continued to file for U.S. patents, including one for a related idea that later became quite valuable. "Magnetic stripe cards had just come out," Katz recalls. The two entrepreneurs had an idea for creating a card-reading processor device to allow people at the point of sale to verify their credit without going to a central database. Goldman then suggested that the cardholder's account data be embedded on the magnetic strips; in this way, cardholders could identify themselves by swiping their cards through the machine, which would read the data and allow cardholders to perform account functions. At the end of the transaction, the system could update the customer's account. No one knew it at the time, but Goldman had invented a core element of what soon became known as the automatic teller machine.

All this work and creativity took its toll. As is typical of hard-driving entrepreneurs, both Katz and Goldman were physically burning out. "We had run this incredible, leading-edge business—we caught crooks, and we allowed honest customers to move through the lines faster," Katz says. "But it was extremely demanding. We were sleeping on the floor of the office some nights, and we were cash-poor." Goldman was looking to retire and soon did, and Katz was looking to raise more money and bring in professional management.

On a fund-raising trip in 1968, Katz was riding an elevator in New York when he was introduced to an investment banker and former Marine named Lee Ault. "He told me about his company and convinced me to attend a presentation," Ault recalls.[5] Instead of just helping to raise money for Telecredit, Ault also signed on to become its CEO. The company was still considered a hot technology start-up, Ault says, with stock trading in the 50s, but it desperately needed to start turning a profit.

Soon after Ault joined the company, however, Telecredit was hit with a nasty class action lawsuit. To recoup the rising costs of the Telecredit service, grocers had begun charging customers ten cents per check if they wanted to get cash back, continuing to charge customers nothing to cash a check to buy groceries only. Lawyers grouped some outraged customers and filed suit against Safeway, Ralph's, and other supermarkets, an action that prompted those grocers to drop the Telecredit service. The news sent the company's stock below $2, and Telecredit was forced to lay off four hundred workers. "We're lucky we didn't go broke," says Ault.

In dire need of cash, Katz came up with a plan to license Telecredit's patents to other companies. "Since I had a good understanding of the technology," Katz says, "I believed I could engage in useful discussions."[6] By then, however, many of the technologies that Telecredit had pioneered were coming into widespread use. Online, real-time telephone credit authorization was becoming popular.

The point-of-sale authorization terminal and the automated teller machine were already on the market from a variety of banks and manufacturers. Naturally, no one wanted to pay to license a technology they were already using.

"I remember one meeting with the CEO of major bank," Ault recalls.[7] Ault was there with Katz in the hope of striking a patent licensing agreement when the CEO lost his temper. "He was shouting obscenities," says Ault. "The veins were sticking out of his neck. I thought he was going to have a coronary." Katz backed off, allowing the CEO to cool down. Katz later returned with a counterproposal. Instead of subjecting himself to a possible infringement action, the bank CEO decided it was better to pay for a license.

Ault was amazed at Katz's negotiation skills. "He's the best negotiator I've ever seen, and I've been told by lawyers that he has the best mind for patent law that they've ever seen. He can read a patent and decipher it and know it backwards and forwards. He knows the field in the way that a Wayne Gretzky or a Larry Bird knows which way all the other players are going at any given moment." When people would ask Ault whether Ron Katz was at all like his Oscar-winning brother, Ault would say, "The difference between Ron and Joel is that when Ron is on his stage, he doesn't need a script."

In one negotiation after another, Katz not only prevailed and reached settlements with leading financial and technology companies but also usually did it in a way that preserved a cooperative relationship going forward. "He would always end up with them in his back pocket," says Ault. Telecredit got virtually every maker of ATMs—including Diebold, Docutel, and IBM—to license its patents. The few legal actions Telecredit initiated were settled under favorable terms.

Katz's patent-licensing program brought in $10 million from more than twenty companies over two years in the early 1970s, revenue that put the company on track for steady profitability. "This was a good thing," Katz says. "Payment was recognition of the inventions. We were able to capitalize on our innovative status for the first time."[8] Only when he started to license the patents did Ronald Katz begin to consider himself first and foremost an inventor.

EXTRACTING VALUE FROM INSIGHTS

Now Katz accelerated the pace of his inventions. He stepped back from day-to-day involvement in Telecredit, leaving the company in the hands of Lee Ault, and focused on building upon his ideas. "Ron always had a great fascination with online systems," says Ault.[9] (Ault eventually sold the company to Equifax, which spun it off as Certegy Inc., which remains a profitable, billion-dollar company that trades on the New York Stock Exchange.) "Ron learned a lot in building Telecredit, and what he did after naturally evolved from it," adds Ault. "It was a cumulative thing."

It was also a legal thing. Inventors need an incentive to keep following up on their ideas. Patents are their legal tool for protecting their ideas and extracting value from those insights. In the preceding decades, patents had become notoriously difficult to enforce. Judges in certain parts of the country were considered pro-patent, and judges in other parts of the country were considered anti-patent. Corporations in danger of being sued by outside inventors tended to locate themselves in anti-patent jurisdictions or, better yet, to influence the process so that politicians appointed anti-patent judges. This uneven and capricious system of patent enforcement had endured for the previous half century, to the point that it became exceedingly rare for an independent inventor to win a case against a corporation. That's one reason Katz had always aimed to negotiate and avoid going to court.

But in 1982, everything turned around. That's when the U.S. Court of Appeals for the Federal Circuit was established to hear all appeals of federal patent cases. With far more knowledgeable judges and uniform guidelines for patent enforcement, for the first time inventors now had something akin to a level playing field. This new central authority sent a clear message to the corporate world. This was the court that ended up ruling, in 1991, that Kodak had infringed on Polaroid's instant photography patents. The judge ordered Kodak to exit that business immediately and pay Polaroid nearly $1 billion in damages, a record. "This was a clarion call to the marketplace," says Katz. "Patents would be enforced uniformly.

You now got a fair shot to make your case, and if you won you got money, and the other guy had to stop what he was doing."[10]

Katz familiarized himself not only with patent law but also with the new field of alternative dispute resolution. Based on some of the negotiation principles he put in practice at Telecredit in the late 1970s, Katz codeveloped the nation's first minitrial, *Telecredit v. TRW.* Following that, he led a project called the UCLA Minitrial Experimental Program, a joint undertaking of the schools of law and business at UCLA. The two-day program involved twenty CEOs and their general counsels, half of them representing the plaintiff in a mock trademark dispute, and the other half representing the defendant. After completion of both sides' presentations and comments from the adviser, one CEO for the plaintiff was paired with one CEO for the defendant, and the pairs were asked to try to resolve the matter. Nine of the ten teams ended up resolving the dispute in the same way. "It showed that these senior business guys are problem solvers," Katz says. The minitrial concept caught on and saved companies millions of dollars. It also gave Katz unique insight into what motivates corporations to resolve disputes quickly.

Armed with this insight, emboldened by the favorable changes in the patent laws, and again looking for something new to invent, Katz set up shop in his home office in Holmby Hills, California. Sketching ideas on yellow legal pads, he began to think more broadly about the ideas he had pioneered with Telecredit, especially the ramifications of marrying computers with telephones. He homed in on the computerized call center. The advent of the touchtone phone, caller identification, advanced database software, and other technologies, he thought, would lead to new applications at such call centers. Customers contacting companies to buy products, receive service, request information, or obtain check balances and transfer money could be presented with a whole new set of services. According to Katz, these are the thoughts that he had in the mid-1980s, ideas that formed the basis of the most creative time in his career.

"Inventions often germinate from an initial idea, but they encompass many ideas," Katz says. "It's like a cluster bomb. After jotting down the initial idea, almost overnight you'll have more and more ways to make it more exciting and more interesting. With me, it was a sine wave—the number of ideas going up, then settling down, then going up. You may think you've got it, and you give it to the patent lawyer, but that's only the start. Then the explosions begin again."

Among the first patents in this new group was a "Statistical Analysis System for Use With Public Communication Facility." This was a system "to provide digital data that is identified for positive association with a caller and is stored for processing," according to one of Katz's patent disclosures. The facility, or call center, would contain a database that served individual callers. The callers would use their touchtone keypads to input choices over the telephone. The database would process those responses, providing callers with a wide range of interactive services. Accessing the caller's file, the system would transfer the caller to a live operator, who would view the data on file and provide additional services. This was not only an extremely broad concept but also a potential platform for thousands of interactive call-center features and applications.

In the mid-1980s, when Katz was working on these patent applications, such features and applications were not yet in use. If they had been proven to have been in commercial use for more than a year, the patents would have been rendered invalid. There's no question that Katz exploited an open window for a set of technologies that his critics would later say were inevitable, no matter who was filing patents to disclose these ideas first. Among the many other methods that Katz disclosed was a process that relates to what happens after customers receive a new credit card. Customers call the credit card company from their home phones to activate their cards. That triggers a remote computer to match the cardholder's phone number on file with the incoming caller-ID number. The system then requests that callers enter the last four digits of their social security number. With that, the card is activated once and only once for use. "That was my idea, the underlying technology to make it happen," Katz says. But it was only one of hundreds of interrelated ideas that Katz kept having, one after another.

DERIVING IDEAS FROM THE MARKETPLACE

After the first three patents that covered this broad system of ideas were issued, Katz decided that it was time to put these ideas into action. Paper patents are one thing, but patents that are actually being exploited by a major corporation have far more economic value. The corporation using such patents would have a financial incentive to protect its edge in the marketplace. Katz needed a big corporation not only to recognize the value of his ideas but also to work with him to commercialize and enforce his patents. He went searching for a corporation that fit the bill, and he found a willing partner in American Express.

In 1988, Katz met with Henry "Ric" Duques, the chief of an information services unit at American Express that soon was spun off as First Data Corporation. Duques already knew about Katz because he had been approached about acquiring Telecredit a year earlier. At the time, Duques was on the verge of becoming one of the most powerful figures in the multitrillion-dollar credit card industry. After First Data was spun off from American Express, Duques had built it into a giant with a $30 billion market capitalization and twenty-eight thousand employees. First Data provides the behind-the-scenes technology for banks and retailers to verify and process the transactions of two-thirds of all U.S. credit card holders. "Some speculate that First Data now has enough scale that it could bypass the Visa and MasterCard networks if it wanted to," said *Credit Card Management* in 2002, the year Duques retired from First Data.[11]

In 1988, though, Duques was only a rising executive looking for new ideas. "I loved his energy," recalls Duques. "When Katz got on a project, he would call you every day to follow up."[12] Duques also appreciated Katz's sense of humor. "When I found out his brother is Joel Grey and I asked him about it, Katz said, 'Yes, I was the one who changed my name.'"

The two formed a joint venture, FDR Interactive Technologies (later named Call Interactive), half of it owned by the First Data unit of American Express and half of it owned by Ronald Katz. The new company set up an interactive call-processing center in

Omaha, Nebraska. In 1989, it signed up clients ranging from the New York Times Company to Philip Morris to CBS News. ABC's *Monday Night Football* used the technology to conduct live polls, asking millions of viewers their opinions on various gridiron matters. After a phone number was flashed on screen, the Call Interactive systems processed the calls automatically and then tabulated and flashed the results back to the viewer. Candymaker Mars Incorporated used the service to stage a nationwide vote on the next new M&M color. "We are the reason that there are blue M&Ms today," says Duques. "This was cutting-edge stuff at the time."

The joint venture brought in millions of dollars of revenue, but again it wasn't profitable because the costs of starting the business and deploying the new technology were high. The technology itself, though, was a big hit, and it attracted rivals. After a small competitor brought out similar interactive call-center technology, FDR filed an infringement suit; the case was settled with a modest cash payment plus a permanent injunction enjoining the competitor from further use of the patented technology. Then a much larger rival, West Interactive, got into the market, undercut Call Interactive on price, and began attracting a lot of business. "The market got commoditized," says Duques. "The technology was easily duplicated."

When Katz and Duques approached West Interactive about taking out a license for the technology, threatening a lawsuit if it refused, the West executives were furious. They drew a line in the sand, according to Duques. "You think you can patent air!" Duques recalls the executive saying. "We will never pay you for this!" But after the litigation and negotiations were over, it was a different story. "They paid," says Duques. West Interactive eventually paid $4.4 million as an initial payment plus ongoing royalties for the patent license. "Katz had an intellectually sound argument," says Duques. "The law says that you can indeed patent a process." Ironically, as is Katz's bent, he developed an excellent relationship with the West executives after the suit, and he and West recently jointly developed and patented a new technology "Methods and Apparatus for Intelligent Selection of Goods and Services in Telephonic and Electronic Commerce."

The West episode served as a source of additional insights. Practicing your ideas and enforcing your ideas in the marketplace naturally lead to follow-on ideas. Craving to devote himself again to full-time invention, in 1990 Katz sold his interest in the joint venture, which included his existing call-center patent portfolio, to First Data, netting more than $4 million. Meanwhile, he was again furiously working for FDR as a consultant, prosecuting patent claims for customizing automated call services and enhancing the FDR-owned patent portfolio. "If you call a company . . . and they ask you if you want chicken powder and you say no, the next time they shouldn't have to ask you if you want chicken powder," Katz says. "This shortens the call. It's intelligent and efficient."[13] Katz patented a method of performing these kinds of customized call-processing services. He stayed on as a consultant for a couple of years, continuing to enlarge First Data's portfolio of his patents. By the time he left in 1992, Call Interactive was bringing in about $80 million in annual revenue.

What Katz did next was probably the riskiest and most unusual move in his career. He saw far more value in the patents than did anyone else. He saw that many of the ideas had been commercially demonstrated and enforced in the marketplace. The settlement with West Interactive had set a legal precedent. Katz saw years of value, and he knew that only he could provide the critical testimony that could confirm those new concepts in courtrooms and boardrooms.

At the end of 1993 he bought back the patents. He paid First Data several million dollars under his agreement to buy the rights, and the deal provided a limited license to American Express and First Data for their own continued use. Moving his office into two small rooms in Beverly Hills, with a secretary and a colleague, he set up Ronald A. Katz Technology Licensing, L.P. "At that time, I wanted to retire, but it was an opportunity to really have something," Katz says.

His actions didn't receive much notice in the business world except for the patent column in the *New York Times* on October 31, 1994, which referred to the man who was "stockpiling the technologies that allow telephones and computers to talk to one another."[14]

The article continued, "By pressing buttons on their touch-tone phones, customers can ask a computer on the other end of the line what their bank balance is, when the next flight from Chicago is expected or whether that burgundy handbag currently being peddled on the television screen is also available in chartreuse." The article noted the recent West Interactive settlement and quoted Katz as saying that he expected royalties to be "in the tens of millions, if not hundreds of millions of dollars." So far, Katz hadn't personally collected a dime from patent litigation. But his insights had multiplied to such an extent that the accumulated value was becoming unmistakably large.

TURNING INSIGHTS INTO MONEY

For Ronald Katz, the time to vigorously enforce his patents had come. At first, he sought small licensees. He personally wrote letters informing companies of his claims, stating that "we would like to offer you a license" to use a group of forty-nine issued and pending patents covering the key operations of automated call centers. He would request a meeting and "an open discussion." After successfully landing a couple of small licensees in this way, he went after some big fish, most notably the Home Shopping Network (HSN), one of the largest and most high-profile users of interactive phone services.

Needless to say, no corporation is thrilled to receive such a letter. "We were already investing heavily in the technology," recalls Barry Augenbraun, who was the general counsel for HSN at the time. "The need to fill orders kept exceeding the limits of our capacity."[15] HSN was using this call-center technology "before we had heard of Ron Katz," he says. "There were plenty of inventors who would come along and said we owe them money, and we would say, 'This is bullshit and we're not going to pay.'"

But Ron Katz, Augenbraun says, was different in two respects. He was "nonconfrontational," and "he said that he wanted to 'educate us' about his patents, and he would come to town at his own expense." Augenbraun adds, "He said that he was going to keep educating us. It became clear he wasn't going away." The other thing that distinguished Katz was his enclosure of a letter from a large and reputable law firm that was willing to take on any of his litigation on a contingency basis. "That was unusual," Augenbraun adds, "because these kind of cases can cost millions." It was a classic liver and stick approach.

As discussions began, Augenbraun found out that Katz's brother was Joel Grey. "I said, 'Are you Mickey Katz's son?'" Augenbraun recalls. "I was a Mickey Katz fan from the time I was a kid. I went home to my wife, and I said, 'I got a call from Mickey Katz's son!' This gave us something to talk about outside our normal relationship of claimant and claimee." After studying the issues, HSN agreed to pay for a multimillion-dollar license, mainly because it would be better than fighting Katz in court but also because of a touch of idealism. "Our Constitution is such a work of genius," Augenbraun notes, "and it says that the best way to promote useful industry is to give inventors an incentive to develop new ideas, and if you don't, it will frustrate progress." Paying someone a "tariff" for a technology you're already using is "counterintuitive," he says, but it's "an anomaly inherent in our system."

Using the same approach, Katz landed other big corporations as licensees, among them MCI, Sprint, Charles Schwab, and the Gallup Organization, which used the technology for automated poll-taking. But there was one corporation that wouldn't be swayed by Katz's arguments, and it was the single biggest fish in this entire sea: AT&T.

The telecom giant simply wouldn't budge. Ironically, AT&T had been a minority owner in the Call Interactive joint venture with American Express, so it had already recognized the value of some of these very same patents. But apparently there was too much at stake, given that AT&T not only used this technology to serve millions of customers but also that it sold call-center technology. This is common in the world of patents, where the motto is "where you stand depends on where you sit."

After months of hitting up against a stone wall from AT&T, Katz saw that this would be his career-defining showdown. If he lost, his patents were at great risk of being weakened and perhaps even overturned. If he won, everything would break loose for him. This was clearly going to take an enormous amount of money. Even Katz, who was already worth tens of millions of dollars, couldn't risk the $25 million or more it would likely cost to complete a lawsuit against AT&T, a civil action that would likely drag on for years. This is the reason big companies are very rarely sued successfully by individuals for patent infringement. "Enforcement is kinder to larger companies," Katz says. "Big companies can outlast and outspend the individual. In very few cases can an individual collect the full value of his innovation."[16]

In 1997, Katz filed his patent infringement lawsuit against AT&T in federal court in Philadelphia. But the trial opened after an interesting twist took place. To help cover the costs and to bring in more potent legal firepower, Katz struck a deal with MCI to join his side as a full party to the litigation against their common foe. "It's always nice to have a big company—one that was wealthy at the time—on your side," Katz says. Why did MCI join the lawsuit? It was already being sued by AT&T for infringement of patents on toll-free calling services. This case presented a way of striking back, says Tim Casey, the former chief technology officer with MCI. "We had no counter-tool," says Casey, now a partner in a Washington, D.C., law firm. "I couldn't sue AT&T because I didn't have anything to sue them on. It occurred to me that if we needed a license [from Katz], why wouldn't AT&T?"[17]

The issues were so contentious and complex that the judge appointed a special master to manage the process of discovery—collecting and organizing the evidence—a task that took a full year. During the trial, Katz's case seemed to get stronger as he continued to rack up new licensees. Among them were IBM and Microsoft, which licensed his patents for use at their own customer-service call centers. "In the technology world," Katz says, "these guys are the Holy Grail."[18] Did Katz give those two companies a deeply discounted rate to fortify his roster? Katz says he did not. "Our patent licensing is consistent," he says. "We don't cut breaks for people just to get their names."

The presence of MCI in the lawsuit set off a remarkable clash. "Everyone knew that AT&T was the nine-hundred-pound gorilla," says Casey. "AT&T could afford to fight it to the death, and it had a reputation for doing so. But we weren't afraid to get into it. They were our archenemy." [19] As it turned out, the Katz patents were stronger than anyone might have expected. "Back in 1984, no one was doing this," Casey says. "It's easy now to say, 'Of course!' But Katz didn't try claiming rights to basic technologies like the audio response unit or to cover computer-based telephony in general. His patents were directed to the nuances that made the technology valuable—the applications—just like computers weren't valuable until there was good software. Ron had the good software, and he had the presence of mind to file patent applications early on, to keep the applications alive, and to keep adding new ideas" to the portfolio.

In the end, AT&T buckled. After almost three years of litigation, a preliminary finding by the court was issued in favor of Katz. AT&T didn't appeal the finding. The settlement happened on December 20, 1999, only a few months after MCI merged with WorldCom. "The resolution was a major event," Katz says. [20] Other than that, Katz won't comment on the litigation or the reports that the payments from AT&T will total $100 million over several years. "I'm precluded from saying anything about the AT&T settlement," he says. But it was clear that Katz had slain a giant. After the deal was finalized, AT&T's chief intellectual property counsel, Francine Berry, jumped ship and accepted a top position with Ronald A. Katz Technology Licensing, L.P.

Such are the potential rewards for having the foresight to multiply insights in a key area of technology. In Katz's case, he was rewarded with a constant stream of licensing checks. Katz used some of his windfall to develop new inventions for interactive customer services over the Internet, a new area of his patent activity. He also expanded the scope his licensing efforts. "We're continuing to knock on doors and visit people," he says. He's going after the top two thousand companies in the United States, and he has already landed financial giants such as Bank of America, First Union, T. Rowe Price, and Vanguard as licensees. By 2002, he had surpassed $750 million in license fees collected, and he expects to reach $2 billion by the time his call-center patents expire in 2009—an all-time record for an independent inventor.

Has Katz received more money than he deserves? Perhaps. But we may be able to say the same about just a few others in our economy. Would this set of technologies have come into existence anyway, even if Ron Katz hadn't come along? Probably. But that is true of almost any technology. Patents are a bargain between inventors and society. They serve as an incentive to innovate as quickly as possible and to disclose all the details of the invention so that others can build on the ideas. Why didn't AT&T's Bell Laboratories itself—with its thousands of researchers, its thousands of patent filings, its proclaimed synergies between phones and computing—come up with these inventions in its core business? For whatever reason, it failed to do so, and the company paid a hefty price for this failure.

Nowadays, everyone seems to take this set of applications for granted, but at one point none of this stuff existed. "Press 1 for this, 2 for that, and 3 for the other thing. Like it or not, that's Ron Katz," concludes Ric Duques, now retired from First Data. "He's everywhere."[21]

CHAPTER 11

Thinking Systematically

*All parts of the system must be constructed with reference to all
other parts, since, in one sense, all the parts form one machine.*

—THOMAS EDISON

INVENTIONS RARELY EXIST IN ISOLATION. No matter how
clever the idea or great the implementation, an invention typically
lives or dies depending on how well it can be integrated into a larger
social and technological context. That context is made up of systems. Systems have many parts and join together many related inventions. We have multiple systems for transportation, systems for
computing and telecommunications, systems for healthcare. We have
systems for developing, processing, and delivering everything from
food to pharmaceuticals to music. That's why the greatest inventions
of all are systems inventions and why every new system needs to
work with or replace existing systems.

Thomas Edison thought in terms of systems. That's why he's remembered more readily than Joseph Swan, who demonstrated his
incandescent lamp in Newcastle, England, many months *before* Edison did. Of the two, why did Edison achieve far more wealth and
fame? Was it because Edison was a better promoter or fund-raiser, or

hired better patent attorneys? Perhaps. But there's no question that Edison's greatest achievement was in seeing that the lightbulb was not an end result but the beginning, and that it would require the creation of a vast power generation and delivery system that would span entire cities. The lightbulb was a vast improvement over gas lamps. But by itself it couldn't have won out. The gas lighting industry fought Edison in court and on every other front. It wasn't an easy battle. A lightbulb alone doesn't convince a city to rip up its entire network of street lamps and replace it with something else. In fact, Swan lost that battle in his country, and England stuck with gas lighting for nearly three decades afterward.

Edison knew he had to develop a complete system. He needed a way to get the light to the people. He needed to integrate electric turbines, power relays, endless miles of wiring, and an entire logistical infrastructure. He knew that if he could link an electric power plant to the home of J. P. Morgan and give the banker illumination on demand, he'd have a much better chance of raising money than if he just went around with a neat lightbulb demo. Swan, meanwhile, tried to retrofit his lightbulb into existing systems. It didn't quite work, investors turned away, and the politicians aimed to protect the status quo. Asked late in life what his greatest invention was, Edison didn't name the electric light alone but "the incandescent electric lighting and power system." That's why those who wish to replace Edison's system with an LED lighting and power system must draw upon this same sort of thinking.

The same principle applied to the automobile. Many inventors created cars before Henry Ford came along. In 1885 Karl Benz invented the first motorcar, and his future business partner, Gottfried Daimler, built the first motorcycle the same year. French inventors took the lead shortly thereafter. In 1893, the Duryea brothers held the first U.S. demonstration of a gasoline-powered car. Two years later, a Duryea car won the famous Chicago motor race, with an average speed of 6.66 miles per hour. At the time, Ford was working as a power station supervisor at the Edison Illuminating Company in Detroit. Ford idolized Edison, and later in life they became close friends.

Inspired by magazine articles that showed how to build your own gasoline engine, the twenty-three-year-old Ford set aside an area of the plant as his workshop. In 1896, he transferred his tinkering to a shed behind his house, where he created a five-hundred-pound contraption he called the quadricycle. But Ford wasn't yet thinking like a systems inventor. The car was bigger than the shed's door frame, and he had to hack down the frame with an axe to get the vehicle outside. Once he did, though, the machine clocked in at twenty miles per hour.

What happened next distinguished Ford from the pack. He became the first successful carmaker not because he built the fastest car but because he invented a system that embraced all the complexity of making cars. Between 1900 and 1906, more than five hundred car companies cropped up in the United States alone. Ford's cars were only one of many makes. But as he began designing the first Model T, Ford started focusing on a way to produce more cars more quickly and at a lower price than anyone else. "The proper system, as I have it in mind, is to get the car to the multitude," he declared.[1]

He came up with four principles: division of labor, interchangeable parts, continuous flow, and reduction of wasted effort. These principles pointed Ford to his greatest invention: the moving assembly line. First installed at his Highland Park plant in 1913, Ford's assembly line grew into the defining business system of the century. Ford was able to produce more cars in a day than other companies could make in a month. By 1927, the Ford Motor Company had mass-produced fifteen million Model Ts. The rest of the industry adopted his system and consolidated into a handful of companies.

EMBEDDING SYSTEMS WITHIN SYSTEMS

Large-scale systems such as these transformed invention itself. The most powerful systems naturally led to monopolies or oligopolies, and other systems sprang up to support these concentrated power structures. Independent inventors trying to apply new products to alter these systems found it increasingly difficult to break in. They soon learned that they had a better chance if they invented a completely new system and formed a new industry. With the introduction of large-scale systems, the companies that originally created them tended to grow conservative, seeking only those improvements that supported their systems. Radical ideas tended to be suppressed.

Suppression is still common, but recently big corporations have become more willing to look outside their own R&D labs for inventions to improve or extend their systems. Whereas the corporation of yesteryear typically trampled independent inventors or tied them up in patent court, corporations today are much more inclined to view crops of smaller companies as their own R&D labs.

That's why it is key for inventors to think systematically. Whether your idea is radical or conservative, big or small, if you fail to think systematically you won't get very far in a world of interdependencies. "Our world is systems within systems," says business systems inventor Jay Walker. "When people ask me what I do for a living, I tell them that I invent commercial systems. That loses people right there, because most people don't know what 'commercial' means or what 'systems' means."[2] So Walker gives examples: A car is a system. A computer is a system. A sewing machine is a system. A casino is a system. A lever is not a system. A hammer is not a system. Anything new, he says, must be compatible with existing systems in order to be viable in the marketplace. That's why it's the inventor's job to consider all the interface points in which a new system interlaces with existing ones. "The reason we use systems," adds Walker, "is because systems are the most powerful ways in the universe to address problems."

Two of the most recent systems inventions in the universe of entertainment serve as prime examples of this integration challenge. The digital video recorder (DVR) addresses problems common to millions of television viewers: They often miss their favorite shows, they can't keep up with hundreds of channels, and they don't like to waste time watching commercials. Systems such as TiVo and ReplayTV are sophisticated set-top computers that store gigabytes of programs preselected by the viewer. These machines enable the time-shifting and the avoidance of ads that viewers crave. But because television habits are governed by inertia, fewer than 2 percent of viewing households purchased these new systems in their first five years on the market.

The stumbling block is that these machines haven't been integrated into the existing systems governing television viewership. To boost their customer base, the companies that make TiVo and ReplayTV have sought to build their technology into the set-top boxes distributed by the major cable companies. The idea is to embed the *new* system into the *predominant* system.

But as DVRs get integrated into the existing cable television system, there will be ramifications for even larger systems. What happens when forty or sixty or eighty million people start time-shifting and ad-skipping? To survive, the major broadcast networks would be forced to change their business model, perhaps turning to subscription models similar to those of the cable networks. Moreover, if advertisers of a thousand types of products have trouble reaching a mass audience in the way they've grown accustomed to, they might have to change the way they make and market their products. The ripple effect of a simple integration of a new system into a dominant system could be tremendous.

Another example of this kind of ripple effect is Apple Computer's iMusic system. The problems stemming from the free downloading of copyright-protected music have been in the headlines for more than five years. Record industry officials have become, by turns, fatalistic, exasperated, and defensive, lashing out by filing lawsuits against young and old alike. "How do you compete with free?" say executives at the major music distributors.

The answer, of course, is with invention, a concept that is remarkably foreign to the recording industry, which seems to have forgotten that it was founded by Thomas Edison. As the record companies litigated and merged with one another out of fear of disappearing, Apple Computer designed an ingenious system that interlaces well with the way people actually listen to music in the Internet age. Apple struck experimental deals with all the major record companies to sell individual songs online, initially for ninety-nine cents each, and ended up selling seventy million such songs in its first year. The company not only developed the online iMusic store, but it also has distributed tens of millions of free iTunes play-back programs for desktop computers, and it has sold tens of millions of its portable iPod digital music players, which hold ten thousand songs or more. While the record companies were still lamenting the end of their world, Apple was building a multibillion-dollar franchise. This systems invention adapted so well to the changing behavior patterns of consumers that the invention caught on with remarkably little friction.

Similarly, PayPal very quickly found a way to interlace its online, person-to-person payment system into eBay, the predominant system for person-to-person online auctions of collectibles and consumer goods. When they were founding PayPal, chief technology officer Max Levchin and CEO Peter Theil identified eBay as the most logical buyer of the company. Only three years after introducing their system to customers, Levchin and Theil indeed struck a deal with eBay, selling their start-up for $1.5 billion. At age twenty-seven, Levchin and the other founders were rewarded for their systems invention efforts to the tune of nine figures' worth of eBay stock.

As all these cases show, the creation of modern systems requires that the inventors consider the most logical way the market will attempt to acquire, reject, or integrate their ideas. Dean Kamen's Segway, for example, is a complex and radical system unto itself. Every part has a purpose, and if you remove one part, the system no longer functions as designed. But it doesn't stand alone. And that fact may help explain why early sales have been disappointing. To make his system successful, Kamen must invent new ways of integrating it within the larger systems of society. For example, a new system needs to be developed for customers to purchase and finance the product. Very rarely will consumers pay cash for something that costs $3,000 to $5,000, but they do buy things that cost, say, $87 per month. The consumer credit system is only one system that virtually all sellers of new products must embrace in creative ways.

An unknown amount of clever system-level invention needs to happen before multitudes of Segways or its successors can coexist with, or displace, existing systems. Industrial clients, for example, can jump-start the early acceptance of a new system. In the case of electric lighting, Edison's General Electric company got entire factories to convert from steam to electric turbines on the basis of cost, safety, and flexibility. Industrial acceptance, in turn, can drive consumer acceptance. That's why Kamen has spent a lot of time with letter carriers, police officers, amusement park operators, and other potential large clients to find ways of matching his system to their needs, desires, mobility patterns, and existing business systems.

To popularize the automobile, Ford and other early pioneers needed to integrate their inventions into the political system, convincing government not only to pave dirt roads but also to construct a new network of interstate highways. Similarly, Kamen launched an intensive state-by-state lobbying effort to pass legislation explicitly permitting motorized vehicles such as his on sidewalks. By the time he introduced the Segway, he had been successful in twenty-six states, with others falling into line shortly thereafter.

Sales and service constitute another system. To popularize television, early makers of TV sets layered a vast network of independent dealers and repair shops on top of the existing radio dealership network. Tens of thousands of people were retrained to demonstrate the new technology for consumers and take care of the new television infrastructure. People need to test drive a product before they want it. Kamen says that's a good analogy for what might have to happen for the Segway.

Turning to his next invention, Kamen is now marketing new systems that solve localized problems in developing nations, such as the problem of contaminated water, which kills millions of people every year. Billions of people lack electric power and clean water, and many inventors are working on this mammoth problem. Kamen's Project Slingshot water purification and power generation system is roughly the size of a small washer and dryer. To sell or even donate these machines to families and villages in the developing world, he must interlace these systems into existing systems throughout Africa, Asia, Latin America, and the Middle East. It's a daunting challenge, and it is going to require thinking systematically.

INTEGRATING RADICAL SYSTEMS

Geoffrey Ballard has learned about the challenges of this kind of systems integration the hard way, over the course of a decades-long struggle to transform the world's most stubborn transportation and energy systems. Born near Niagara Falls, Ballard is a dual citizen of the United States and Canada. After earning a degree in geological engineering in 1956, Ballard embarked on a career in oil exploration, working first for Shell and then for Mobil. The jobs took him to drill sites around the world, including the Mediterranean and the Persian Gulf. After going back to school for his Ph.D., Ballard became a civilian scientist with the U.S. Army. He worked on a wide range of research projects. He received such a high security clearance that the Pentagon would not permit him to fly on commercial airlines out of concern he would be held hostage in a terrorist hijacking.

In 1973, with Ballard working at an Army base in Arizona, the OPEC crisis hit the energy markets. Oil prices skyrocketed, and motorists nationwide lined up at service stations to buy rationed gasoline. The U.S. government created a new office of energy conservation, and Ballard was tapped as its director of research. He rented an apartment in Washington, D.C., while his wife and three sons stayed in Arizona.

Ballard was asked to create a long-term plan under which the United States would achieve energy self-sufficiency, an ambitious task of systems design. His staff studied solar panels, wind turbines, geothermal energy, hydroelectric power, and new battery technologies. He developed a range of proposals and began pitching them to politicians, but his ideas got lost in the congressional bureaucracy and went nowhere. He grew disillusioned and then disgusted. He wanted to prove that new technology could solve the problem. But the energy independence effort, he concluded, wasn't being taken seriously. During the Watergate scandal, everyone around him seemed to lose interest.

Ballard only grew more determined. The entire system needed to change and perhaps even be replaced, he thought. To him, the main obstacle was obvious: the internal combustion engine. The transportation sector was responsible for consuming more than half the world's crude oil and for generating about half the urban smog in U.S. cities. It was becoming clear to him that no politician had the will to fight the might of the car companies. "I didn't think the government was going to make a concerted effort to change the internal combustion engine," Ballard recalls. "The gestation period for developing a new energy system is twenty-five years. And there were no politicians interested in that sort of time frame."[3]

Not only were his ideas for alternative energy rejected, but also he became less and less convinced that conservation was a practical answer. "Social progress is dependent on the consumption of energy," he says. "That is a correlation that has been established since the amoeba began to emerge." What is going to happen as the population keeps increasing and developing countries such as India and China start to generate immense numbers of people who want many of the middle-class trappings that Americans have, especially cars? Ballard became convinced that the seeds of a long-term, multidimensional, global catastrophe were being planted. "The lesson we should have learned [from the OPEC crisis] was that we were going to increase our dependence on foreign oil, and that [oil interests] were going to control our economy, and this would lead to de facto control of our foreign policy," he says.

Ballard decided to take on the task of searching for alternative energy and transportation systems himself. In 1974, he told his wife he wanted to resign his position and his Army research post to become an inventor and entrepreneur. He was looking for a technological silver bullet, and a vision was already forming in his mind. "I thought that a fast-recharging, high-energy-density battery would be the answer," Ballard recalls. As he points out, battery-powered cars were common before Henry Ford's mass-produced Model T. Sporting a new gasoline-fueled internal combustion engine, the Model T began proliferating rapidly beginning in 1908, and within ten years the game was over. Or was it? "I wanted to look at battery systems that might have emerged had oil not taken over," he says. Ballard already knew the limitations—that batteries had sharply limited range and had to be recharged regularly—but he was convinced that there had to be some sort of chemical combination for creating a revolutionary new battery, one with a much higher power-to-weight ratio.

Ballard began casting about for ideas. With two colleagues, he formed Bluestar Battery Systems. The headquarters for the venture was an abandoned, dilapidated, filthy motel they purchased for $2,000. It was located south of Tucson, Arizona, near the Mexico border, in an area known as Miracle Valley, so named because a religious cult was based there. The name may have been a coincidence, but it perfectly fit the mission of the new company.[4]

The founders fumigated the motel and converted it into a battery invention laboratory. Their experiments centered on a cutting-edge composite based on the lightest metal, lithium. After three years of intense work, however, Ballard and his team weren't getting anywhere. They seemed to have come up against a barrier, and they didn't know how to get past it.

Ballard began looking for other systems to explore. He relocated the company to his native Canada and regrouped. Along with one of his partners, Keith Prater, and a new associate named Paul Howard, in 1976 Ballard formed Vancouver-based Ballard Power Systems. They put the Bluestar battery project on the back burner. Responding to a request for proposals from the Canadian National Research Council, the new company embarked on a project to research the viability of the hydrogen fuel cell, another technology that had been around for a long time but was thought to have serious limitations. Like the Stirling engine, the fuel cell was a nineteenth-century conception, and there were few viable applications. In the 1960s, for example, GE had built some for NASA's Gemini space program. In the course of their research, Ballard and his partners became convinced that hydrogen fuel cells held even more promise than the rechargeable lightweight battery, if only they could detect the right barriers and work through them systematically.

And so this is what Ballard did—for the next quarter century and beyond. "I decided to put the company behind fuel cells and make that our major objective," he recalls. But Ballard soon realized that the barriers were not only technological. There were business barriers, economic barriers, political barriers, and social, behavioral, logistical, and financial barriers. He was determined to do whatever it took to think systematically about replacing the internal combustion engine with the fuel cell, to get an entire society to give up crude oil and embrace hydrogen.

CHALLENGING THE SYSTEM

First, Ballard needed proof of the concept. He put an initial team of four engineers on the fuel cell. Quite simply, fuel cells work through electrochemistry rather than combustion. There's no piston or any other moving parts, and there are no exhaust fumes containing pollutants. The only inputs are hydrogen fuel and oxygen from the air, and the only outputs are electricity and water. Ballard's proton-exchange membrane (PEM) fuel cell uses thin electrodes to split the hydrogen into electrons and protons. The electrodes sit on either side of the membrane, essentially a plastic-like film. Only the protons can travel through the membrane on their way to combining with the oxygen to form water. The blocked electrons, meanwhile, are released. These moving electrons are the electricity that powers a motor.

The technology worked in the laboratory. But like any source of power, fuel cells needed to be made efficient and economical. It was all about power density, boosting the power-to-weight ratio, decreasing the size so that dozens of units could be easily stacked together, and finding ways to make engines as cheaply as possible. The Ballard team made an astounding amount of headway in these areas in its first few years, leading Geoffrey Ballard to believe they could build a fuel-cell-powered bus. "Nobody really wanted to do the bus except me," he recalls. "I didn't see any other way of demonstrating to the public what we could do with a fuel cell vehicle. We needed money. And it would be a long time before we'd ever make a profit. I persuaded everyone that this is something we could do."

The day in 1983 that Geoffrey Ballard drove the fuel cell bus through the streets of Vancouver was one of the proudest days of his life. A framed photo of the original Ballard bus taken on that day still hangs in his house. The photo shows the hydrogen fuel tanks sitting on a roof compartment, with the stacks of fuel cells fitted into the back of the vehicle. Politicians, businesspeople, and ordinary citizens came to see it in action. Ballard presided over a ceremony in which champagne glasses were filled with the exhaust water from the bus. The politicians and the engineers toasted as they drank the exhaust. On that day, Ballard declared, "We've seen the beginning of the end of the internal combustion engine."

Ballard became the leading voice for the fuel cell, and his approach was to cajole Detroit and Japan into seeing things his way. "You'll run into a point here when you'll find I'm at odds with the car industry," he says. He began calling those who disagreed with him "pistonheads." But his invention teams continued to make steady progress, to the point that the auto companies started coming around to the concept. "By the time we put out the bus, we were getting three to five kilowatts per cubic foot [of engine volume]," he says. "We do ten times that now."

Daimler Benz was the first to license the technology and build a prototype fuel cell car. It debuted in 1995. Toyota and Honda also became customers and built their own models. So did Ford. There was a crush of posturing and prototyping and a struggle for power over the new technology. Ballard Power Systems formed joint ventures with both Ford and the newly merged DaimlerChrysler. (Ballard Power would later acquire both ventures outright in exchange for providing the two auto giants with a combined 44 percent ownership stake in the parent company.) All this provided validation. Geoffrey Ballard had challenged a powerful system, and the system had come to him. Vancouver was positioned to become the new Detroit.

That turned out to be a problem. The car companies that came on board wanted to turn Ballard into a manufacturing company. Geoffrey Ballard wanted to keep focusing solely on invention, R&D, and building the patent portfolio, keeping his company relatively small and licensing the technology to the big automakers. He knew that manufacturing would require a huge amount of capital, with little chance of payoff in the short term, and he wanted the auto giants themselves to take on the cost and risk of manufacturing.

Geoffrey Ballard lost this power struggle. When it was over, he resigned from the company that still bears his name. He no longer sits on the board of directors. "I felt the company was making the wrong moves," he says. "I felt that Ballard should be a technological company. Management felt they should become a manufacturing company, going head-to-head with General Motors. That's a completely different approach. That's why I didn't want to stay around."

ENVISIONING THE SYSTEM OF SYSTEMS

A visit to the headquarters of Ballard Power Systems in suburban Burnaby, British Columbia, reveals that the company is struggling to remain a world leader in hydrogen fuel cells. The massive R&D center is overflowing with evidence that the technology is still moving forward, but Geoffrey Ballard disputes whether it's advancing fast enough, and he says that the most cutting-edge innovation is now happening elsewhere. Nevertheless, cool prototype cars sit in the vast lobby. Dozens of researchers are scampering around from project to project. Engineers here can demonstrate a stationary, 29-pound fuel cell unit that can power a home with 1.2 kilowatts of electricity, as well as a 212-pound fuel cell engine that can power a small car with 85 kilowatts of electricity. The company continues to pile up patents. "There's still room for breakthroughs to happen," says David Wilkinson, director of R&D.[5] He sees fuel cells getting smaller, lighter, and more powerful, in a process not unlike the trajectory of personal computers.

Across a giant parking lot filled with internal combustion vehicles, the finishing touches are being put on a massive manufacturing facility. Ballard Power's entry into large-scale manufacturing has indeed required massive investment. Its losses have been escalating, to nearly $200 million in its most recent fiscal year. So much money had to be raised that the company was forced to dilute the value of its stock. Investors haven't been happy. The CEO was ousted and replaced. And the big payoff still seems to be a decade away. It's clear that the company will be at the mercy of its largest investors: Ford and Daimler. The big auto companies are really running the show, learning everything about the technology while keeping the expenses of building it off their own balance sheets.

Geoffrey Ballard credits the company with making him what he is today: bitter and angry about what happened. He wants to see his namesake remain viable, but he has moved on to the bigger issues. Now in his early seventies, the gray-haired Ballard is just as active as ever. He plays tennis to keep in shape, and he's still inventing, but at the system level rather than the engineering level. Along with his old partner, Paul Howard, he runs a start-up company, General Hydrogen, also based near Vancouver. The new company doesn't make or market fuel cells. "I don't work on fuel cells," he says. "If we need fuel cells, we buy them. I don't want any possibility of conflict of interest."[6]

Instead, Ballard researches and designs systems, specifically the overall structures that are required if we are to make the grand switch to the "hydrogen economy" that Ballard envisions more clearly than ever. This more expansive mission energizes him. "We've changed the way people think about power," he says. "We've got the entire automotive industry convinced that there is going to be a new engine, a new fuel. It's an amazing thing to have achieved. We're educating people about the hydrogen economy. We've demonstrated that you don't have to have the internal combustion engine polluting our cities. Nor do we have to have the United States dependent on foreign oil. Since September 11, that also means you don't have to have the same fuel threatening homeland security."

Taking it to the next level requires systematic thinking of the highest order. Now that fuel cell systems work well, there are at least three major systems that need to be designed to make everything come together: hydrogen fuel production, hydrogen fuel delivery, and vehicle management and maintenance. Hydrogen is one of the most plentiful substances on Earth, but it comes bundled as part of other things, such as water. Hydrogen isn't free. Other forms of energy are required in order to separate the hydrogen from the oxygen through, for example, electrolysis. Hydrogen can be refined as a solid, a liquid, or a compressed gas. But what are the best energy sources to produce the fuel in the first place?

Options are plentiful. Obviously, it would be counterproductive to use oil. Coal is also a poor choice, given the pollution factor. Methanol and natural gas can be reformulated into hydrogen, and these are realistic alternatives, given an abundant domestic supply.

But Geoffrey Ballard prefers nuclear power, which now quietly supplies 17 percent of the world's electricity. He knows that the safety issues are still politically sensitive in the United States, but he believes that the fear is irrational and overblown. Hydrogen production plants, he notes, need not be located near population centers. In any case, all the sources we've mentioned can be used, and the various ways of making hydrogen fuel can be ramped up or phased out as desired, with no effect on the vehicles or the home power units themselves. That's not true with oil, which must be made through geothermal pressure over centuries.

Building a system for delivering and dispensing hydrogen is also a huge undertaking. "It's a Catch-22," Ballard says. "You can't sell fuel cell vehicles unless there is an infrastructure for refueling. And you can't persuade the oil industry to put a hydrogen refueling station at every gas station until there are customers to drive in and buy the hydrogen." Once this system is designed, however, hydrogen will likely cost the same as gasoline, he says. But it's better than gas for three reasons: There are no limits on supply, consuming it causes no pollution, and it's twice as efficient as gasoline, so the car can go twice as far on the same tank.

The third big system is a gnarly constellation of safety and liability issues. The driving public will need to be retrained to care for and operate new kinds of vehicles. To work out the kinks, Ballard has always maintained that he wants centrally managed fleets of buses and trucks to be the first to convert to hydrogen. From a pollution perspective, replacing one big rig is equal to replacing one hundred cars. After doing that, we'll know more about handling any safety risks, such as installing proper ventilation in garages and making sure that people don't smoke near hydrogen fuel tanks in enclosed areas.

This systematic thinking about the coming hydrogen economy isn't a theoretical exercise. Ballard has brought in a strategic partner, General Motors, to fund and execute his new systems invention effort. Under a twenty-five-year partnership, the auto giant has made a "strategic investment" in General Hydrogen. Led by R&D vice president Lawrence Burns, GM has created the industry's most radical design of a fuel cell vehicle. Known as the Hy-wire car, it has more in common with a laptop computer than a traditional automobile. Except for wheels and a place for passengers to sit, everything else about this vehicle is new. The entire engine block under the hood has been eliminated, replaced by a safety system. The car doesn't have a drive train; instead, it has a "drive-by-wire" system for steering, braking, and throttling. The entire body can be unhitched from its "skateboard"—which includes the wheels, fuel cells, and fuel tanks—and replaced with another body. GM's Burns considers the fuel cell a disruptive technology, and he is in a position to do something about it before it's too late. "The goal is to reinvent the automobile and reinvent the industry," says the GM executive. In fact, he sees the transportation and power industries merging into one.[7]

The ramifications for other systems are virtually endless. Because a car requires far greater bursts of power than does a home, a fuel cell engine sitting idle in a garage could literally power a house. Indeed, it could probably power the entire block. "If only one in twenty-five cars in California were fuel cell cars," says Ballard, "it would exceed the entire capacity of state's electricity grid."[8] Both Ballard and Burns agree that homes of the future will likely generate their own power, obviating the need for the home to be hooked up to the electrical grid, an especially attractive option for developing countries. Another option is to use electricity from the grid to produce hydrogen fuel in your garage. If any of this happens, other large technological and social systems will have to change dramatically. By thinking systematically, inventors could generate hundreds of inventions and ideas that people will need in such a world.

THINKING BIOLOGICALLY

The ultimate system is the biological system. That the human body is a system of systems has been known for ages. The respiratory system, the circulatory system, the immune system, the cardiovascular system, the neurological system, the metabolic system—all these and more have been identified and studied extensively, but mainly on the level of the cells and molecules that constitute them. "In a general sense, biological systems have been understood for one hundred years," says Leroy Hood.[9]

Three fairly recent developments, however, have given rise to the possibility of thinking systematically—holistically—about the human body in a far more profound way than ever before. First, there's the mapping of the entire human genome, a project that was completed ahead of most predictions, thanks in large part to the inventions of Hood and his colleagues. The massive gene sequencing endeavor has yielded a fine-grained "parts list" of the genetic codes that program the workings of those systems, says Hood.

Second is the Internet, which globalized biological invention to an unprecedented level, enabling far-flung groups of investigators to use and contribute to mind-blowing arrays of biological data. "The Internet gave us the ability to deal with an enormous global set of data," Hood says.

Third, the transdisciplinary approach that Hood helped pioneer is finally catching on. "We need to invent new technology, new math, and we need to integrate everything with biology and medicine," he notes. "We need people who speak this new common language."

This new language is the language of systems. In Hood's view, the new systems approach to biology has such radical implications that to pursue it, entirely new types of organizations are required. Even though he created a cross-disciplinary department at the University of Washington, Hood became convinced that he could no longer work within the confines of a university, with its rigid tenure, employment, and intellectual property policies governing work with other institutions. When he decided to leave, in 1999, the man who had invested the money to establish Hood's department there wasn't happy. "Bill Gates said to me, 'Isn't there any way of working this out?' I said, 'No, systems biology creates a completely different culture. It's different in every dimension.'"

That's why Hood and two other UW researchers—Alan Aderem and Ruedi Aebersold—left to establish the nonprofit Institute for Systems Biology, and it's why Hood now spends much of his time raising tens of millions of dollars in government grants and private donations to keep it going. Housed in a three-story brick building overlooking Seattle's Lake Union, the institute is located near the university campus for a good reason: It employs many of the school's students and graduates. All three floors of the institute are populated by people who are smart, young, and typically sport white lab coats and green gloves. They're laboring away at lab benches, analyzing mysterious-looking liquids using a wide array of sophisticated machinery, especially DNA sequencing and analysis instruments. Presiding over his new place, Lee Hood is finally doing exactly what he wants in exactly the way he wants. Nearly a half century after becoming fascinated with the double helix, Hood says that the really exciting stuff is being invented now.

The history of medicine, he says, has been about diagnosing and treating disease. The future, by contrast, is all about predicting and preventing disease. We already know that gene sequencing is the key to unlocking the secrets of each person's biological systems. So if you know the basic code, you can invent the ultimate form of healthcare: personalized medicine. These days, Hood says, we can sequence an entire human genome one hundred times as fast as his original gene machines could do, and at half the price. "In ten to twelve years," he says, "we'll be sequencing entire genomes in twenty minutes for under $1,000." He cautions, however, that many companies will claim that they have this technology before it's ready, and so patients need to make sure that both the maternal and the paternal chromosomes are being mapped out for the data to be meaningful.

The implications of this technology are astounding: "We'll be able to look at thousands of genes that may predispose you to late-onset diseases such as cancer and cardiovascular disease," he says. "We'll be able to write out for you a predictive health history, what your course is likely to be if unperturbed. It might say you have a 60 percent chance of getting prostate cancer at age sixty-five, or a 30 percent change of getting cardiovascular disease at forty-five." The way Hood sees it, these genetic reports should be available for everyone. "Everyone will get them," he says. "Everyone will be able to get this readout. It will be paid for by health insurance because it will save everyone a lot of money."

Like Geoffrey Ballard's hydrogen economy, Hood's vision triggers systematic thinking of the most radical kind. Inventors listen for these triggers. They are compelled to spend their time imagining what this new world will be like. To do this, you need to go right back to the beginning of the cycle of thinking strategies: creating new opportunities, pinpointing new problems, recognizing new patterns, detecting new barriers, and so forth.

Hood has no doubt that the new systems approach to biology will not only spawn hundreds of lucrative new companies but will also render today's giant pharmaceutical companies obsolete. "There will be enormous intellectual property generated from this," he says. "It will spin out a whole series of new companies. The pharmaceutical industry won't be able to do systems biology. They are too siloized," meaning that they are separated into isolated divisions. He adds, "They are too driven by immediate profit. They don't hire cross-disciplinary people." He foresees the industry moving from its current state of vertical integration—in which the corporations discover, develop, test, and market every kind of drug—to one of horizontal integration, in which corporations do only one of these tasks, but they do it across an entire systems domain. Instead of Glaxo-SmithKline, we'll have Heart Systems Corp.

Getting down to the business of creating this new world, Hood returns to the advice that his mentor, Bill Dreyer, gave him forty years ago: Always practice biology at the leading edge, and if you want to change biology, invent a new technology. One opportunity that Hood and many others have created in their minds is the idea of capturing an instantaneous genetic health snapshot of an individual, to see whether any genes are mutating and whether any cancers might be forming in the near future. Doing this requires the invention of something new. "If you ask me what the technology of the future will be in biological medicine," Hood says, "it is utterly clear: microfluidics coupled with nanotechnology."

That may sound complex, but it's just a systematic approach to the problem of getting an instant genetic health status report. To obtain tremendous amounts of information from tiny samples of blood, you create groups of submicroscopic robots, essentially reducing an entire laboratory to the size of a fingernail. And so that is the invention effort that Lee Hood has instigated. This new project is being conducted as an alliance between his institute, UCLA, and

Hood's alma matter, Caltech. Based at a hospital in Pasadena, the NanoSystems Biology Alliance is led by physicists Stephen Quake and Michael Roukes, chemist James Heath, PET scan inventor Michael Phelps, and prostate cancer expert Charles Sawyers. The project was launched with a $20 million annual budget, and the group is already testing nanochips less than one hundred microns wide—smaller than the dot made by a pencil.

The goal is to invent something akin to a true "cell" phone. "We're working on a systems biology nanochip that's going to be able to take thousands or even tens of thousands of measurements from proteins and RNA molecules," Hood says. "In five to ten years, you'll have a small, handheld device. It will prick your finger, take a small amount of blood, take those ten thousand measurements, plug them in to the Internet, go to a server, and analyze and test those ten thousand elements against one another. So it gives you a ten thousand dimensional space, which is incredibly sensitive to change. That will determine your instant health status."

Naturally, this technology has already led to a vast new category of discovery and invention: the therapies that repair, correct, or modify our genes before any symptoms appear. We need to find new ways to flip our bits.

Inventors typically shy away from making bold predictions about the future. As the saying goes, it's easier and safer to invent the future than to predict it. Inventors are often so caught up with pinpointing problems, overcoming barriers, crossing boundaries, analogizing and visualizing that they often don't see the point in making wild claims about where everything is heading. But Leroy Hood is so confident of the end result that he matter-of-factly makes this prophecy: This new systems approach to medicine will extend the average human life span by ten to thirty years. If he's right, we or our children may be the world's first mass generation of people who live past a hundred. If so, we are going to cause a lot of problems. Luckily, we may have some extra time to invent our way out of them.

Scaling Up and Out

WE NEED MORE INVENTIVE PEOPLE turning on more juice for
the simple reason that there's so much that needs to be invented
and improved. The number of problems facing the world is mush-
rooming at the same time that massive amounts of new knowledge
are being created that could serve the process of invention. Inventive people are fueled by their ability to redefine those problems
and imagine ways to apply knowledge to the solution. Of course,
new technology can't solve all the world's woes. Misapplied inventions make some problems worse. But as you've seen, an individual
inventor can have a disproportionately positive impact. If we were
able to tap the powers of a million new inventors of all types, we
would have a fighting chance of remaking the world in one human
lifetime, just as every generation of inventors has done since the
Enlightenment.

As Nathan Myhrvold says, there's never been a better time to have
big ideas. We have collective brains now. People all over the world
are coming up with inventive new ideas, and they're using the Internet and new communications tools (whose prices are falling
every day) to share these ideas more quickly and more richly than
ever before. Even corporations that are focused on their existing

markets are realizing that they're better off trying to capitalize on all this creativity rather than trying to fight it. As a result, inventive people can greatly increase their economic power, if they choose to exercise it. Inventors have a better shot than ever before at getting the best of their creations embraced by a world that has become accustomed to constant change.

The smartest corporations have learned that they must lead the charge. "The only long-term source of profit, and the only reason to invest in a company, is your confidence in its ability to innovate," says General Electric CEO Jeffrey Immelt.[1] Like most corporate leaders, Immelt seems to embrace the widely known equation from economist Joseph Schumpeter: Invention plus capital equals innovation. "Good leaders," Immelt adds, "pick the right areas to innovate, and they place big bets." He says he's tripling the number of engineers in executive positions in the company and reducing the number of lawyers. To grow the company, he'll rely less on mergers and finance and more on creating new technologies such as wind turbines, photovoltaic and hydrogen fuel cells, and new instruments for detecting disease at the molecular and genetic levels. Most auspiciously, Immelt has revived the image of GE founder Thomas Edison in the company's branding, and its new credo is "imagination at work." He promises to again make GE's century-old R&D laboratory "a hub for cultural change."

This may be the first time that the heads of some of the world's biggest corporations are on the same page with the quirkiest individual inventors. "Right now, there is an explosion of new ideas in every field," says Woody Norris.[2] He believes that almost anything written about the state of the art in energy, transportation, physics, electronics, medicine, biology, and other fields can become obsolete in three months. Big corporations are more vulnerable to invention than they've ever been, he says. That's why companies are keeping a close eye on individuals like Norris. IBM, for example, recently invited Norris to address its R&D groups all over the world so that its researchers can glean thinking strategies from him. "We're just getting started," Norris tells them. "Fundamental new stuff is coming."

THE RESTLESS AND THE RELENTLESS

On a personal level, Woody Norris was hit with the unexpected. A great fire swept through Southern California in the fall of 2003 and consumed thousands of homes. Norris and his wife had enough warning to evacuate in time, but their twenty-thousand square foot house in Poway, outside San Diego, was engulfed by flames. Among the possessions they lost were their collection of fifteen thousand record albums and one thousand DVDs, a half million dollars' worth of rare books, millions of dollars' worth of paintings, and a collection of framed letters signed by Thomas Edison, Alexander Graham Bell, and Nikola Tesla. Luckily, Norris's nearby company headquarters remained unscathed, and his wife had taken out one of the largest private insurance policies in the state, with a monthly premium of $3,200. "My attitude is this: I enjoyed all those things for all these years," he says. "Now, I'll get new stuff."

That brings us to the basic character trait that all the inventors profiled here have in common: They're relentless and restless. Only an inventor would see a destructive fire as a chance for renewal. Inventors are focused on what's next. Once cultivated, their compulsion to create is too strong for anyone or anything to contain. As long as they're able to think well, they keep inventing. Inventors see too many possibilities for their process of invention to stop or even slow down. Inventors don't believe in the general concept of retirement or resting on their riches. Even if they did, they wouldn't be able to stop themselves.

PayPal cofounder Max Levchin, still in his late twenties, invented a follow-up program to his Igor financial fraud detection software. Whereas Igor looks for thousands of possible anomalies in online transactions, Levchin's newer Ilya program "covers millions of events."[3] Levchin tried to take some time off after selling Igor and Ilya, along with his entire company, to eBay. But he began brainstorming new invention ideas almost immediately. Over lunch recently in a San Francisco dim sum restaurant, Levchin wore a Japanese edition of a Bart Simpson T-shirt and dropped hints about his latest start-up idea, which is based on pattern recognition and machine learning. "I think in images all the time," he says.

At the other end of the age spectrum, kidney dialysis machine inventor Willem Kolff, now in his early nineties, has a new girlfriend, and he's working feverishly to bring out his latest invention: a portable artificial lung. Again, he's planning to give his ideas to the world. "I don't have the money or the time for patent applications," he says. "If it can benefit mankind, they can have it."[4]

Some of our inventors have been genuinely surprised by their creations. Carl Crawford, the coinventor of the spiral CT scanner, left GE Medical Systems in 1995 and became a vice president at Analogic Corporation, a Peabody, Massachusetts, company whose culture focuses on inventing across a half dozen domains. Founded by Bernard Gordon, an illustrious inventor of analog-to-digital signal-conversion chips, Analogic has never posted a loss in its three decades as a public company, but it has also never been known as a high-flying company. In 2000, Gordon received a call from Lockheed Martin about adapting its CT scanners for possible applications in airport baggage scanning. Gordon put Crawford in charge of the project. Not long after 9/11, the government decided to buy these new machines in bulk to scan checked baggage at U.S. airports for the first time.

Analogic won a big part of the business, and it delivered hundreds of these machines in December 2002. Sitting in Gordon's corner office only a few days after the *Boston Globe* named Analogic Massachusetts's best-performing company in its annual "Globe 100" survey, Crawford took it in stride. This was pretty much a one-time gain, he said. Gordon agreed: "We probably can't grow profit margins by 10,872 percent every year."[5] Stephen Jacobsen, of Sarcos Research in Utah, was surprised by one of his inventions for another reason. Over the past several years, he's been successful in building learning programs into robots. Using pattern recognition software, he created a humanoid robot that learned to bounce a ball after watching a person do it about three dozen times. Jacobsen then created a robot that learned how to juggle three balls after watching someone do it only five times. But it was the robot that learned to play air hockey that freaked him out. "When the robot plays, he looks like my son," Jacobsen says. "He's very earnest."[6] One day, when the robot missed the puck and allowed a goal, it made a pronounced human-like twitch and snarl. "It scared the hell out of me," Jacobsen says. "He had all the mannerisms of someone who is pissed off and is going to come around and beat the hell out of you. He seemed kind of angry."

Such stories tend to revive the debate over intelligent machines, whether humans will one day build robots with human-like cognition and consciousness. Some robot inventors still hold that out as the ultimate goal. But Jacobsen doesn't buy it. What that air hockey–playing robot was experiencing was more like a mechanical response to an unexpected change in a pattern. Jacobsen is more worried about the state of the art of human cognition than he is about building true human intelligence into a bunch of sensors, actuators, and microprocessors. As B. F. Skinner once said, "The real question is not whether machines can think, but whether men do."[7]

COPYCATTING, PIGGYBACKING, AND LEAPFROGGING

Successful invention tends to scale upward. Invention spawns continuous and endless improvement. The technology gets better and better. Computers become faster, medical equipment more precise, engines more powerful, communications devices more versatile, robots more dexterous, and so on. People who use these new inventions and improvements can do more work and enjoy life in new ways. Their increased living standards stimulate further economic growth, which in turn supports invention and innovation.

But invention also needs to scale *outward*. There are those who can't afford any of the technology described here, and therefore they receive few or none of the benefits of invention. More than 1.3 billion people—about one out of every six people in the world—live on less than $2 per day per day, and billions of others live only marginally less impoverished lives. Can invention do for the developing world what it has done for the developed world?

Answering this question requires a different frame of reference. Amy B. Smith, a biomechanical engineer who spent four years in Botswana with the Peace Corps, has invented simple but sturdy machines that don't require electricity, such as mechanical grain grinder and an incubator for developing antibiotics. Now a professor at MIT, she teaches her students how to think about problems that are out of their own world. "Engineers tend to be at the very top of the economic pyramid, so we tend to design for ourselves," she says. "But what about the other 90 percent of the world?"[8] She takes her students on trips to places like Honduras and sub-Sahara Africa. Back in Cambridge, Massachusetts, she assigns them the task of trying to eat for less than $2 per day for an entire week. "No one is able to do it," she says. "But even if you try it for a short time, you never forget it."

Even better, more and more inventive thinkers in the developing world are responding to the challenges around them. One of the most successful is an inventor named Ashok Khosla. Born in India, Khosla was educated at Cambridge University and received his Ph.D. from Harvard University, where he lectured on the topic of the environment. He enjoyed the American lifestyle and his apartment overlooking the Charles River. But after ten years at Harvard, he decided to return to India. "I just packed up my stuff one day and went back home," he recalls.[9]

In the 1970s, Khosla helped the Indian government set up the first national agency for environmental protection in the developing world. Then in the mid-1980s, he struck out as an entrepreneur, starting a New Delhi company called Development Alternatives. Khosla aimed to do what he believed foreign aid and government antipoverty policies were failing to do: lift up entire civilizations. His goal was to create what he calls "sustainable livelihoods": jobs that produce basic products and services for the local economy, generate income and purchasing power, and provide dignity and meaning to people's lives. As the old saying goes, "Give a person a fish, feed them for a day. Teach a person to fish, feed them for a lifetime." But something is almost always left out of that equation: First, you need to invent a system for creating and distributing the appropriate fishing rods.

Khosla sees three proven models that can turn poor nations into rich ones: copycatting, piggybacking, and leapfrogging. Copycats steal ideas, technologies, and techniques from other countries and improve and adapt them. During its first few decades, the United States ripped off the key secrets of the Industrial Revolution from England, Scotland, and France and launched its own industrial economy. Two centuries later, Japan and then Korea developed by copying American manufacturing, raising the quality and lowering the cost of goods. Now China is doing it again. In contrast, India is practicing the art of piggybacking: riding on the backs of rich nations by doing an increasing share of their manufacturing and service work at far lower costs. Finally, leapfrogging involves skipping over inappropriate technologies and embracing new ones; an example is Finland's sudden break from backward Soviet domination and its adoption of inventions such as wireless networks.

Khosla believes that developing nations need to employ all three models at once. "Industrial countries have made some lousy technology choices," he says. "Why should we adopt what we already know is bad? We need to invent on our own, thinking everything through from scratch."

As the world's largest democracy, with a diverse population of more than one billion, India is a fascinating experiment in economic development. Most of the attention has been focused on the country's pockets of urban, English-speaking university graduates, who are capitalizing on the Internet and decreasing telecommunications costs to capture hundreds of thousands of software and customer service jobs from overseas, at a fraction of American or European wages. The high-tech start-ups of Bangalore have been heralded in the business press. Corporations such as GE and IBM have even opened gleaming R&D centers there, employing brilliant engineers who are helping to scale up technologies in the domains of infotech, biotech, and nanotech.

But Khosla is focused on the rural poor, the 70 percent of India's population who are almost untouched by any of this so-called "offshore outsourcing." He's focused on scaling the global process of invention outward to as many people as possible.

To do this, Khosla is marshaling the same thinking strategies as other world-class inventors. Creating an ambitious opportunity in his own mind, he envisions bringing seven hundred million people in India out of impoverishment or subsistence living. The problems he has pinpointed are quite specific: People need places to live, but they can't afford most construction materials. They need to produce their own clothing locally. They need ways to cook food, but electric service is spotty at best. They need ways to purify water. They need cheap, renewable energy.

The pattern Khosla recognized is that the most successful inventions in such environments are the ones that use locally available materials. Borrowing ideas he has seen all over the world, Khosla has invented a series of new products: a hand-operated press that converts mud into hard bricks for low-cost housing; a vertical kiln that rapidly and continually bakes and churns out higher-quality bricks made from native clay; a machine for making cheap roofing tiles out of industrial waste; a process for turning local weeds into a fuel that can burn in a diesel engine that can provide power to an entire village; woodstoves that dramatically reduce smoke inhalation and early cancer death; and hand-powered looms and paper-making machines based on radically simple designs. These are only some of his company's successful inventions. Along the way, Khosla has embraced failure, creating many technologies that flopped, such as solar-powered water heaters that were too expensive for most people. "We use failures as building blocks for success," he says.

Above all, Khosla thinks systematically. One of his biggest innovations is a franchising system. Borrowing a page from Ray Kroc of McDonald's fame and rewriting it, Khosla has created a network of dozens of profitable local dealerships that set up their own businesses distributing dozens of these technologies and training people how to use them. Just as important as the jobs created at the franchise level are the jobs created by the inventions themselves. Each of Khosla's products, once it is up and running, creates an enterprise that requires the hiring of four to four dozen employees. The entrepreneurs, who use credit to invest in the company's kilns, looms, paper-making machines, and energy systems, now have a sustainable way to make goods that they can sell. These products do well in local markets because they serve as simple, cheap ways to fill basic needs.

As Khosla sees it, this systematic strategy is the best way to give people the chance to escape the cycle of poverty. At the same time, the impact on the environment is low. Using its own cheap mud bricks, Development Alternatives built a massive, orange-hued head-quarters for 150 employees that consumes the same amount of electricity as a single American household. With those same bricks, one of the company's customers built the Indira Gandhi National Centre for the Arts in 180 days at a cost of $40,000; the center hosts dozens of exhibitions every year. Khosla's company is signing up franchises in hundreds of new locations, collecting ongoing royalty and training fees from each one.

Khosla also makes money by data mining and by running an Internet portal, called tarahaat.com, for communicating with franchisees and customers. He uses low-tech and high-tech ways to gather and sell market data on these new households to corporations interested in selling products into developing markets. In all these ways, invention is leading to economic growth in the areas most in need of it.

THINKING OPTIMISTICALLY

By nature, inventors are optimists, and why wouldn't they be? They know they can light up the world with the mere twenty watts of electrical energy that fuels their gray matter. By applying thinking strategies to their surroundings, inventors can convert mud and weeds into an economy. At the very top of the scale of technology, inventors can convert the information from a drop of blood into time itself. Today's high tech will eventually become tomorrow's low tech, but it's all the result of invention.

Considering all this, why is invention often taken for granted, and why isn't exposure to inventive thinking a central goal at all levels of the education system? Instead of losing our innate inventiveness as we grow older, we should instead become more inventive with time. That's why living a long life and having fun are often of primary importance to inventors and those around them. Inventors need to enjoy themselves, and inventors need to live long enough to see as many of the effects of their work as they can. For thousands of years, societies have risen and fallen due in large part to their inventiveness, so we shouldn't be shocked that it continues to happen, only faster. Knowledge can now be dispersed around the globe more cheaply and rapidly than ever. Any company and any country can conceivably jump up to a new level of economic success if it is able to harness the inventiveness of its own people. So let's turn on the juice and see what shakes loose.

Notes

Prologue

1. For a powerful correlation between invention and market performance, see "Investing in Invention Pays Off," *Technology Review*, May 2004, 38. The study by CHI Research Inc. shows that the top twenty-five S&P companies with patents that are most highly cited by papers and other patents, and that yield marketable products the fastest (quick "cycletimes"), have far outperformed the S&P 500 since 1990. $1,000 invested in the S&P 500 in January 1990 was worth $4,500 in January 2004, while $1,000 invested in the 25 most "inventive" corporations was worth nearly $40,000. Correlations aren't proof of cause and effect, and there may be counterexamples of successful companies that aren't innovative and inventive, but these correlations are remarkably consistent over time.

2. Numerous studies have shown an extremely high correlation between patents per million people and a nation's standard of living. One of the most comprehensive annual study is "Ranking National Innovative Capacity: Findings from the National Innovative Capacity Index," by Michael Porter of Harvard Business School and Scott Stern of the Kellogg School, Northwestern University, and the National Bureau of Economic Research. Rankings are based on the following metrics: U.S. patents per million people, proportion of scientists and engineers, innovation policy, number and size of technology hot spots, degree of connection between those hot spots and other institutions, and other metrics. See "Global Invention Map," *Technology Review*, May 2004, 76-77.

3. Leslie Aiello and Peter Wheeler, *Current Anthropology*, vol. 36, no. 2 (April 1995), 199–221. "The expensive-tissue hypothesis: the brain and the digestive system in human and primate evolution." (PET is positron emission tomography,

MRI is magnetic resonance imaging, and EEG is electroencephalograph.) Also see John Morgan Allman, *Evolving Brains* (New York: W.H. Freeman & Co, 1999).

4. Thea Singer, "The Innovation Factor: Your Brain on Innovation," *Inc.* magazine, September 2002.

5. Observation at Edison's laboratory made by Joyce Bedi, historian at the Smithsonian Institution's Jerome and Dorothy Lemelson Center for the Study of Invention and Innovation.

6. Nick Holonyak Jr., the John Bardeen Professor of Electrical and Computer Engineering and Physics at the University of Illinois, interview by the author, Washington, D.C., 22 April 2004.

7. The blue LED turned out to be one of the most useful and most difficult to produce, because blue has the shortest wavelength (highest frequency) of the visible colors. Japanese inventor Shuji Nakamura, while working for Nichia Corp. in the early 1990s, achieved the breakthough. He is now a professor at the University of California at Santa Barbara. Under a recent intellectual property trend in which Japanese inventors are demanding a share of corporate patent royalties for their inventions under the "fair compensation" rule of the patent code, Nakamura sued his former employer in Toyko District Court. In January 2004, he won a judgment of 20 billion yen (about $200 million), a record sum for a corporate inventor. Also see David Talbot, "LEDs vs. the Lightbulb," *Technology Review*, May 2003, 30.

8. Ralph Waldo Emerson, quoted from "Letters and Social Aims," 1876.

9. See QuoteDB.com, the Quotations Database, or www.davebarry.com.

10. "Over Time, America Lost Its Bullwackers," *Wall Street Journal*, 24 2002, 1.

11. "The Architecture of Invention," report on the Lemelson–MIT workshop, March 2003, 14–15. See <http://web.mit.edu/invent/report.html>.

Chapter 1

1. Elwood "Woody" Norris, interviews by the author, American Technology Corp., Poway, CA, 19 January 2004, and by telephone 19 May 2003 and 4 June 2003.

2. Carlo Cipolla, *Before the Industrial Revolution* (New York: W.W. Norton, 1980).

3. Carl Jung, *Memories, Dreams, Reflections* (London: Fontana Press, 1983).

4. Norris, interviews.

5. Donald A. Norman, *Things That Make Us Smart: Defending Human Attributes in the Age of the Machine* (Cambridge, MA: Perseus, 1994).

6. Gerald Messadié, ed., *Great Inventions Through History* (Edinburgh: W&R Chambers, 1991).

7. Stuart Campbell, "History of Ultrasound in Obstetrics and Gynecology," OBGYN.net Conference Coverage, FIGO 2000: International Federation of Gynecology & Obstetrics, Washington, D.C., 2000.

8. Donald W. Baker, interview by the author, 4 June 2003.

9. Norris, Elwood. 1972. "Phase-Lock Doppler System for Monitoring Blood Vessel Movement," U.S. Patent 3,631,849, issued 4 January 1972.

10. David Perkins, interview by the author, Harvard Graduate School of Education, Cambridge, MA, 12 February 2003. Perkins cites these four basic types of inventions.

11. Robert V. Bruce, *Alexander Graham Bell and the Conquest of Solitude* (New York: Little Brown, 1973).

12. Edwin S. Grosvenor and Morgan Wesson, *Alexander Graham Bell: The Life and Times of the Man Who Invented the Telephone* (New York: Harry N. Adams, 1997).

13. Norris's most lucrative inventions were probably not his cleverest ones. He created one of the first flash-memory voice recorders as well as a series of car audio systems that ended up being spun out as part of a start-up called e.Digital Corp. The stock in the company rose from a low of 8 cents in 1999 to a high of about $24 in early 2000, netting Norris an eight-figure windfall. He also invented the Jabra headset for cell phones, which embeds a microphone in an earpiece, an invention that fetched about $7 million in the early 1990s and was later resold for much more.

Chapter 2

1. Robert Scott Root-Bernstein, *Discovering: Inventing and Problem Solving at the Frontiers of Scientific Knowledge* (Cambridge, MA: Harvard University Press, 1989).

2. Ernö Rubik, Tamas Varga, et al., *Rubik's Cubic Compendium* (Oxford, U.K.: Oxford University Press, 1987).

3. Jay Walker, interview by the author, Walker Digital, Stamford, CT, 19 August 2003.

4. Peter Corr, presentation at *Technology Review*'s Emerging Technologies Conference, MIT, Cambridge, MA, 24 September 2003.

5. In addition to gambling, other behavioral superforces on Walker's list include: beauty, acceptance, religion, tribalism, security and safety, greed and fear, self-expression, and voyeurism. His four superforces for the Internet are: saving money, entertainment, being informed, and convenience. Inventions that tap into these and other primal urges and desires have a much better chance of success.

6. Neil Baldwin, *Edison: Inventing the Century* (New York: Hyperion, 1995); Paul Israel, *Edison: A Life of Invention* (New York: John Wiley, 1988).

7. Walker, interview.

8. Jay S. Walker, Bruce Schneier, and James Jorasch. 1998. Method and apparatus for a cryptographically assisted commercial network system designed to facilitate buyer-driven conditional purchase offers. U.S. patent 5,794,207, issued 11 August 1998.

Chapter 3

1. Abbot Payton Usher, *A History of Mechanical Inventions* (New York: McGraw-Hill, 1929).

2. Christopher Alexander et al., *A Pattern Language* (New York: Oxford University Press, 1977).

3. Victor K. McElheny, *Watson and DNA: Making a Scientific Revolution* (Cambridge, MA: Perseus, 2003).

4. Leroy Hood, interviews by the author, Institute for Systems Biology, Seattle, 20 November 2002, and Boston, 24 April 2003; Leroy Hood, "My Life and Adventures Integrating Biology and Technology," commemorative lecture for the 2002 Kyoto Prize in advanced technologies, Kyoto, Japan, 5 December 2002.

5. Richard P. Feynman, *The Meaning of It All* (Reading, MA: Addison-Wesley, 1988).

6. Neil Baldwin, *Edison: Inventing the Century* (New York: Hyperion, 1995).

7. Reese Jenkins, in *Inventive Minds: Creativity in Technology*, eds. Robert J. Weber and David N. Perkins (Oxford, U.K.: Oxford University Press, 1992). See also Baldwin, *Edison: Inventing the Century*, and Paul Israel, *Edison: A Life of Invention* (New York: John Wiley, 1988).

8. Baldwin, *Edison: Inventing the Century*; Israel, *Edison: A Life of Invention*.

9. Baldwin, *Edison: Inventing the Century*, 84.

10. Max Levchin, telephone interview by the author, 20 July 2001, and in San Francisco, 11 August 2003.

11. Evan I. Schwartz, "Digital Cash," *Technology Review*, December 2001.

Chapter 4

1. *Oxford Dictionary of Modern Quotations*, ed. Tony Augarde (Oxford, U.K.: Oxford University Press, 1991).

2. Bernard Meyerson, telephone interview by the author, 28 January 2003, and at IBM Watson Research Laboratories, Yorktown Heights, NY, 5 March 2003.

3. Ira Flatow, *They All Laughed: From Light Bulbs to Lasers—The Fascinating Stories Behind the Great Inventions That Changed Our Lives* (New York: Harper-Collins, 1992); Mitchell Wilson, *American Science and Invention: A Pictorial History* (New York: Bonanza/Crown, 1954). This book is also the source of the quotation that opens this chapter.

4. George Polya, *How to Solve It: A New Aspect of Mathematical Method* (Princeton, NJ: Princeton University Press, 1945).

5. Harold "Doc" Edgarton, as quoted by Claire Calcagno, Lemelson-MIT Workshop, "Historical Perspectives on Invention and Creativity," Cambridge, MA, 15 March 2003.

6. David Perkins, *The Eureka Effect: The Art and Logic of Breakthrough Thinking* (New York: W.W. Norton, 2001). Originally published as *Archimedes' Bathtub* (New York, W.W. Norton, 2000).

7. Wilson, *American Science and Invention.*

8. Ibid., 125.

9. Ibid., 126.

10. Ibid., 127.

11. Lillian Hoddeson and Michael Riordan, *Crystal Fire: The Birth of the Information Age* (New York: W.W. Norton & Co., 1997).

12. Meyerson, interviews.

13. Ibid.

14. John Markoff, "IBM Researchers Increase Speed of Silicon Transistors," *New York Times*, March 15, 1990, D5. The story stated that the IBM breakthrough almost doubled the world speed record for silicon-based chips, to 75 billion cycles per second.

15. "The Nobel Prize in Physics 2000," <www.nobel.se>, interview with the 2000 Nobel Laureates in Physics by Joanna Rose, science writer, December 13, 2000.

Chapter 5

1. Arthur Koestler, *The Act of Creation* (London: Arkana, 1989).

2. Isaac Asimov, *Biographical Encyclopedia of Science and Technology: The Lives and Achievements of 1510 Great Scientists from Ancient Times to the Present* (New York: Doubleday & Co., 1982).

3. Nathan Rosenberg, Lemelson-MIT Workshop on Historical Perspectives on Invention and Creativity, Cambridge, MA., 15 March 2003.

4. Ibid.

5. Leroy Hood, interviews by the author, Institute for Systems Biology, Seattle, 20 November 2002, and Boston, 24 April 2003; Leroy Hood, "My Life and Adventures Integrating Biology and Technology," commemorative lecture for the 2002 Kyoto Prize in advanced technologies, Kyoto, Japan, 5 December 2002.

6. William Dreyer, telephone interview by the author, 2 April 2003.

7. Applied Biosystems Inc. was acquired by Perkin-Elmer Corp. in 1993, which changed its name in 2000 to Applera Corporation, which also includes Celera Genemics Group. ABI reported sales of $1.7 billion in fiscal 2003.

8. Jerry E. Bishop and Michael Waldholz, *Genome: The Story of Our Astonishing Attempt to Map All the Genes in the Human Body* (New York: Simon & Schuster, 1990).

9. Hood, "My Life and Adventures Integrating Biology and Technology."

Chapter 6

1. Quoted in Michael Kanellos, "Intel Unfurls Experimental 3D Transistors," CNET News.com, 16 September 2002.

2. Kathryn Wilder Guarini, interview by the author, IBM Watson Research Laboratories, Yorktown Heights, NY, 5 March 2003.

3. Isaac Berzin, interview by the author, GreenFuel Inc., Cambridge, MA, 23 May 2003.

4. Evan Richman, "The Smartest Man in Boston," *Boston Globe Sunday Magazine*, May 25, 2003.

5. Isaac Asimov, *Biographical Encyclopedia of Science and Technology: The Lives and Achievements of 1510 Great Scientists from Ancient Times to the Present* (New York: Doubleday & Co., 1982).

6. James Tobin, *To Conquer the Air: The Wright Brothers and the Great Race for Flight* (New York: Free Press, 2003).

7. Fred Howard, *Wilbur and Orville: A Biography of the Wright Brothers*, (New York: Knopf, 1987), 19.

8. Ibid., 33.

9. Carl Crawford, interviews by the author, Analogic Corp., Peabody, MA, 22 February 2003 and 22 May 2003.

10. Ibid.

11. Ibid.

12. Sandy A. Napel, "Basic Principles of Spiral CT," in *Spiral CT: Principles, Techniques, and Clinical Applications*, eds. Elliot K. Fishman and R. Brooke Jeffrey (New York: Raven Press, 1995), 1:1–8.

13. Carl R. Crawford and Kevin F. King, assigned to General Electric Co., Milwaukee, Wisc. 1993. Extrapolative reconstruction method for helical scanning. U.S. Patent 5,233,518, issued 3 August 1993. Willi A. Kalender et al., "Spiral Volumetric CT with Single-Breath-Hold Technique, Continuous Transport, and Continuous Scanner Rotation," Thoracic Radiology, July 1990, 176:181–183.

14. "Cardiac and Preventative Diagnostic Imaging Markets," Feed-Back.com's TeleMed E-Zine, July 2001, <www.feed-back.com/july01ezine.htm>.

15. M. M. Morin, Pauline A. Mysliwiec et al., "Screening Virtual Colonoscopy —Ready for Prime Time?," *New England Journal of Medicine* 349, 4 December, 2003, 2261–2264; published at www.nejm.org on Dec 1, 2003 (10.1056/NEJMe038181), as part of a series of articles on virtual colonoscopy. Nathan Seppa, "No Scope: CT scan works as well as colonoscopy," *Science News*, 6 December 2003.

Chapter 7

1. Elwood "Woody" Norris, interviews by the author, American Technology Corp., Poway, CA, 19 May 2003, 4 June 2003, and 19 January 2004.

2. James McLurkin, speech given at the Lemelson–MIT ceremony for the Student Prize for Inventiveness, Boston Museum of Science, 26 February 2003; David Arnold, "MIT Student Honored for Robot Design," *Boston Globe*, 27 February 2003.

3. For the latest work from Rodney Brooks and his lab at MIT, see <http://www.csail.mit.edu/>.

4. Robert Langer, interview by the author, MIT Langer Laboratories, Cambridge, MA, 29 October 2002; David Brown, *Inventing Modern America: From the Microwave to the Mouse*, (Cambridge, MA.: MIT Press, 2003), 37.

5. David Perkins, *The Eureka Effect: The Art and Logic of Breakthrough Thinking* (New York: W.W. Norton, 2001). Originally published as *Archimedes' Bathtub* (New York: W.W. Norton, 2000).

6. Ibid.

7. Evan I. Schwartz, *The Last Lone Inventor: A Tale of Genius, Deceit, and the Birth of Television* (New York: HarperCollins, 2002).

8. John L. Vaught et al., assigned to Hewlett-Packard thermal inkjet printer. U.S. patent 4,490,728, issued 25 December 1984.

9. "Spitting image: Engineering insight, dogged determination and a dash of serendipity have made the lowly inkjet imaging device the king of computer printers," *The Economist*, 19 September 2002.

10. Robert and Michéle Root-Bernstein, *Sparks of Genius: The 13 Thinking Tools of the World's Most Creative People* (Boston: Houghton Mifflin, 1999).

11. Norris, interviews.

12. Evan I. Schwartz, "The Sound War: two very different inventors are locked in a head-to-head battle to tame sound. At stake are billion-dollar markets and lasting fame as the one who redefined how we all think about audio," *Technology Review*, May 2004.

Chapter 8

1. Daniel Gilbert, Harvard University, as quoted from his presentation at the TED conference in Monterey, CA, on 27 February 2004.

2. Stephen Jacobsen, interview by the author, Sarcos Research, Salt Lake City, UT, 15 November 2002.

3. John Warnock, telephone interview by the author, 14 January 2003.

4. Ibid.

5. Jacobsen, interview.

6. Richard P. Feynman, *The Pleasure of Finding Things Out* (Cambridge, MA: Perseus Books, 1999).

7. Jacobsen, interview.

8. Ronald W. Clark, *Einstein: The Life and Times* (New York, Avon Books, 1984).

9. Elwood "Woody" Norris, interviews by the author, American Technology Corp., Poway, CA, 19 May 2003, 4 June 2003, and 19 January 2004.

10. Max Tegmark, "Parallel Universes," *Scientific American*, May 2003.

11. Jacobsen, interview.

12. Willem Kolff, telephone interview by the author, 6 January 2003.

13. Jacobsen, interview.

14. Kolff, interview.

15. Jacobsen, interview.

16. Kolff, interview.

17. Jacobsen, interview.

Chapter 9

1. Linda Stone, talk given at "The Architecture of Invention: Cognitive Aspect of Invention and Creativity" workshop, Lemelson-MIT Program, Harvard Graduate School of Education, Cambridge, MA, 21 August 2003.

2. Gary Wolf, "The World According to Woz," *WIRED*, September 1998.

3. Kenneth Brown, *Inventors at Work: Interviews with 16 Notable American Inventors* (Redmond, WA: Microsoft Press, 1988).

4. Ibid.

5. Ibid.

6. Wolf, "The World According to Woz."

7. Michael A. Hiltzik, "Woz Goes Wireless," *Technology Review*, May 2004, 42–45.

8. Dean Kamen, interviews with the author, DEKA Research, Manchester, NH, 8 July 2002, and Boston, 15 February 2002.

9. Steve Kemper, *Code Name Ginger: The Story Behind Segway and Dean Kamen's Quest to Invent a New World* (Cambridge, MA: Harvard Business School Press, 2003).

10. William P. Murphy Jr., interview by the author, Boston, 24 April 2003.

11. John Morrell, interview by the author, Manchester, NH, 8 July 2002.

12. Kemper, *Code Name Ginger*.

13. Kamen, interviews.

14. Doug Field, interview by the author, Manchester, NH, 8 July 2002.

15. Kamen, interviews.

16. Field, interview.

17. Morrell, interview.

18. Stephen Jacobsen, interview by the author, Sarcos Research, Salt Lake City, UT, 15 November 2002.

19. Kemper, *Code Name Ginger*.

20. Kamen, interviews.

21. Nathan Myhrvold, interviews by the author, Intellectual Ventures, Bellevue, WA, 5 December 2001 and 20 November 2002.

22. Linda Stone, talk given at "The Architecture of Invention: Cognitive Aspect of Invention and Creativity" workshop.

23. Kamen, interviews.

24. Stone, "The Architecture of Invention" workshop.

Chapter 10

1. Georg Pólya, *How to Solve It: A New Aspect of Mathematical Method* (Princeton, NJ: Princeton University Press, 1945).

2. Joel Grey, telephone interview by the author, 4 December 2002.

3. Ronald A. Katz, interview by the author, Ronald A. Katz Licensing, L.P., Los Angeles, 18 November 2002.

4. Ibid.

5. Lee Ault, telephone interview by the author, 9 November 2002.

6. Katz, interview.

7. Ault, interview.

8. Katz, interview.

9. Ault, interview.

10. Katz, interview.

11. James J. Daly, "Masters of the Payment Domain," *Credit Card Management,* August 2001, vol. 14 no. 5.

12. Henry "Ric" Duques, telephone interview by the author, 9 December 2002.

13. Katz, interview.

14. Teresa Riordan, "Stockpiling Technologies That Allow Telephones and Computers to Talk to Each Other," *New York Times,* 31 October 1994.

15. Barry Augenbraun, telephone interview by the author, 9 November 2002.

16. Katz, interview.

17. Tim Casey, telephone interview by the author, 10 November 2002.

18. Katz, interview.

19. Casey, interview.

20. Katz, interview.

21. Duques, interview.

Chapter 11

1. Robert Lacey, *Ford: The Men and the Machine* (New York: Little Brown, 1986).

2. Jay Walker, interview by the author, Walker Digital, Stamford, CT, 19 August 2003.

3. Geoffrey Ballard, interview by the author, General Hydrogen, Vancouver, BC, Canada, 19 November 2002.

4. Tom Koppel, *Powering the Future: The Ballard Fuel Cell and the Race to Change the World* (New York: Wiley, 1999).

5. David Wilkinson, interview by the author, Ballard Power Systems, Burnaby, BC, Canada, 19 November 2002.

6. Ballard, interview.

7. Lawrence Burns, speech at *Technology Review*'s Emerging Technologies Conference, MIT, Cambridge, MA, 23 September 2003, as quoted by the author.

8. Ballard, interview.

9. Leroy Hood, interviews by the author, Institute for Systems Biology, Seattle, 20 November 2002, and Boston, 24 April 2003.

Epilogue

1. Jeffrey Immelt, as quoted at *Technology Review*'s "Emerging Technologies Conference," MIT campus, Cambridge, MA, 25 September 2003.

2. Elwood "Woody" Norris, interviews by the author, American Technology Corp., Poway, CA, 19 January 2004, and by telephone 19 May 2003 and 4 June 2003.

3. Max Levchin, telephone interview by the author, 20 July 2001, and in San Francisco, 11 August 2003.

4. Willem Kolff, telephone interview by the author, 6 January 2003.

5. Bernard Gordon, conversation with author, Analogic Corp., Peabody, MA, 22 May 2003.

6. Stephen Jacobsen, interview by the author, Sarcos Research, Salt Lake City, UT, 15 November 2002.

7. B. F. Skinner, *Contingencies of Reinforcement* (New York: Appleton-Century-Crofts, 1969.

8. Amy B. Smith, faculty member at MIT, interview by the author, 22 April 2004.

9. Ashok Khosla, interviews by the author, London, 20 November 2003, and Boston, 15 December 2003. Khosla talk given at "Invention and Innovation for Sustainable Development" workshop, Lemelson-MIT Program, LEAD International, London, 20 November 2003.

Acknowledgments

MY FIRST TIP of the hat goes to those who dedicate their lives to solving other people's problems. Most of the inventors I met while researching this book are multitalented, transdisciplinary people who could have more easily gotten normal jobs. Well, maybe not. Nonetheless, I'm grateful to all the inventors whose stories are told herein for inviting me into their laboratories and into their minds, and for spending time showing me what they do and how they do it. Thanks also go to their many co-inventors and colleagues, and to the inventors who gave of their time but who didn't end up in the book—they enriched it nonetheless.

Writing is invention too: There's the initial inspiration, the research into the prior art, the gathering of all the needed materials, the moments of frustration, the unlikely breakthroughs, and the long process of trying to make it better and better until it's time to send it out into the world. Sometimes writers also build on their earlier work. My fascination with inventive personalities took hold while I was researching my previous book, which concerns an invention that the average person gawks at for more than four hours per day. In many ways, invention itself has changed dramatically since Philo T. Farnsworth demonstrated the first electronic television system, but in other ways invention hasn't changed much at all.

In my quest to delve deeper, I turned early on to the people at the Massachusetts Institute of Technology who run the Lemelson-MIT Program, which aims to inspire the next generation of inventors. Special thanks to program director Merton Flemings, and to Kristin Finn, Kristin Joyce, Melissa Makofske, Kari Thande, Marissa Wozniak, and the rest of the staff for being so supportive from start to finish. Thanks also goes to Julia Novy-Hildesley at the Lemelson Foundation.

These people gave me the unique opportunity to attend and report on a series of two-day workshops on invention. These workshops covered the history of invention, cognitive and educational aspects of invention, and intellectual property, as well as global sustainable development. These were all mind-expanding experiences that enabled me to consider how "enhancing inventiveness" is so vital for "quality of life, competitiveness, and sustainability," as the title of our final report declared. (The document is available at <web.mit.edu/invent/report.html>.) Thanks to the National Science Foundation for supporting the effort, and to the chairs of each of those workshops: MIT's Merritt Roe Smith and Christopher Magee, Harvard's David Perkins, Wharton's Mark Myers, and LEAD International's (London) Julia Marton-Lefèvre. Special thanks to the more than fifty professors, inventors, and other world-class experts who participated in these discussions and shared their research and perspectives.

Thanks to the entire staff of MIT's *Technology Review*, especially to Bob Buderi, David Rotman, Wade Roush, and Rebecca Zacks. I must put in a plug for the incredible community of people at the TED conference in Monterey, California, including Andrew Bein, James Daly, Malcolm Gladwell, James Hong, Joe Pine, and Linda Stone, who were so willing to brainstorm a fresh and punchy book title. Additional thanks to Kristen Collins, who always gets the word out, and to Steven Latham for his talent and enthusiasm.

Thanks to Elyse Cheney at Sanford J. Greenburger, as well as to Stephanie Hanson, Peter McGuigan, and Kirsten Neuhaus. My appreciation goes to all the talented people at Harvard Business School Press, especially to Hollis Heimbouch, Zeenat Potia, Sharon Rice,

Astrid Sandoval, and Jennifer Waring, and to Jacqueline Murphy, who has been there for me from the start and has guided the book through each stage of its evolution.

To Shelby Barnes, for being an enormous help ever since December 2001, when I first showed up at Intellectual Ventures in Bellevue, Washington, for an early peek at Nathan Myhrvold's and Edward Jung's invention factory in the making, now known as Invention Science. To me, what Nate and Ed are doing shows that there is something new and exciting happening in the world of invention, and I thank them for their role in inspiring this book.

Finally, great gobs of gratitude go to my friends and family, especially to my parents, and to Lily and Michaela, who fill life with wonder and imagination. And to Amy, for your love, support, and patience. No way does it happen without you.

Index

About the Author

EVAN I. SCHWARTZ is the President of Creative Juice, LLC, which advises companies on how invention and innovation strategies can fuel market leadership and growth. Mr. Schwartz is a former editor at *Business Week*, where he was part of a team that won a National Magazine Award. He is currently a contributing writer for MIT's *Technology Review*.

Mr. Schwartz's previous book, *The Last Lone Inventor: A Tale of Genius, Deceit, and the Birth of Television* (HarperCollins, 2002), tells the story of electronic television inventor Philo T. Farnsworth. The book follows Farnsworth's battle against RCA tycoon David Sarnoff, and shows how their clash symbolized a turning point in the way innovation happens in our economy. A *Discover* magazine top 10 bestselling science book, it has been optioned by Miramax for development as a feature film.

Mr. Schwartz's first book, *Webonomics* (Broadway Books, 1997), anticipated the emergence of the Internet economy. It ranked among Amazon.com's top 25 overall bestsellers for the year and was chosen as a finalist for a Global Business Book Award as well as a Computer Press Award. His second book, *Digital Darwinism* (Broadway Books, 1999), anticipated the Darwinian shakeout among the dot-com species and offered seven survival strategies. Also named a finalist for a Computer Press Award for nonfiction book of the year, it ranked among Amazon.com's top 15 bestselling business books for the year, and it appeared on the *New York Times*'s extended best-seller list.

While researching and writing *Juice*, Mr. Schwartz served as a consulting editor for the Lemelson-MIT Program for Invention and Innovation at MIT's School of Engineering. Mr. Schwartz received a B.S. in computer science from Union College in Schenectady, New York. He lives with his wife and two daughters in Brookline, Massachusetts.